The Kings & Queens of Anglo-Saxon England

About the Author

Timothy Venning received his PhD in History from Kings College, London. His previous books include *If Rome Hadn't Fallen* and *The Kings & Queens of Wales*. He lives in Hampshire.

The Kings & Queens of Anglo-Saxon England

TIMOTHY VENNING

AMBERLEY

This edition first published 2013

Amberley Publishing
The Hill, Stroud
Gloucestershire, GL5 4EP

www.amberley-books.com

Copyright © Timothy Venning, 2011, 2013

The right of Timothy Venning to be identified as the Author
of this work has been asserted in accordance with the
Copyrights, Designs and Patents Act 1988.

All rights reserved. No part of this book may be reprinted
or reproduced or utilised in any form or by any electronic,
mechanical or other means, now known or hereafter invented,
including photocopying and recording, or in any information
storage or retrieval system, without the permission in writing
from the Publishers.

British Library Cataloguing in Publication Data.
A catalogue record for this book is available from the British Library.

ISBN 978-1-4456-0897-6

Typesetting and Origination by Amberley Publishing.
Printed in Great Britain.

Contents

Introduction: The Problem of the Sources	7
Early Settlements to *c.* 560	12
c. 550 to *c.* 620	21
c. 620 to *c.* 655	38
c. 655 to *c.* 690	61
c. 690 to 756	79
756 to 796	92
796 to 860	107
860 to 899	124
899 to 959	141
959 to 1016	158
1016 to 1066	172
Notes	201
List of Illustrations	223

Introduction

The Problem of the Sources

It has become the fashion in recent decades to emphasise the development of the Anglo-Saxon kingdoms of post-Roman England in terms of social and economic (and cultural) developments, as opposed to a lineal narrative of their leadership. The latter was long the established mode for recording history, as was the overall sense of a progressive pattern of development from 'primitive' and local polities to the unity of a single English state. Indeed, the fashion for this was set as far back as the Northumbrian monastic historian Bede's pioneering *Ecclesiastical History of the English People*, written in the early 730s, where he traced the development of the kingdoms founded by those Germanic peoples who migrated to England after the 'fall' of Roman Britain in tandem with their conversion to and promotion of Christianity and the heroic role of such Christian warrior-kings as Edwin and Oswald of Northumbria. Indeed, Bede first mentioned the concept of Anglo-Saxon England, describing the three peoples who came to England from the north-west of continental Europe in the fifth and sixth centuries as the Angles, the Saxons and the Jutes, the latter being less successful than the first two and gradually being eclipsed[1]. (By contrast, the more contemporary Byzantine historian Procopius referred in the 550s to Angles, Britons and 'Frissones', presumably Frisians[2].) Bede also mentioned a concept of a line of 'over-kings' from Aelle of the South Saxons *c.* 490 to Oswy of Northumbria *c.* 655–70, recognised as overlords by their allies or vassals, the problematic *bretwaldas* – also called *brytanwaldas*, 'wide rulers'(?) – which is also argued over by historians[3]. Bede, on whom all subsequent accounts of early English history rely, was indeed writing a 'positive' account of the development of Germanic-settled, Christianised 'England' – land of the Angles. He was partly reacting to the previous great account of post-Roman Britain, written from a 'negative' and British/Welsh point of view – *De Excidio Brittaniae, On the Ruin of Britain*, by the 540s (?) British monastic writer Gildas, whose account is equally invaluable but even more problematic[4]. The progressive tone of Bede towards developments in Christian England was followed by the other main source for the period, the *Anglo-Saxon Chronicle*, compiled at the court of Alfred the Great's Wessex in the 890s, which arguably sought to present an inspiring history of the West Saxons (and to a lesser extent the other kingdoms) to unify the peoples under attack by the Vikings in the later ninth century and rally them under Alfred's leadership[5]. All were thus subjective histories, writing for a socio-political purpose – and perhaps bending or ignoring the 'facts' if the latter did not fit the narrative? In addition, there is the problem that kingdoms of little interest to the West Saxon-led 'narrative' in the *Chronicle* tended to be left out of their account, as with the East Saxons, East Angles, and to a certain degree Mercia, and Bede significantly downplayed the role of pagan rulers of whom he disapproved, both predecessors of the Christian kings in his native Northumbria (e.g. the sixth-century kings of Deira and Bernicia) and seventh-century foes of his heroes Edwin and Oswald, such as the ferocious and successful Penda, the first great king of Mercia (*r. c.* 626–55). In view of the known evidence, can we really agree with Bede that Penda was not a *bretwalda*, i.e. the main over-king of the English, in the period of his greatest success in 642–55, or that Oswy rather than the Christian Mercian Wulfhere was not more powerful in southern England in the 660s?

The linear narrative of history and its concentration on politics, war and 'national' leaders was duly followed by subsequent historians after the Norman Conquest, e.g. Henry of Huntingdon and William of Malmesbury[6], and was taken up too by the great 'Whig historians' of the nineteenth century at the peak of the British Empire. It was the fashion to look back nostalgically to the creation of the basic structures of British – which in this context meant English, not Welsh or Scottish – greatness in the Anglo-Saxon period, not least the 'Mother of Parliaments' and the navy, and a cult of the learned, pious, 'muscular Christian' warrior-hero Alfred duly emerged. This coincided with European (mainly German) historians' enthusiasm for nationalism and tracing the origins of nineteenth-century nation-states in the post-Roman period, a model followed in England by writers such as Bishop Stubbs, and the notion of a 'free' and 'democratic' Anglo-Saxon people unjustly subdued after 1066 by a Frenchified 'Norman yoke' (a staple of anti-monarchic, anti-authoritarian seventeenth-century radical polemic) was revived to extreme lengths. The exhaustive account of late Anglo-Saxon history by E. A. Freeman in the later nineteenth century duly presented Earl Godwine and his son Harold II as authentic English/British heroes in a stirring narrative with the Normans as the villains[7]. This version of history was followed in a simplified form by generations of school textbooks well into the mid-twentieth century, and was bound to meet a reaction quite apart from careful research studies of particular events providing contradictory evidence and showing that the real picture was not that simple. To the Marxist historians, social and economic developments had a far greater effect than the choices of individual rulers, who were 'class enemies' in any case. Was the ruling class only able to act within the constraints of its society's social and economic systems and its cultural traditions? And how much were the lives of ordinary people really affected by high politics and wars, except in an overwhelming catastrophe such as the landing of the Viking 'Great Army' in 865 or the Normans in 1066?

The nineteenth- and early twentieth-century historians' enthusiasm for history as the lives of kings and queens has been downplayed in recent decades, and in education the textbooks have ignored learning names of rulers by rote – to the extent that many kings have dropped out of the public consciousness, even if they were only dimly there anyway. Children have been encouraged to empathise with the lives of ordinary people, as more relevant to them than politics and battles, and Anglo-Saxon archaeology has tended to reveal far more about the details of life in farming homesteads than about royal halls (the palaces of the era). In addition, greater knowledge of the intentions of, and literary constraints on, the writers of the early sources has raised problems about their reliability. Were they really writing objective or trustable 'history' in the modern sense? And were kingly genealogies created for contemporary political purposes and capable of inventing or bending facts about earlier generations to suit the intended objective?

This issue is particularly relevant for the era of 'conquest' – itself a problematic concept at variance with the evidence of archaeology. The picture of fifth-century mass murder by land-grabbing Germanic immigrants on a genocidal scale, the burning of towns and farms alike, and the flight of the post-Roman British populace to the hills of Wales presented by Gildas c. 540[8], just does not tally with the archaeological discoveries. The amount of fire-related damage to post-Roman sites in southern Britain is not that great, and not every fire can be attributed to picturesque bands of plundering Germans. In addition, the careful investigation of land-use patterns shows that many estates were taken over as Anglo-Saxon agricultural land without a break, not left desolate and eventually resettled as Gildas would imply[9]. Is every wooden fifth- or sixth-century construction necessarily the work of incoming Germans, as opposed to post-Roman British who had abandoned working in stone for lack of skill or materials? Do the 'Germanic' artefacts found in (mainly south-eastern at first) fifth-century graves or the new forms of inhumation, a sharp cultural 'break' from 'sub-Roman' practices, imply the work of new settlers or just the adoption of new fashions – from Germanic traders? – by a people cut off from centuries of Roman culture? And what of the DNA evidence that the vast majority of modern English people have ancestral ties (at least in the maternal line) with the pre-Roman Neolithic peoples of Britain, rather than being descended from new settlers in a land de-peopled of post-Roman 'Celts' by Anglo-Saxon invasions? Indeed, can the DNA evidence of south-eastern 'English' blood-ties with the peoples of the Low Countries be attributed to fifth- and sixth-century incomers or to an earlier influx of such people in pre-Roman times?[10] (DNA evidence of 'genocide' is only found in the Viking-settled Hebrides.)

In recent years the fashion seems to be moving back to more narrative history and to the at least partial study of leadership, not least to provide a basic sequential study of the development of the English 'nation' and how a series of small, local states came to merge into one kingdom of the southern and central parts of the British mainland. The obscure history of minor Anglo-Saxon states therefore does matter, as the building-blocks of the English state which emerged as the kingdom of Wessex forcibly unified both Anglo-Saxon and 'Viking' Scandinavian states in the 910s. The basic narrative can be reconstructed, albeit with many caveats, particularly for the earlier centuries, and with a need to point out the limitations of the sources. There is much that we do not know and much that has been misconstrued, not least the amount of survival of post-Roman 'Celtic' British people in southern and central England. There sems to have been more than a transfer of political power and cultural leadership to a new, alien elite as in 1066 – not least as the pre-'conquest' indigenous language of the ordinary people broadly vanished in seventh-century official linguistic terminology (e.g in the *c*. 700 Wessex law-code), but survived and re-emerged after 1066. There was little sign of any surviving British land-owning class in Anglo-Saxon England, unlike in Germanic-conquered Gaul; and the term for the previous inhabitants in the Wessex law-code, *Wealh* (i.e. 'Welsh'), doubles up for 'slave' and 'foreigner' which is an indication of contemporary attitudes[11]. The majority of place names across England are Germanic, except for some geographical features such as rivers (e.g the commonly used 'Avon', from the Welsh *Afan*); and not many towns have recognizably Latin, Roman-descended names. There was no surviving structure of a post-Roman Christian Church in the pagan-ruled kingdoms of *c*. 600, unlike in Gaul, and at most one local Christian church was in use in Kent when St Augustine landed – though Bede may have deliberately ignored surviving 'Celtic' Christians to emphasise the heroic conversion work of the Roman missionaries, and complains that the British did not convert anybody[12]. Yet the names of some early 'Germanic' rulers are British, including those of the West Saxon dynastic founder Cerdic and two successors, Cynric and Caedwalla.

It may be impossible to do more than guess at the element of British/Welsh contribution to rulership and society after 500, but it is easier to point out the equal importance of sheer chance or what we would call 'leadership skills'. Even with the advantages of geography and resources, would Northumbria ever have emerged as a major player in seventh-century politics but for a line of dynamic leaders, such as Aethelfrith (largely ignored by Bede as a pagan), Edwin, Oswald and Oswy? Or Wessex have emerged but for the (brief) career of the warlords Ceawlin and Caedwalla, or Egbert's assumption of national leadership as Mercia – perhaps ground down by exhaustive wars against the Welsh – faltered after the unexpected extinction of Offa's dynasty in 796 and the death of Coenwulf without a son in 821? Did its isolation from central England and inability to keep its rivals short of resources after 616 doom Kent despite the success of

Aethelbert as leader of the southern English? Would East Anglia – briefly the leader in southern affairs in the late 610s – have been able to outmatch its rivals but for the unification of Mercia and the weakness of Raedwald's successors? Was Northumbria doomed as a leader of south-central England as it was too isolated in the north, and what would have happened had its military power not been weakened by Ecgfrith's downfall at the hands of the Picts (685) and the constant civil strife of the eighth century? At a later date, would all England have been Scandinavianised but for Alfred? Did the autonomist tendencies of Viking York – aided by help from Dublin – only delay English unity in the mid-tenth century due to the early deaths of Athelstan (939) and Edmund I (946)? Did Edgar's early death (975) doom England to another round of Viking attacks, and the unexpected extinction of Cnut's dynasty (1042) give Edward the Confessor an unlikely chance to rule? Above all, what of the 'near misses' of the complex events of 1066? Much could depend on the outcome of a single battle, whatever the likelihood that greater resources would 'inevitably' cause a particular kingdom to prevail; the ruin of Edwin's dynasty after the battle of Hatfield Chase in 633/4, the death of Penda at Winwaed in *c.* 655, and the defeat of Guthrum at Ethandun in 878 are particularly important. It is hoped that the following narrative will show that the handling of leadership problems and the characters of individual rulers in pre-Norman England certainly mattered to the long-term development of English – and British – history.

Early Settlements to *c.* 560

KENT

HENGEST (*fl.* 440s – 60s (?)) Traditionally the founder of the kingdom, which unlike all the other Anglo-Saxon states (apart from Wight), was 'Jutish' by race as defined by Bede. Hengest was supposed to have been the first Germanic captain to come to England, as stated by both Anglo-Saxon and British sources (Bede, *c.* 732, and Nennius, *c.* 829). The legend of Hengest and his foundation of Kent is unclear beyond the essentials, with different versions, none of which is contemporary, and some of it is shared with stock Germanic hero-tales. The dynasty was called after his 'grandson' Aesc/Oesc, not the founder himself, according to Bede – which is unique and may mean that he was later annexed from legend by enterprising dynasts as a prestigious ancestor and Aesc, *c.* 500, was the real founder. Hengest's name translates as 'Stallion', which could be a nickname but also appears to have been the ancient Kentish standard of a white horse; his so-called 'brother' Horsa translates as 'Mare'. Many modern historians (led by David Dumville and Patrick Sims-Williams) declare that he probably never existed and was a legendary hero brought in to give extra lustre to the founding of the kingdom.

The written evidence for Hengest is all of later date, with an independent Continental saga reference in *The Fight at Finnsborg* to Hengest as a half-Danish warlord who commanded mercenaries and led a revolt against the Danes in Jutland. The earliest English version is the story told by Bede (*c.* 732), who presumably derived it from oral Kentish accounts known to the monks of Canterbury. He dates the arrival of the first Germans (three races – Angles, Saxons and Jutes) at 449–50, the consulship of Marcian and Valentinian. According to Bede the Jutes settled Kent and the Isle of Wight (plus the New Forest area); but it is not clear if these people were from the land the Scandinavians were later to call Jutland in Denmark. A force of mercenaries, led by Hengest and Horsa, sons of Wihtgisl, came to aid the British King

Vortigern against the raiding Picts and achieved great success but outstayed their welcome, brought in their countrymen, and eventually revolted against their employer. Bede's story agrees with that of Gildas, c. 540, on the summoning of and treachery to Vortigern by Germanic mercenaries; but did his Kentish sources obtain the story from a copy of Gildas' book or from their own local oral history? The various versions of the *Anglo-Saxon Chronicle* (late ninth-century) agreed that Hengest and Horsa were brought in during the reign of Marcian and Valentinian (449/50 to 455/6) to defeat the Picts, but revolted and seized their own kingdom.

The version in the Bodleian Library names their place of landing at Ebba's Creek (Ebbesfleet near Sandwich), as in Bede's account. The continuing story then has them fighting Vortigern at 'Aeglesprep' or 'Agelesford', which has been traditionally interpreted as Aylesford, in 455; Horsa was killed there, and Hengest and his son Aesc then 'took the kingdom'. (Aesc is alternatively called Hengest's grandson, and supposedly lived to 512 which makes this unlikely.) In 456 they won a victory at 'Crecganford', supposedly Crayford on the River Darent, and the British fled to London, leaving all Kent to them. A further victory followed at 'Wippa's Creek' in 465 and after a final victory in 473 the Welsh (the word used here for the first time) fled 'like fire'.

A slightly different story is given in the *Historia Brittonum*, the Gwynedd version of the events written by Bishop Nennius in the 820s. This dates the Saxon arrival as 428, three years into Vortigern's reign, and has Hengest arriving with three ships to fight the Picts and being granted land at 'Ruym', 'river island' (river-surrounded Thanet in Kent?). The date is twenty years before Bede's. In due course, Hengest persuades Vortigern to allow him to bring in sixteen more ships – and his daughter Ronwen (Rowena), with whom the king becomes besotted. Hengest arranges their marriage, and is granted Kent; forty more ships arrive under his son Octa and their kinsman Ebissa, and are sent north. The Saxon revolt follows, with Hengest and Horsa beng driven back to Thanet three times by Vortigern's son Vortimer and besieged there. A long war occurs, with the main battles of the campaign at 'Derguentid', 'Episford' or 'Rithergabail' ('Horse Ford'), and by the 'inscribed stone' on the shore of the Gallic Sea. Horsa falls at Episford, and after the final battle Vortimer evicts the Saxons. He soon dies and Vortigern invites them back. This time the treacherous Hengest invites Vortigern and his nobles to a parley where both sides promise to come unarmed, and the Saxons pull knives out of their long sleeves on Hengest's signal to kill all the Britons except Vortigern. He is forced to hand over more territory before he is released, and is deposed by his countrymen. This detailed story may derive from a British written source, but equally likely from legend; some modern historians think that Nennius acquired it from Kent as the Saxon name of the battle of 'Episford' is given first and then translated into Welsh. Its independence from the Bede/*Chronicle* version cannot be verified. The clues in the names of the battles have been reinterpreted in modern times to assert that they need not refer to Kent at all and could be related to warfare on the lower Humber, also settled in the fifth century (which is nearer to the presumed sites of conflict with the Picts). The 'Gallic Sea' reference seems to indicate a battle near a Roman memorial near the Straits of Dover (Richborough?).

The archaeological evidence for extensive early Germanic settlement in Kent seems to show widespread undefended villages in the first half of the fifth century – and even perhaps a few artefacts from earlier. One argument has it that Germanic artefacts need not have been owned by incoming Germans, merely bought from them by traders and used by Britons after trade with the Roman Empire declined; this would invalidate a lot of archaeological theses on the nature and date of 'conquest'. The fact that settlers lived close to towns such as Canterbury would imply that it was by arrangement with the locals, probably as mercenaries. There is no evidence of the battles and massacres alleged by the *Chronicle* (and by Gildas on the British side), and some Germans may even have arrived in Kent to man the Saxon Shore fortresses in the fourth century. According to this interpretation the whole story of Hengest was a later fabrication, imported from a Continental saga to give a heroic past to the kingdom of Kent.

Assuming that there was a real 'founder' of Kent in the 420s to 450s, a mercenary captain who revolted against a British employer decades before Aesc reigned, he may have been unrelated to him. The traditional name for Hengest's father, Wihtgils/Wihtgisl, sounds Jutish – from the Danish mainland – and has a similarity to the names of the dynasty of Wight, also settled by Jutes. This has been alleged to have been a 'back-formation' by later propagandists to play up the link between the two kingdoms. The practice of using Germanic federates was common practice in the fourth and fifth centuries and a later, Anglo-Saxon fabulist would not have known this authentic detail. Logically, Vortigern could even have placed Hengest in Kent *c.* 450, to oppose a crossing from the Continent by his Roman enemies, backers of his nemesis Ambrosius Aurelianus; a mercenary settlement on Thanet was militarily valuable. The Nennian claim that Hengest forced Vortigern to hand over all the kingdom of Kent to him and dispossess the British ruler is possible, as the Roman provinces of Britain – the administrative system which the fifth-century British inherited – was based on pre-Roman tribal regions and the pre-Roman 'Cantii' had occupied Kent, as described by Julius Caesar. The Germanic incomers seem to have retained a version of the local name. Bede's statement that a notable monument existed to Horsa in Kent in his time may be a reference to a local story about the Roman triumphal arch at Richborough, which was a possible site for one of Hengest's battles.

The *Chronicle* states that Hengest died in 488, which is not beyond the bounds of possibility for a young war-leader of the 440s, but is unlikely for a man who entered Vortigern's service in 428. The entry may rest on a vague memory that he ruled for forty years (a suspiciously round number, also used for the reign of Wessex's founder Cerdic). If Aesc can be dated at around 490–510, Hengest was clearly supposed to have been one or two generations older. In the twelfth century, Geoffrey of Monmouth describes him being defeated, captured and executed by Ambrosius at 'Caer Cynan', probably Conisborough in Yorkshire, on uncertain evidence. Hengest remains as much an object of controversy and denial of his existence as does the British Arthur, and in both cases centuries of literary invention are to blame.

OCTHA (I) (Mid-fifth century) The shadowy 'son' of Hengest, cited in later legend, which may derive from a Kentish and/or a Welsh source. Bede does not even mention him; the ninth-century Welsh historian Nennius has his story. He was supposed to have been summoned to Britain by his father some time after the latter arrived as a mercenary commander to King Vortigern, along with his kinsman Ebissa, and to have brought reinforcements. He campaigned in the north of Britain against the Picts and according to one story settled there, which may be a reference to early Anglian settlements in the fifth century around the lower Humber. He then came south to his father's kingdom when the latter died, *c.* 488. This may be a vague folk-memory of genuine Germanic campaigns against raiding Picts on the east coast, with their leader Octha incorporated into Kentish dynastic sagas as an ally of Hengest and rationalised as his son. The *Chronicle* makes it clear that it was Aesc, not Octha, who assisted Hengest in his battles and succeeded as king, and the Kentish dynasty was named after Aesc not Octha. He may have had no connection with Kent at all.

AESC/OESC (Alternatively known as Oeric (Eric), with Aesc/Oesc as his surname or nickname (Bede), *c.* 488 – 512 (?)) The king of Kent after whom the later dynasty (Aescingas) was named. The fact that he was the dynastic progenitor is at odds with the legends that make Hengest the founder of the kingdom; he was said to be Hengest's grandson, the son of Octha, father of a second Octha and great-grandfather of Aethelbert (d. 616). Hengest was recorded as dying in 488, with Aesc succeeding him directly for a reign of either twenty-four or thirty-four years. Aesc's father Octha was supposed to have ruled Anglian settlements in the north-east. One version of the *Chronicle* has Aesc becoming co-ruler with Hengest as early as *c.* 455, on the death of his uncle Horsa, and assisting Hengest at the battles of Creganford (Crayford [?]) *c.* 457, and Wippesfleot *c.* 465. This would suggest a clear 'saga' linking Hengest and Aesc from an early date. If he lived until thirty-four years after his accession (i.e 522), it gives him an active career of over sixty years, which is unlikely; 512 is more plausible. Alternatively, Aesc's early career before his accession may have been backdated by panegyricists, keen to associate the dynastic founder with Hengest in the 450s, and Aesc was not in fact active until later.

Aesc is the first solidly-grounded ruler of Kent and may have been a lieutenant rather than a relative of the founding leaders of the 450s. He was certainly important enough to his descendants to have the dynasty named after him, and consolidated the kingdom securely enough to survive the British military revival around 500. There is one reference to him fighting at Mount Badon *c.* 516, and the nearness of this date to his death in the *Chronicle* has been interpreted as a 'cover-up' of his possible death there. His military experience and resources would logically make him a likely recruit to any Germanic coalition for a major attack on the British.

OCTHA (II) (Early sixth century (?)) Allegedly the son and successor of King Aesc, the eponymous founder of the Aescingas dynasty, who traditionally died around 512. If he is not an invention, muddled up with Hengest's 'son' and lieutenant Octha, he could have been called after the latter. The recorded name of his alleged son and successor, Eormenric, is Gothic and refers to the greatest hero-king of their people: the Gothic ruler on the steppes before the catastrophe of the Hunnic invasion of *c.* 375. This may indicate ambitious pretensions or a pride in the Germanic past on the part of Octha, more likely for a senior king than a mere local sub-ruler.

SUSSEX

AELLE (*c.* 477 – ?) The founder of the dynasty of Sussex. According to the *Chronicle* he landed at 'Cymensora' with his sons Cissa, Cymen and Wlencing in 477; the site may be on the Selsey peninsula.

His 'sons' may have been his lieutenants rather than relatives and not even named as in the record; Cymen is linked to the place-name 'Cymensora' and Wlencing to Lancing near Worthing, so they may have been the chiefs of the settlers in those two areas. Aelle's initial settlement on the Selsey ('Seals' Island') peninsula is logical, given that it was linked by a relatively narrow 'neck' to the mainland and so easily defensible; due to erosion much of the fifth-century area has been lost to the sea, so the absence of discovered settlements are not surprising. Aelle drove the British, presumably the 'Regni' tribe who Roman records state inhabited Sussex, into the Weald, thus securing coastal West Sussex for settlement. The nearby ex-Roman district capital of Noviomagus was renamed after Cissa by the Saxons, which may indicate its seizure by Aelle's family.

In 485 Aelle defeated the British at 'Mearcreadesburn', translated as 'border stream'. This may have been the River Adur or Arun as the Saxon/British border, given the discovery of early Saxon settlement around Worthing and the lack of any known sites to the west – but if so, Aelle's kingdom was based in East not West Sussex. Some historians believe the association of Aelle with West Sussex is only legendary. Aelle's next victory is dated as 491 and involved the capture of the late-Roman Saxon Shore fortress of Anderida (Pevensey) at the far eastern end of the South Sussex coastal strip, a rare recorded conquest of a fortified British position adding immensely to Aelle's prestige. No more military activity is recorded for his kingdom for 180 years, suggesting that this victory rounded off the establishment of a small but secure kingdom.

Bede records Aelle as the first *bretwalda* of the Saxons – probably meaning 'wide ruler' and implying a military command over a number of kingdoms. Aelle – a ruler of a small and isolated kingdom – likely acquired a degree of (informal?) leadership over other incoming Saxon commanders by military prestige and attracting a large following of warriors. It is only guesswork for modern scholars to imply that his dating means he is the likeliest Saxon commander to have led a coalition of rulers to face the resurgent British under Ambrosius Aurelianus *c.* 480–500, or to have been the losing commander at the battle of Mount Badon. It is unclear if it was defeat, the comparative military weakness of inferior heirs or the geographical position of Sussex which led to the kingdom's eclipse after Aelle. It is unknown if 'Cissa' succeeded him, and the kingdom is next recorded as fighting the West Saxons around 600.

WESSEX

CERDIC (Trad. 494/514 – 534) The founder of the kingdom of the 'Gewissae' or West Saxons, and according to the genealogy of his line in the *Chonicle*, the son of Elesa, son of Esla, son of Gewis, the eponymous dynastic ancestor. He was allegedly the direct ancestor of the kings of England and Great Britain, whose line still sits on the throne 1,500 years later. But he is also a major figure of controversy and his story was clearly embellished in later centuries. Why should the founder of a Saxon kingdom have a British name (the same as the Welsh 'Ceredig'), and was this due to a British mother or a British father? The neat story in the *Chronicle* of his advance across battle sites identified as being in Hampshire supposes that the kingdom he founded there was in that area, but no Saxon remains of the early sixth century have been found except scattered settlements around Winchester and the south-west; 'Ytene', west of Southampton Water, where he may have 'landed', was settled by Jutes, as testified to in late eleventh-century references.

Archaeology indicates no sharp break in British settlement in south-central England around 500–50, as the conquest recorded in the *Chronicle* suggests; the centre of Saxon settlement was in the upper Thames valley. Some historians have declared the entire *Chronicle* narrative to be fiction, a heroic saga about the dynastic founder created in later centuries and possibly derived from that of Kent. Cerdic, like their equally dubious Hengest (q.v.), landed with a colleague, 'took the kingdom' six years later, and reigned for forty years. In recent times, there have been Welsh claims that his father's and grandfather's names indicate a British origin; 'Elesa' or 'Esla' might be a mysterious son of the deposed early to mid-fifth-century Powys ruler Vortigern – or the Saxon warrior 'Osla of the Knife', a military opponent of 'King Arthur' in twelfth-century Welsh literature. The 'Gewissae' – a unique, non-ethnic sobriquet for Cerdic's kingdom – might have a connection to the 'Guentissae' (Gwent), to the kingdom of 'Ewias' or to a word meaning 'confederates'. Cerdic might have been the son of an exiled British prince – a mercenary warlord who seized new territory far from his homeland – and he ruled a predominantly British-inhabited kingdom which imposed its rule on local Jutes and Saxons.

The later West Saxons, leading the remaining Germanic peoples in England in the later ninth century, would want to present Cerdic in the *Chronicle* as a respectable Saxon to add lustre to their own dynasty – and may not even have known that the early sixth-century kingdom was a complex, mixed British/Germanic personal fiefdom. Moreover, the first 'Germanic' remains in Hampshire are from an evidently tolerated settlement close to the post-Roman town at Winchester (Venta Belgarum) – suggested as belonging to mercenaries, more likely to traders, and from around Cerdic's date. The 'Meonwara', the people of the area east of the River Itchen around the Meon valley, where it has been suggested that Cerdic could have operated if he landed and fought around Netley, were a distinct people from the West Saxons in the seventh century. Indeed, their main cemetery at Droxford has been analysed as Jutish, not Saxon, in culture.

The *Chronicle* story may thus be worthless, but it probably presents a garbled account of what the ninth-century West Saxons believed to be their origins. It records Cerdic and his son Cynric (possibly a mistake for Creoda) landing at 'Cerdic's Shore' in 494/5 with five ships; the site is possibly Ower, near Calshot on the west shore of Southampton Water, but the area was settled by Jutes not Saxons. The creation of the kingdom is dated at 500, possibly indicating the winning of enough (British and Saxon/Jutish?) military support for Cerdic to claim royal status as an equal of powerful neighbours such as Aelle. The incorporation of the victories of Aelle into the West Saxon records may indicate an early alliance; similar guesswork must mark the connection of Cerdic to the recorded landing of Port (a suspicious name, logically back-formed from Portsmouth) and his sons in 501 at 'Portesmutha', i.e Portsmouth Harbour. (There was a nearby Roman Saxon Shore fortress at 'Portus Adurni', Portchester, but the current town was not founded until the twelfth century, by Richard I.) The alternative date for Cerdic's landing suggested by the tenth-century chronicler Aethelweard, a West Saxon prince, is 500.

In 508, Cerdic defeated a British ruler with the name of Natanleod at the eponymous 'Natan leaga'; the personal name sounds Pictish (Nechtan?) and has been suggested as a back-formation from the site, either Netley Marsh near the head of Southampton Water or Netley to the east. Allegedly, 5,000 Britons fell with their king, and logically Cerdic annexed the land named after 'Natan' stretching west to Charford on the Avon. (If Netley, east of the Itchen, is meant, annexation of the Itchen valley is logical.)

Another victory followed at 'Cerdic's leag' or 'Cerdic's ford', probably Charford, in 518 – logically against the British of Dorset, to the west. But confusingly, the *Chronicle* also states that the 'West Saxons' – not Cerdic in person – landed at 'Cerdic's Shore' in 514, with their leaders as Stuf and Wihtgar (later rulers of the Jutes on Wight) and Cerdic's Saxon kingdom was created in 519, seemingly a duplication from the 494/5 entry. This may reflect two rival traditions of the date, with the *Chronicle* compilers unable to decide so they entered both of them; the twenty-year gap may imply that the original entries were made in a cyclical 'Easter table' under two separate 'cycles' of years, commencing in 494 and 514, and are only approximate.

Another battle by Cerdic and Cynric at 'Cerdic's Wood' (or 'leag') follows for 527, and in 530 they and Cerdic's 'nephews' Stuf and Wihtgar defeated the inhabitants of the Isle of Wight at 'Wihtgaresbyrg', probably Carisbrooke Castle as the main fortification. The conquest of Wight is presumed to have followed, though Cerdic's (superior) relationship and rank compared to Stuf and Wihtgar may be West Saxon propaganda justifying their kingdom's conquest of Wight in the 680s. Indeed, when the *Anglo-Saxon Chronicle* was compiled, *c.* 890, the government of Wessex was keen to assert the kinship of the Jutish dynasty of Wight, from whom King Alfred descended via his mother Osburh, to Cerdic's line; is the evidence unsafe? Cerdic is recorded as dying in 534, forty years after his landing; if he was buried at 'Cerdic's Barrow' this is in the north of Hampshire, near Hurstbourne Tarrant, and indicates probable rule of the entire county. This area has no 'Germanic' remains for the first half of the sixth century.

The extent of Cerdic's kingdom's Germanic, as opposed to British, nature and the truth of his career have been hopelessly muddled. But his role as 'founder' of the royal line of England and Great Britain has preserved his importance, and he was even the subject of a twentieth-century historical novel by Alfred Duggan. (*The Conscience of the King*, which made him a renegade British prince of part-Saxon descent.) Some historians have argued that the British writer Gildas' account of a generation of peace after the battle of Badon (*c.* 516 [?]) means that Cerdic could not have been forging a kingdom then, but more likely the campaigns were so minor that the majority of the British did not take note of them.

CREODA The son of Cerdic according to some accounts, which make him the father of Cerdic's successor Cynric. This is the version in the West Saxon royal genealogical lists, but the *Anglo-Saxon Chronicle* does not mention him. His name is Saxon; his father's and son's are not. Putting two generations, not one, between Cerdic and Ceawlin (acceded *c.* 560) makes more sense than Cynric, who allegedly reigned to 560, being the son and lieutenant who fought at Cerdic's side in 514 (let alone in 494). If the *Chronicle* is correct that Cerdic was joined in the new kingship by Cynric in 519, Creoda was presumably dead by then, but this may be another mistake. Creoda may only have been Cerdic's lieutenant, subsequently placed in the royal genealogy in order to fit him into the dynasty.

CYNRIC (Trad. 534–60) The son or grandson of Cerdic. For an account of the problems of the traditional story of the sixth-century kingdom, see Cerdic's entry. Cynric is a British (or Irish- influenced) name, 'Cunorix', which may indicate that his mother was British. Cynric is supposed to have been Cerdic's co-commander at his arrival, which is unlikely if he landed in 494; 514 is more logical if Cynric, rather than the mysterious 'Creoda' (possibly Cynric's father), is meant. Nor is it clear that Cynric was really Cerdic's son, and that this connection was not inserted later to formalise a less direct relationship and link Cynric's son Ceawlin, founder of the extended kingdom and *bretwalda*, to the dynastic ancestor.

Assuming that the record used by the *Chronicle* was accurate and that the new kingdom was established in Hampshire not the Thames valley, Cynric supposedly fought alongside Cerdic against the British at 'Cerdic's Ford' (Charford?) in 519 and 'Cerdic's leag' or 'Cerdic's Wood' in 527. They then fought against the British of Wight at 'Wihtgaresbyrg', probably Carisbrooke, in 530. Co-ruler since 519, Cynric then succeeded Cerdic in 534; the archaeological record is almost devoid of Germanic remains in Hampshire for this period, so if Cynric ruled this area it must have been a multi-ethnic realm of British and Germans. The New Forest area and Wight had Jutish culture and linguistic identity, as testified by Bede. His reign lasted for twenty-six years according to the Corpus Christi College, Cambridge ('A'), Peterborough ('E') and Canterbury ('F') versions of the *Chronicle*.

Wihtgar, co-ruler of the Isle of Wight and allegedly Cynric's cousin, died in 544 and was buried at 'Wihtgaresbyrg'. In 552, Cynric defeated the British at 'Searobyrg', Old Sarum, and put them to flight. There had been a Romano-British town at this fortified site (Sorviodunum), which remained the political centre of Wiltshire through the Saxon period, and its conquest as the crucial stage of annexation of Wiltshire is logical. The severe plague in Britain, dated at 547/9, would also have diminished the manpower of the British, with the West Saxon advance coming at the end of what Gildas implies was a generation of peace after *c.* 516. A further military success for Cynric and his 'son' Ceawlin came in 556, at the site of 'Beranbyrg' which appears to be Barbury Castle near Swindon. This is in northern Wiltshire, and if the attribution of the sites is correct it more logically suggests an advance northwards from a Hampshire base than from the Thames. As there is little record of settlement in sixth-century Wiltshire, the invaders' manpower may well have consisted of local British as well as Germanic allies.

Cynric is supposed to have died in 560. It is unlikely that he was really adult in 494 if he was able to command an army in 556, but even if the dating is approximate he seems to have been active since *c.* 520 and so was probably in his fifties or sixties. Ceawlin succeeded him, and took the kingdom to even greater success.

c. 550 to *c.* 620

KENT

EORMENRIC (? – *c.* 560) Given in the royal geneologies of Kent as the father of its greatest king, Aethelbert, and son of the obscure Octha (probably the son of Aesc/Oesc, *fl.* 488–512). His name is that of the great Gothic hero Eormenric, semi-mythical king of their people in their days of prosperity on the Ukrainian steppes before they were forced into exile by the Huns in *c.* 375; its use for a scion of the Kentish royal family indicates high pretensions and future hopes of prosperity. Nothing is known of him except his name, and his dates can only be calculated from his son's; the *Chronicle* gives Aethelbert as being born in 552, though some historians have disputed this. Referring to the latter's marriage in *c.* 581, the Frankish chronicler Gregory of Tours calls him the son of a king of Kent, which confirms that Eormenric did hold royal rank; this does not mean that Eormenric was still alive in 581. Possibly the absence of a need to lead armies in battle led to a degree of decentralisation and decline of royal power amidst a mass of peaceful farming settlements, with the king only needed for pagan religious rites or legal judgements. His date of death is usually taken as 560, when the *Chronicle* says that Aethelbert commenced his fifty-six-year reign, but it is possible that the two men ruled jointly for a time as only a few details of contemporary events survive.

AETHELBERT (*c.* 560 – 616/17) The greatest ruler of the Kentish kingdom, recorded by Bede as its sole *bretwalda* and overlord of the other kings of southern England. His reputation was built up by Church writers as the man who had invited the first Catholic mission to England and was the first king to be converted, but his achievement is undeniable. He was the son of Eormenric, either sole or one of a number of rulers in Kent in the third quarter of the sixth century, and himself grandson of Aesc-Oesc. Division into realms of East and West Kent divided by the Medway, visible in Kentish custom for centuries, is also possible.

The Canterbury version of the *Anglo-Saxon Chronicle*, presumably transmitting Church records at Canterbury to the late ninth century, gives Aethelbert as born in 552, as he died aged 65/6 in 616/17, and as succeeding to the throne in 560/1 for a reign of fifty-three years; this is presumably a mistake for fifty-six years, as stated by Bede using Church records. It has him baptised in the thirtieth year of his reign, which working back from 597 gives his accession at 567/8. An alternative version gives the date of accession as 565 and death as 618/19, given that Bede says that Aethelbert died twenty-one years after receiving the Christian faith (which must be in 596/7).

This length of reign, the longest in Anglo-Saxon history if accepted, has been reckoned unlikely for a ruler in the sixth century by some historians, and Gregory of Tours calls Aethelbert 'the son of a king of Kent' when he married his Frankish wife *c.* 581. Accordingly, it has been suggested that the *Chronicle* mistook the length of his life for the length of his reign, and that he was born *c.* 560 and reunited a divided, decentralised realm in the 580s.

The dating of Aethelbert's first battle, at 'Wibbandun' against Ceawlin of the West Saxons, as '568' may be inaccurate. If the battle-site has been correctly placed at Wimbledon, a struggle over Surrey (north of the impenetrable Wealden forests) is probable. Whoever won, Aethelbert's subsequent emergence as the next *bretwalda* after Ceawlin probably followed the latter's overthrow by his subjects in 591/2; it is to this period that Bede's statement that he was recognised as overlord by all the kings south of the Humber belongs.

Aethelbert seems to have expanded his influence over the lower Thames valley and into Essex, whose late sixth-century king, Sledda, married his sister Ricula; he did not annex London and his power seems to have been enforced more by influence than by conquest. The extent of current Saxon settlements along the lower Thames, the scattered nature of their small political units, and the lacuna in our knowledge of their rulership until the rise of Mercian power would make it likely that much of Aethelbert's influence was exercised here.

Aethelbert's promulgation of the first law-code in the Germanic kingdoms in Britain indicates his desire for order and justice and a concept of leading a settled government. The precedents for such a move lay within the Roman Empire, most recently the codification by Justinian in the 530s, and the more stable and settled Germanic successor-states such as the Gothic kingdoms (Aethelbert's father had had a Gothic name). The promulgation of the code followed the arrival of the mission from Rome led by Augustine, which would have been able to show him how the plan worked and its advantages for the ruler; the methodology followed for the terminology was that of the Franks. Bringing the idea to England and adapting it acted as a unifying factor for a Kentish 'state' probably unused to strong rule by one leader. In practical terms, the requirement to pay compensation to the king as well as the victim boosted royal financial power (providing money to hire warriors and lavish gifts on dependants) as well as bringing the sovereign into local affairs as guarantor of justice. The increase in the usage of coins, arising from extended trade with the Continent, reflecting a prosperous realm, led to the establishment of the first post-Roman mint in Britain, at Canterbury; the coins were designed in the Frankish manner. Canterbury, the principal royal 'vill', where Aethelbert was to settle the Christian mission in 597, was arguably the first Germanic 'capital' in England – using a Frankish (ultimately Roman) urban concept alien to his ancestors.

Aethelbert formed his own marital alliance in *c.* 581 with the Frankish kingdoms across the Channel, with whom the Kentish peoples had close trading and cultural contacts through the sixth century, as apparent from archaeological sites. His wife Bertha was the daughter of Charibert (d. 567), late ruler of Paris, and niece of the latter's surviving brothers, Chilperic and Guntramn. Confusion has been caused by Bede's statement that Aethelbert received Bertha from her parents, as that would imply that the marriage occurred before Charibert died in 567; the contemporary historian Bishop Gregory of Tours, however, places the marriage at *c.* 581. This would be more logical, given that Aethelbert and Bertha's daughter was married to King Edwin of Northumbria after 617 and so was probably born around 590–600. However, Gregory only calls Aethelbert 'a man of Kent' at the first mention of the marriage and 'son of a king of Kent' at the second, which some commentators have taken to mean that Aethelbert was not yet king at the time.

Contrary to the version of events propagated by Bede, the first Catholic missionary in Kent was Bertha's Frankish chaplain, Bishop Liudhard, to whom Aethelbert seems to have granted the surviving Romano-British church of St Martin's in Canterbury for his devotions. The nature and extent of conversions was probably more extensive than Bede claimed. Aethelbert was interested in prestigious Continental connections, and in 596/7 he momentously accepted the arrival of a larger group of missionaries, this time from the Holy See and led by Pope Gregory's nominee, (St) Augustine. It was probably the practical advantages of Church support for kingship as well as the theological arguments which eventually convinced him to convert and be baptised in 601; after this, Bede records that he enthusiastically encouraged large-scale conversions among his subjects. He allowed the creation of the mission's first residential see at Canterbury, the only large settlement within a former Roman town in Kent and probably his principal royal residence. A second see was set up at Rochester, probably to fit in with the political division between east and west Kent, and work began on converting the neighbouring East Saxons in his brother-in-law's vassal kingdom with a see at London. Augustine set up the principal see at Aethelbert's court, not in the more 'historic' former Roman see of London, despite Gregory's intentions. Aethelbert also backed Augustine in a journey to the far west of Britain to meet the senior leaders of the British Church, within their own lands – traditionally at Aust near Bristol – in 604. This was a failure, but Aethelbert's political influence was wide enough to assist the attempt and protect the travellers. Augustine gave the king valuable advice in the creation of his new law-code, and in return Aethelbert granted the Church and its officials comparable legal rights to those they possessed in other Catholic-led kingdoms.

Aethelbert died on 24 February 616 or 617, the most influential and probably most militarily powerful ruler in southern Britain. A case has been made out that the year was 618, given that Bede refers to him dying twenty-one years after receiving the Christian faith, but that would complicate the fixed later Kentish regnal lengths. Possibly aged around sixty-six and at least fifty-six, he had been the first Germanic ruler to establish a state with a political and cultural level akin to that of the sixth-century Frankish dynasts, but unlike the latter his achievement was ephemeral. His alliance of crown and Church, and promulgation of a law-code, set the template for future Anglo-Saxon rulers; his kingdom, however, lost its influence over its neighbours: firstly to Raedwald of East Anglia and then the kings of Northumbria.

WESSEX

CEAWLIN (*c.* 560 – 592 (?)) The son and successor of Cynric as king of the West Saxons (or 'Gewissae'), and thus supposedly great-grandson of Cerdic. There are major discrepancies over the length of his reign, with the *Chronicle* dating his accession as 560 and his deposition as 592 while the West Saxon regnal lists give him a reign of seven or seventeen years. The logical explanation is that the latter refers to his rule of the larger, extended kingdom created by his victories over the British (and unrecorded groupings of Saxon or Jutish settlers?). There is also doubt over the record of the West Saxon kingdom presented by its heirs in the *Chronicle* (see article on Cerdic), as the archaeological record does not tally with the idea of a West Saxon 'nucleus' in Hampshire expanding northwards through the mid-sixth century. The main areas of settlement were in the upper Thames valley, and the locations of Ceawlin's battles have been interpreted as implying that this was the centre of his power, not Hampshire. Possibly the early kingdom consisted of a mixture of Saxon, Jutish (south-west Hampshire) and British residents, and its expansion through Wiltshire in the 550s brought it control over the Saxon settlements in the Thames valley and the manpower to expand further.

The course of Ceawlin's career is thus unclear, with the patchy record of the *Chronicle* written down 300 years later and possibly giving his successes a cohesive structure which hides much of the reality. He was remembered by Bede as the next *bretwalda* after Aelle of the South Saxons, i.e. a powerful king who could call on rulers beyond his immediate kingdom and was the major military power of his day. According to the *Chronicle*, his first battle was at 'Beranbyrig', Barbury Castle in northern Wiltshire, in 556, assisting his father Cynric. The West Saxons are traditionally supposed to have been advancing gradually northwards from their Hampshire 'power-base', with this victory gaining them access to the Thames valley area. Probably either Cynric or Ceawlin took over control of the upper Thames in the years after the battle of Barbury.

Ceawlin traditionally succeeded to Cynric's kingdom in 560. He is recorded as fighting against Aethelbert of Kent, his main rival in southern England, at 'Wibbandun' in 568 – if this is Wimbledon, a conflict for control of Surrey and the London area is implied and Ceawlin was moving east. Ceawlin and his 'brother' (or ally) Cutha/Cuthwulf were the winners and drove Aethelbert back into Kent; Oslaf and Cnebba, two 'ealdormen', a term later used for the royal officials governing counties, were killed. The subsequent victory which Cutha/Cuthwulf won over the British in the Chilterns at 'Bedcanford' in *c.* 571, annexing four royal 'vills' (Limbury, Aylesbury, Benson and Eynsham), suggests a Saxon advance along the Icknield Way on the British enclave in the Chilterns, but it is less clear if this success was part of Ceawlin's expansion from the upper Thames. Was 'Cutha' his close relative and lieutenant as stated in the *Chronicle*, or an ally whose connection to him was 'tidied up' by later memory to annex him to the dynasty of Cerdic? Was Cutha's force advancing east from the upper Thames, or arriving south-westwards from the Fenland settlements – and was Ceawlin thence overlord of the Chilterns?

Ceawlin had enough resources by the later 570s to challenge the surviving British states of the Cotswolds – a rich agricultural area with surviving (if truncated) urban settlements. Traditionally in 577, he won a major battle over the British at 'Deorham', probably Dyrham near Chipping Sodbury, thus implying an advance as far as the western edge of the Cotswold escarpment. Three British kings (Coinmail, Farinmail and Condidan) were killed, and three fortified towns – Bath, Cirencester and Gloucester – were conquered. It is not certain if the three rulers were their lords or allies from further afield, and Condidan may have been connected to Powys. West Saxon power now extended to the Severn valley. Saxon settlement in the Cotswolds seems to have been minimal for decades after 577, and to have been small-scale in the Severn valley in the early seventh century; probably the surviving local British remained as Ceawlin's subjects. There is also a question over whether Ceawlin's probable part-British ancestry (from dynastic names) and/or a claim to the Welsh kingdom of Gwent aided his authority over an area of British settlement, but had been forgotten by the time the *Chronicle* was composed; the kingdom's usual name was the dynastic 'Gewissae', not yet the culturally exclusive 'West Saxons'. Nor is it clear who Ceawlin's fellow-commander at Deorham, Cuthwine, was – he seems to be distinct from his usual ally, Cutha, but the similarities of names suggests he was a close relation to the latter. The 'A' Manuscript of the *Chronicle* for 688 gives a Cuthwine as Ceawlin's son, King Ine's ancestor, so he is the logical candidate – but in that case why did he not succeed his father? Was he dead by, or expelled in, the 592 revolt? (Henry of Huntingdon has him killed in the 584 expedition, as below.)

The reach of Ceawlin's power is unclear, but the regnal record of a seven- or seventeen-year rule implies that his enlarged kingdom only came into existence in the 570s or early 580s. In 584 he is stated as fighting at 'Fethan Leag' (probably Stoke Lyne in Oxfordshire), where his ally Cutha was killed; he took countless towns and loot, but returned in anger to his own country. This enigmatic statement would imply some sort of reverse, probably at the hands of the British, and an inability to hold onto territory; the geographical location would make a conflict over the northern Cotswolds likelier than one modern suggestion that this is a reverse suffered by the invaders at British hands at Tintern in the Wye valley. This may have cost Ceawlin the chance to maintain his power over recent conquests.

In 591 the *Chronicle* states that Ceol, Ceawlin's successor and later identified in the genealogies as his nephew, commenced his reign. It is not clear if this was by agreement with Ceawlin as his co-ruler or was the commencement of the rebellion that followed. If Ceol was the son of Cutha, he may have claimed his father's old lands around the upper Thames. The following year there was 'great slaughter' at 'Woden's Barrow', identified as 'Adam's Grave' at Alton Priors in northern Wiltshire, and Ceawlin was driven out of his kingdom. This was probably a result of civil war rather than a British attack, and any revolt was presumably led by the beneficiary, Ceol. The ousted ruler died, possibly violently and with an unknown Cwichelm and Creoda as stated by the Chronicle ('A' and 'E' versions), in 593; he was probably at least in his fifties if he had been fighting since 556. His evident abilities as a war-leader had established the West Saxon kingdom temporarily as the greatest power in southern England, and had gained control over areas which his successors were not to regain for three centuries. His ambitions may well have overreached his resources.

CEOL (591 (?) – 597 (?)) Successor and probably nephew of Ceawlin, who is recorded in the *Chronicle* as coming to the throne in 591; the *Chronicle*'s reference to his son Cynegils makes Ceol's father Cutha, presumably the Cutha/Cuthwulf, Cewalin's military ally, who died in 584.

The 'A' version of the *Chronicle* gives Ceol a five-year reign, the Canterbury version (where he is called 'Ceolric') six; the uncertainty is probably due to whether his reign was reckoned from his accession (as co-king or rebel?), or from Ceawlin's expulsion. The rebellion of 592 which he led saw Ceawlin defeated amidst great slaughter at 'Woden's Barrow', probably near Alton Priors in North Wiltshire, and driven out of his kingdom. It is unclear if Ceol was initially appointed as his uncle's co-ruler by mutual agreement or by seizure of power in a province, and it is presumed that Ceol led the coalition of rebel West Saxon princes and/or nobles which evicted his predecessor. Was his power-base the region where Cutha had operated around 570, the upper Thames valley?

The crisis of 592 mentioned above saw the end of his kingdom as a major power, as the next *bretwalda* was not Ceol but Aethelbert of Kent. Ceol appears to have been a less successful ruler than his predecessor, with no battles recorded for his reign, and had probably lost control of Ceawlin's large army of subject allies; his reign is recorded as lasting for six years, probably to 597. His death is not recorded, which may mean that he was deposed by his successor Ceolwulf – another nephew of Ceawlin, either Ceol's brother (and son of the mysterious 'Cutha') or his cousin.

CEOLWULF (*c.* 597–611) The successor of Ceol as king of the West Saxons. His dates are unclear; he succeeded Ceol as (sole?) king six years after the latter's accession, i.e. in 597, but if he reigned for seventeen years until his death in 611, this would mean that he was already co-ruler with royal rank from around 594. He was the son of Cutha, but it is not certain that he was Ceol's brother or his cousin. If Cutha was the semi-independent ruler of a West Saxon 'state' based around the upper Thames valley incorporated in Ceawlin's kingdom, i.e. Ceawlin's junior ally, Ceol or Ceolwulf may have inherited this kingdom; possibly Ceolwulf's 'accession' seventeen years before his death was when he took over this region as sub-king to Ceol.

In any case, it is clear that the West Saxon state was far less powerful than it had been under Ceawlin, with no more fighting against the Severn valley British. Given the multiplicity of co-rulers in the early to mid-seventh century and the confusing genealogy recorded for the extensive dynasty, a degree of 'devolution' among sub-kings and a weak central command by a senior ruler is probable. The 'E' version of the *Chronicle* has him fighting continually against Angles (whether in East Anglia or Mercia), British and, more oddly, Picts and Scots/Irish; if this is an accurate reflection of his activities, it would suggest some involvement in northern Britain which was not contiguous with his own territory. Did he send troops to aid allies in Northumbria, most obviously Aethelfrith, whose Bernician dynasty is supposed, in the regnal lists, to be related to the West Saxon dynasty? More logically, Ceolwulf seems to have fought against the South Saxons in 607. He died in or around 611 and was succeeded by Cynegils, probably his brother Ceol's son.

ESSEX

AESCWINE (Mid-sixth century?) An early king of the East Saxons, only recorded by Henry of Huntingdon in the twelfth century, active around 540. Henry calls him 'Erchenwin', son of Offa; the latter might account for the use of that name for an early eighth-century king of Essex. The absence of pre-1066 Anglo-Saxon references to him does not rule out the possibility of his existence, given that the

East Saxon kingdom was not of major importance to later writers. It is unclear if the Kentish nature of Aescwine's name means that he was a relative of his near-contemporary Aesc.

He was succeeded by Sledda, supposedly his son (according to Henry), but not with an alliteratively similar name as would be more usual.

SLEDDA (Late 580s (?) – *c.* 600) Probably the son of King Aescwine, he is said by one source to have acceded in 587. He ruled a reasonably large kingdom, incorporating both the lands west of London (the Middle Saxons) and their 'South District' (Surrey) across the Thames, but was politically eclipsed by his powerful neighbour, Aethelbert of Kent, whose sister, Ricula, he married. As Aethelbert was accounted the most powerful ruler in the south *c.* 600, with vassal kings, Sledda was probably the most senior of these and his (early?) death left his son Saebert under his uncle's influence. He was dead by 604.

SAEBERT (*c.* 600–616) Son of King Sledda and Ricula, sister of Aethelbert of Kent. He probably succeeded his father around 600, and like him was a client of his uncle; any control which the East Saxons had exercised west of London over the disparate settlements of the lower Thames valley was eclipsed by Kentish power. It was Aethelbert's influence that led him to convert to Christianity. In 604, a see, the second in Anglo-Saxon England, was duly set up at Essex's principal town, London, with Justus as bishop. Saebert died in 616, around the time of his uncle's death, and his three sons (Seaxred, Seaxbald and Saeward) returned to paganism.

EAST ANGLIA

WUFFA (Mid-sixth century) Traditionally the dynastic founder of the ruling house, the Wuffingas, and son of Wehha. The grandfather of King Raedwald, who died in the 620s, his date is too late for him to have been involved in the first, fifth-century Germanic settlements of East Anglia. (Historians now disagree how violent and military-led this was; possibly most settlement was relatively unopposed, or else the records of warfare have been lost.) We can only guess that from the local nomenclature, which becomes entirely Germanic in this period, the smaller-scale groupings of the 'North Folk' and 'South Folk' were united into one kingdom by Wuffa and/or his contemporaries. The later centre of royal power was in Suffolk, around Rendlesham – was this the family's original home area? Assuming that he called his son Tytila after the Gothic military hero of the 540s, he presumably had Continental contacts (trading or military?) and was aware of the wars in Italy and wished to name his son after their Germanic war-leader.

TYTILA (*fl.* late sixth century) A very obscure ruler, only known from the genealogies as the father of the *bretwalda* Raedwald. Named after the great Gothic hero who was fighting Emperor Justinian's generals in Italy in 541–52, suggesting an East Anglian awareness of, and inspiration from, Continental Germanic events – and that he was born after 541. Henry of Huntingdon testifies to his bravery.

RAEDWALD (*c.* 595 – 625 (?)) The most obscure of those rulers reckoned *bretwalda* by Bede and the *Chronicle*. His success suggests that he was a man of charisma, energy and ability. The dynasty of the Wuffingas is traced back to the eponymous Wuffa, his grandfather; Raedwald, son of Tytila (a sixth-century Gothic hero's name), was probably the first king to extend the dynasty's power beyond the isolated settlements of the 'North Folk' and 'South Folk' in the East Anglian peninsula. Their pre-620s history is not recorded and is usually assumed to have been largely peaceful. This may be inaccurate, but the amount of sixth-century Germanic archaeological finds in East Anglia show that the area was settled early and relatively thickly; the good agricultural land would have added to prosperity. Raedwald, a pagan, so disapproved of by Bede, probably extended his control over the settlements in the Fenland around 600–10 as Mercia was not yet a military power, and a confrontation with Northumbria over Lindsey would explain how he came into conflict with Aethelfrith. He gave sanctuary to Edwin, exiled prince of Deira, after he had to leave Mercia and in 617 invaded Northumbria on his behalf. Aethelfrith, victor over Angles, Britons and Dal Riadans, and probably undefeated for twenty years, was killed in battle on the River Idle and Edwin was installed as king of Northumbria.

The fact that Raedwald was able to defeat the Northumbrian 'war-machine' in 617 is testimony to his military ability and the size of the army he was able to muster. The death of the most powerful ruler in south-east England, Aethelbert of Kent, in *c.* 616/17, led to Kent's eclipse, and if his rank as *bretwalda* implies any formal recognition by contemporaries as overlord it would have followed this event. He probably took over Lindsey, and as Edwin's patron was in a strong position across the north. He exiled his second son Sigebert (a Frankish name, testifying to overseas links) who had become a Christian, not definitively for that reason.

He died some time around 625, probably after a reign of several decades given the way he had built up his kingdom's power, and was succeeded by his elder son Eorpwald. It is possible that Raedwald was the unknown king buried in the ship-burial found at Sutton Hoo, near a royal manor, as the amount of treasure there (some of it foreign) would indicate a powerful and wealthy ruler.

MERCIA

ICEL The eponymous ancestor of the Icelingas, ruling dynasty of the Mercians, and allegedly the first of his line to rule in England. As he was the grandfather of the first king to unite Mercia, Creoda, *c.* 589, that would place him in the first half of the sixth century. Icel, if he was not invented or was only appropriated as a heroic 'founder' for the ruling dynasty, was presumably a minor chieftain of noble blood. The later genealogies linked him to the legendary fifth-century continental 'king' Offa, after whom the eighth-century king was named, and made him the son of Eomer (a name taken by the Mercian scholar J. R. R. Tolkien for his king of the Anglo-Saxon-like people of the Rohirrim, also living in a 'Mark'). It is possible that the settlement of Ickleton in Hertfordshire took its name from Icel, as does nearby Knebworth from his son (in the *Anglo-Saxon Chronicle*'s Mercian genealogy, at the 626 entry) 'Cnebba', but this is only a guess.

CREODA (*fl.* 590s) The first king of Mercia; son of Cynewald, son of Cnebba, son of Icel, first of the dynasty in England. (The Mercian genealogy is given by the *Anglo-Saxon Chronicle* under the entry for 626.) The extensive nature of Anglian settlement across the eastern Midlands in the sixth century and the existence of many separate 'peoples' in the seventh suggest that the Anglian advance from the Fens was a piecemeal matter. The eventually dominant Icelingas may have suppressed records of their rivals, but it is assumed that those few 'peoples' named after an individual assumed the appellation from a war-leader. The name 'Mercia' means 'Mark' or 'borderlands', and logically the requirements of anti-British warfare on this frontier led to some warlord – probably Creoda – assuming authority as leader of a coalition of minor kingdoms. The probable date for this is the 580s, with some putting the 'accession' of Creoda (formal assumption of leadership of a coalition?) as *c.* 589.

The 'original land of the Mercians' specified by the Tribal Hideage (later seventh century?) is apparently based around Northamptonshire, Leicestershire and eastern Staffordshire; areas of Shropshire (the 'Wreocanseate'), the Arrow valley in Warwickshire (the 'Arowsaete'), northern and eastern Worcestershire (the 'Westerne'), the Peaks area in Derbyshire ('Pecsaete'), northern Oxfordshire (the 'Faerpingas'), Hertfordshire (the 'Hicce' around Hitchin) and southern Lincolnshire (the Fenland 'Gyrwe') are assessed for tax as separate regions. This central area was presumably the nucleus of the kingdom, and the centre of the dynasty's power by *c.* 600. The *Chronicle* gives Creoda's date of death as 593; it is assumed that his son Pybba, father of the first great Mercian king, Penda, succeeded him.

PYBBA (*fl.* 600?) Only known from the Mercian genealogies, Pybba was apparently the second king of the united kingdom, son and successor of the 'founder' Creoda. If the usual date for Creoda, c. 585-90, is accurate and Pybba's son Penda was born around 605 (not 575), he would have reigned around 600. By 616/17 Ceorl was ruling; it would appear likely that Pybba died relatively young, leaving an under-age or untried heir who was superseded by a more experienced war-leader. Pybba also had at least two, if not three, other sons according to the genealogies.

CEORL (*fl.* 610-625) An obscure king of the Mercians in the early seventh century, not in the recorded dynastic descent of the Icelingas. His predecessor was probably Pybba, father of Penda; the 'central' kingship of Mercia as a coherent state seems to have been created in the 580s by Creoda and it is not clear if Ceorl was a usurping sub-king who took power on Pybba's death, or if he was chosen as king as a proved warrior, unlike Pybba's young sons. According to Bede he was the king who gave refuge to the exiled Deiran prince Edwin, enemy of Aethelfrith of Northumbria, c. 616. Presumably the two men formed an anti-Northumbrian alliance against the threat posed by Aethelfrith, with Edwin intended as a Mercian candidate for the throne of Deira, as Edwin married Ceorl's daughter Cwenburh. But within a year or so, Aethelfrith compelled Ceorl to expel his son-in-law. It was Raedwald of East Anglia who aided Edwin in killing Aethelfrith and installing him in Northumbria in c. 617, and Edwin's accession would have ensured better relations with Mercia. Ceorl's date of death is unknown, as the length of his successor Penda's reign is disputed; the most probable version gives Penda a thirty-year reign from 625/6.

NORTHUMBRIA

DEIRA

AELLE (560s (?) – c. 600 (?)) Ruler of the Anglian kingdom of Deira in the last third of the sixth century, traditionally for thirty years. The *Anglo-Saxon Chronicle* puts his accession at 560, and has him succeed (anachronistically) to rule of 'Northumbria' – which did not yet exist – on the death of Ida of Bernicia. Possibly this is due to a tradition that he was the most powerful Anglian ruler in the region. Aelle was probably the son of 'Yffe' (Wuffa?), and a descendant of the fifth-century Soemil who first established the kingdom (the archaeological record agrees with the dating); the *Chronicle* gives his pedigree from Woden in the '560' entry, suggesting that his or his family's 'official' genealogy was of interest to, and recorded by, the West Saxons (though not necessarily in the sixth century). The fact that the distant West Saxons bothered with such an obscure ruler, while ignoring the closer rulers of Mercia and East

Anglia, implies that his dynasty were their allies – though not necessarily in Aelle's own time. The kingdom was centred on the settlements at the mouth of the Humber. Aelle was stated as succeeding in 560, and conquered the British kingdom of York to secure control of lowland Yorkshire (traditionally *c.* 580). His kingdom was wealthy enough to export slave-boys as far as Rome, where Pope Gregory the Great saw them in the slave-market ('not Angles but Angels') and resolved to convert their compatriots to Christianity.

Deira was to lose out to its aggressive northern rival Bernicia, which seems to have borne the brunt of contemporary Anglian/British warfare. The father of the later Northumbrian ruler Edwin, Aelle died either around 588 (as the 'A' version of the *Anglo-Saxon Chronicle* has it) or a decade or so later (as Bede has him still alive when St Augustine landed in 596/7). One tradition has it that he was killed by his Bernician rival Aethelfrith.

AETHELRIC (ETHELRIC) (590s – 604) The elder son and successor of Aelle, he came to the throne in the mid to late 590s, when his kingdom was being militarily eclipsed by its northern rival Bernicia under Aethelfrith. The threat from Rheged to both states was primarily aimed at Bernicia, which fought them off. According to the twelfth-century story told in William of Malmesbury, Aethelric – the king of Deira, or else his namesake in Bernicia – was an old as well as unfortunate ruler. This is likely to be inaccurate unless he was much older than his brother Edwin, who was only born *c.* 585; but he was certainly unfortunate. His reign was estimated at five years by the *Anglo-Saxon Chronicle*, 'A' version, and ended with the extinction of Deiran independence. The destruction of Rheged's military power at Catraeth by Aethelfrith of Bernicia in *c.* 600 doomed Deira as well as the Pennine British kingdoms, and within a few years Aethelfrith overran Deira and killed Aethelric.

BERNICIA

The traditional regnal genealogy of Bernicia gives the following lengths of reigns:

Ida (founder)	12
Glappa	1
Adda	8
Aethelric	4
Theodric	7
Frithuwold	6
Hussa	7
Aethelfrith	24

As will be explored below, the 'safest' dates are *c.* 547 for Ida's arrival in Bernicia and 592/3 for Aethelfrith's accession, the latter being twelve years before he took over Deira in *c.* 604.

IDA (*c.* 547 – (?)) Traditionally the first king of Bernicia, who landed on the Northumberland coast and founded the kingdom at a date ascribed by Bede and the *Chronicle* to 547. The date was reached by adding up the lengths of Bernician kings' reigns, which may have ignored periods of co-rulership and thus been placed too early. It is possible that the major plague recorded for Britain in 547/9, and dateable from Irish sources, helped to weaken resistance and gave him a chance to seize defensible fortresses. His grandfather Oesa is supposed to have been the first of the dynasty to live in Britain, logically in the Anglian settlements on the Humber. The great plague would have been a logical time for an ambitious warlord to seize an easily-defendable coastal fortress from the weakened local British.

Ida supposedly took the local fortress on Bamburgh rock (Din Guairi) and set up his residence there; it became the principal stronghold of his dynasty. The *Chronicle* makes much of his fortifying the place, as if this was his principal achievement in holding onto his new lands. The name of the kingdom came from that of the British kingdom which it superseded, Bryniach. In archaeological terms, the major area of Germanic settlement in the sixth-century North was around the Humber, and Ida may have come from there as an adventurer keen to carve out his own territory; Bernicia seems to have been restricted to a few embattled settlements on the coast for decades. His father Eoppa may be connected to the 'Ebissa' remembered in legend as a fifth-century Germanic warlord operating in the north-east. Ida died after a twelve-year reign, which would 'officially' make it 559 but was probably in the 560s. The West Saxon *Anglo-Saxon Chronicle* puts his death at 560, at the same time as their King Cynric died. Ida was not succeeded immediately by any of his (six or twelve?) sons, suggesting that they were under-age; Glappa was the next king.

GLAPPA (BERNICIA) (560s (?)) An obscure early king only known from the king-lists, traditionally known as the successor of the dynastic founder, Ida. Not listed as one of Ida's sons, he succeeded him after his twelve-year rule – which, if the *Chronicle*'s date for Ida's landing is correct, would put it at 559. (Dates this early can only be approximate.) It is possible that although Ida had a multitude of sons, none were adult or militarily experienced enough to lead in the fierce warfare with the local British of Bryniach, and that Glappa was an older kinsman or allied war-band commander who took control by agreement or usurpation. He either reigned for one year or five, which may mean that after a year he had to share power with his eventual successor, Ida's son (?), Adda. He probably died in the later 560s.

ADDA (570s (?)) Eldest son of Ida, the founder of the dynasty of Bernicia. Traditionally dated as ruling for seven years, though not in immediate succession to his father. He succeeded Glappa, apparently not a brother – which may suggest that Adda was under-age or untried in battle when his father died and was superseded by a relative. Whether he took power by agreement on Glappa's death or seized it once he was old enough is unknown. Adda probably reigned in the 570s; he was possibly the victor of the battle of Caer Greu over Peredur, British king of York.

AETHELRIC One list places him as the next king after Adda; but this is at odds with the statement in the *Chronicon ex chronicis* that he was the Bernician ruler who expelled his namesake Aethelric of Deira. The latter ruled after Aelle, who lived until at least 588 and possibly 597. This version has Aethelric ruling for five years in Deira, but this may be a mistake for his namesake's length of reign.

THEODRIC (Mid- to late 570s (?)) Traditionally thought to have ruled for seven years, after either Adda or Aethelric. Possibly called after the great Gothic king of Italy who ruled from 493 to 526; if so, this would suggest ambitious pretensions by his father (Ida?). According to the ninth-century Welsh *Historia Brittonum*, Theodric was the target of a coalition of North British princes led by Urien of Rheged (Lancashire and Cumbria?), greatest warlord of the region, and was able to respond vigorously, suggesting that he ruled a reasonably-sized kingdom with a sizeable and competent army.

FRITHUWULF (570s or early 580s (?)) One of the very obscure rulers of Bernicia in the regnal lists for the later sixth century, who is not recorded as being a member of Ida's dynasty. He is usually given a seven-year reign and is placed after Ida's son Adda, who appears to have ruled in the 570s. Bede calls him king of Bernicia at the time of St Augustine's landing in 597, but by that time Aethelfrith was ruling; Bede may have been confused over which Christian mission to Kent was meant in his sources, as *c.* 581 a Frankish bishop arrived with a princess who married King Aethelbert. Alternatively, Frithuwold may have been the military leader of Bernicia in a 'power-vacuum' after Adda's death, handing it over to, or being deposed by, a rival from Ida's line, and survived into the 590s as a semi-autonomous local warlord.

HUSSA (580s (?)) One of the very obscure Bernician kings of the later sixth century, not placed in the genealogies as a son of Ida. This presumably indicates that he was a senior warlord of the hard-pressed coastal kingdom who assumed leadership by agreement or by a coup against the 'legitimate' line. Alternatively, he may have ruled with and eclipsed one of Ida's sons at a time when the kingdom was divided. His seven-year reign is usually placed before that of Ida's son Theodric, who ruled for seven years and preceded Aethelfrith's father Aethelric. Aethelric (probably) ruled for around seven years, Aethelfrith succeeding him in *c.* 593. One version has Hussa as Aethelfrith's immediate predecessor, in which case he, not Aethelric, fought Owain of Rheged in the early 590s. His reign is usually assigned to the late 570s to early 580s. Hussa's son, Hering, was recorded as leading an army against the British in 603; the family had enough military and landed power to remain a source of military leadership under the rule of Aethelfrith.

AETHELRIC (Alternative dating) (570s or *c.* 587 – *c.* 593) The father of Aethelfrith of Bernicia, and son of the founder, Ida. He is alternately mentioned as ruling in the 570s, or immediately before his son, i.e. from the mid to late 580s. The dates given in the *Anglo-Saxon Chronicle* for the royal reigns from Ida's arrival in the North (*c.* 547) to Aethelfrith are at variance with other accounts, and several kings may have reigned at once to account for the 'overlap' in the tally of years reigned in this period. Aethelric is supposed to have reigned for six or seven years, and he may thus have been co-ruler for several years with Theodric, king in the mid-580s, probably an older brother whose realm was severely threatened by British counter-attack under Urien of Rheged. In 589, Urien was assassinated by a British rival during his siege of Anglian-held Lindisfarne island, which broke up the coalition; it is not clear which Bernician king was ruling at the time.

The extreme pressure which Bernicia was under from Urien and his son Owain probably continued into Aethelric's reign. If he, rather than his namesake of Deira, was the elderly and unfortunate ruler referred to by William of Malmesbury, this would fit in with the contemporary British poet Taliesin's panegyrics to Owain's successes against Bernicia. Owain's principal Anglian enemy was 'Fflamddwyn', 'the Flame-Bearer'; if this was Aethelric he must have been an active and feared foe. This Anglian ruler was killed in battle by Owain around 593. Assuming that he was under-age in the late 550s, as he was not a contender for the kingship for another thirty years, but had an adult son in *c.* 593, he was probably in his forties or early fifties.

AETHELFRITH (Bernicia, *c.* 593–617; Northumbria, 604? – 617) Successor of either Hussa or Aethelric, Aethelfrith was the dynamic warlord who created the kingdom of Northumbria in the decades around 600, uniting Bernicia and Deira and incorporating portions of the defeated British kingdoms of northern Britain. He was the son of Aethelric, ruler of Bernicia (?) in the early 590s and a younger son of the dynastic founder Ida; he was probably born in the late 560s or early 570s. Aethelfrith succeeded his father (?) in *c.* 593, at a time of danger for the Anglian people from Owain of Rheged. He soon managed to turn Bernicia's fortunes around

– against a much more experienced enemy – and inflicted a decisive defeat on Rheged and its ally Mynydog of Din Eidyn (Edinburgh) at Catraeth *c.* 595. The site of the battle has been debated but was probably Catterick; the British had assembled a force of experienced mercenaries recruited from all over the North. Much of the central and northern Pennines area was either overrun by Bernicia or reduced to vassalage. Bernicia now became the dominant power of northern Britain.

Aethelfrith was to win the sobriquets of 'the Ferocious' and 'the Crafty', suggesting a military reputation for a mixture of direct aggression and subtle tactics. The threat which his power posed caused King Aedan mac Gabhran of Dal Riada to bring an army southwards from Argyll to challenge him, *c.* 603. The battle between Aethelfrith and a Dalriadan-British coalition at 'Degsastan' (Dawston, at Liddlesdale [?]) saw heavy losses for both sides; Aethelfrith claimed the victory and Dal Riada did not challenge him again.

In 604, Aethelfrith overran his weaker southern neighbour Deira, killing King Aethelric and driving his brother Edwin into exile in Gwynedd. This victory provided the crucial cement for the newly dominant power among the northern Angles, permanently united in one state stretching from the Forth to the Tweed; those British rulers who survived (e.g. in Rheged and Elmet) were vassals. Aethelfrith had two wives – Bebba (after whom Bamburgh was named), mother of his eldest son, Eanfrith, and Acha (mother of Oswald and Oswy), daughter of King Aelle of Deira and possibly acquired as a means of legitimising his rule there.

The Anglian state now threatened to cut off the Britons of Gwynedd from their kinsmen in the north, quite apart from tension arising from the presence in Gwynedd of Edwin. Probably in 613 to 616, Aethelfrith advanced west to the Dee and fought a major battle with King Selyf ap Cynan at Chester, 'Legacaestir', as related by Bede. The victory, where Selyf was killed, consolidated control of Cheshire. Before the battle, Aethelfrith massacred a large number of monks (2,100 according to Bede) from the nearby British monastery of Bangor-on-Dee who had gathered near the battlefield to pray; Bede relates that the king said that even if they were non-combatants, they were praying for his foes, so deserved a similar fate. Edwin now fled to the court of Ceorl of Mercia, who married him to his daughter but was intimidated by Aethelfrith into expelling him. He went on to Raedwald of East Anglia, the main military power in southern Britain, who refused a bribe to murder him. Raedwald took up Edwin's cause and marched north in 617; the two states were probably contending for control of Lindsey. The East Anglians withstood Aethelfrith's attack on the River Idle near Doncaster, and he was killed. Raedwald then assisted Edwin's return to York to take over all of Northumbria; Aethelfrith's sons fled to Dal Riada. But despite Aethelfrith's defeat and death his state survived, soon regaining military pre-eminence in the north, and ultimately his heirs, not Edwin's, were to rule it. Notably, he was the first northern Anglian king to be mentioned by Bede, who testifies to his bravery and energy and compares him to Saul (i.e. as creator of the kingdom inherited by 'David', namely Edwin).

LINDSEY

CRITTA/CREODA (Early seventh century (?)) The first king of the royal line of Lindsey according to the eighth-century genealogy; the number of generations involved would make it probable that he reigned in the later sixth century. The kingdom, settled early according to the archaeological evidence and well-populated by *c.* 600, was not yet threatened by its larger neighbours, Northumbria (united *c.* 604) to the north and Mercia (united *c.* 590?) to north and west, and was probably a substantial and independent realm in this period. (The names of some kings indicate a mixture of British and Anglian culture.) Critta may have been the first to unite scattered settlements in a new 'state' under himself as war-leader, logically with the local (ex-Roman) town, Lincoln, as his main residence. Critta's name may indicate that he was actually Creoda, first king of Mercia (q.v.), *fl.* 590. In that case placing him at the head of the Lindsey genealogy may indicate that he was the ancestor of its kings, a junior branch of the Icelingas. Alternatively, by the eighth century, the Lindsey royal family wished to be seen as connected to Mercia, their current overlords, rather than to their early to mid-seventh-century overlords Northumbria, expressing this in genealogical terms.

3

c. 620 to c. 655

KENT

EADBALD (616/17 – 640) Son of Aethelbert, probably by his Frankish wife Bertha, most likely born c. 582–5. He succeeded his father on 24 February 616 (or possibly 617/18), and married his father's widow in defiance of canon law. It may have been to continue political alliance with Francia. He reversed his father's favour to the Church by returning to paganism. The move endangered the future of the Roman Church mission, but Eadbald decided to revert to Christianity; Bede attributes it to his being impressed by the signs of a supernatural scourging inflicted on Archbishop Laurentius, who had been contemplating abandoning his post. If the cleric who baptised Eadbald was Laurentius, this return to Christianity occurred by 619.

Eadbald showed his continuation of his father's international profile and enabled the influence of Canterbury to spread into other English kingdoms. His sister Aethelburh's marriage to Edwin of Northumbria in c. 625 led to the mission of Paulinus, but the extending prestige of Canterbury failed to have secular benefits for the dynasty. Eadbald never attained his father's influence despite the Northumbrian alliance, or was powerful enough to be considered Bretwalda. He failed or did not attempt to save the Church mission in the neighbouring East Saxon kingdom, his father's vassal – a possible sign of military weakness. Following the renunciation of his first wife, his second wife Emma/Ymme was of noble or royal Frankish birth. Eadbald's elder son, Eormenred, died before him; when he died on 20 January 640, probably in his fifties, his second son, Eorconbert, succeeded.

EORCENBERT (640–664) He was the second son of Eadbald of Kent, either by his stepmother or by his second wife, Emma of Francia; the latter would make him born c. 620–25. His older brother Eormenred having died in Eadbald's lifetime, Eorcenbert was chosen king on

20 January 640, excluding his infant nephews. He was raised as a Christian, and on his accession he ordered the destruction of the remaining pagan idols in Kent. He married a fervent Christian, Seaxburgh, a daughter of the evangelizing King Anna of the East Angles, who established a nunnery at Minster in Sheppey during his reign, and in 653 appointed the first native-born Archbishop of Canterbury (Frithuwine/'Deusdedit').

It was the difference between Eorcenbert's date for celebrating Lent in the Roman calendar which the church of Canterbury followed and that of the Iona-backed 'Celtic Church' in Northumbria which helped to lead to the Synod of Whitby. Eorcenbert dispatched Deusdedit to the synod to argue that the Roman methodology should prevail, and this duly won out. Eorcenbert may have been the principal mover in marrying off his daughter Eormenhild to Mercia's new king Wulfhere, c. 658–60; Wulfhere followed his lead as a Christian king but was to use the alliance to interfere in Kent later.

Eorcenbert died on 14 July 664, probably in the plague after the Synod of Whitby, which also claimed Deusdedit that day; his son Egbert, probably adult, succeeded him.

WESSEX

CYNEGILS (611 (?) – 643 (?)) The successor, though not necessarily the son, of Ceolwulf; he probably came to the throne around 611. His reign is set at thirty-one years in the West Saxon regnal list (and the 'A' version of the *Chronicle*), as is that of his successor Cenwalh which ended in 673/4. The *Chronicle* makes him son of (King) Ceol, son of Cutha, son of Cynric; though later, under the 676 entry for King Centwine, it makes Cynegils the son of Ceolwulf. The West Saxon regnal genealogical list makes him Ceolwulf's nephew. His reign marked the resumption of the expansion halted in 592, against the British if not the English, and in 614 he and his co-ruler (brother or son?) Cwichelm fought successfully against the British at 'Beandun'. If this is Bindon near Wareham, it would have marked the conquest of the archaeologically-attested area of British settlement around Cranborne Chase, possibly the eastern part of the kingdom of Dumnonia; if it is Bindon near Seaton, it would have marked the annexation of western Dorset and/or eastern Devon to the River Axe. Cynegils had less success against the Anglian powers, as Cwichelm's attempt to murder Edwin of Northumbria in 626 led to the deaths of assorted Wessex sub-kings in a retaliatory invasion, and in 628 the weakened Cynegils and Cwichelm were defeated by Penda of Mercia at Cirencester. This may have led to the loss of the Cotswolds, annexed by Ceawlin in 577, and the emergence of the ferocious Penda halted any West Saxon expansion northwards. Cynegils' main residence may have been in the upper Thames valley, where the new Christian bishopric (usually found near a court) was to be founded; if so, Mercian aggression was especially dangerous.

In 635, Pope Honorius dispatched a group of missionaries to Wessex, independently of the Church in Canterbury. Cynegils was soon baptised by Birinus, apparently in the presence of the evangelizing Christian king, (St) Oswald of Northumbria, who was a West Saxon ally. Oswald had come to Cynegils' court to marry his daughter Cyneburh as part of an anti-Mercian alliance, and may have insisted on his father-in-law's conversion. Birinus became the first bishop of the West Saxons, based at Dorchester-on-Thames. Cynegils' son Cenwalh, Cwichelm and the latter's successor did not convert yet. He died in 643 and was succeeded by Cenwalh; it is not clear if Cwichelm, presumably his senior co-ruler in the 620s, given his prominence in campaigns, was originally intended as his heir. The choice of king seems to have been down to the senior nobles and/or sub-kings, and to have favoured the most able or best-supported adult prince of the royal house ('atheling') – which would imply Cwichelm as the logical next king. But Cwichelm had apparently died around 636, soon after Birinus' arrival; did Cenwalh succeed him as the heir to Wessex?

CENWALH (643 – 644 (?), 648 (?) – 672/4 (?)) Son and successor of Cynegils; he probably came to the throne around 643 as his reign is stated in the *Chronicle* as lasting for thirty-one years to 673/4. The kingdom of the West Saxons seems to have consisted of a senior king as overlord of a number of sub-kings in the seventh century, and in particular Cynegils' kinsman Cwichelm (king of northern Wiltshire, d. *c.* 636) and his son Cuthred had a substantial domain and military strength. Cynegils had refrained from converting to Christianity in *c.* 636 with his father and Cwichelm. Cenwalh's main problem was the threat posed by his most powerful neighbour, Penda of Mercia, and at some point he had married Penda's sister (in an abortive attempt at alliance?). After his accession he risked alienating his brother-in-law by repudiating her in favour of another wife, and around 645 Penda invaded Wessex and drove him out of his kingdom. He took refuge in East Anglia, and Penda probably assumed some form of authority over Cuthred and other assorted sub-kings.

Cenwalh was now converted and baptised at the court of the determinedly Christian King Anna of the East Angles. He was able to return to Wessex after a three-year exile, *c.* 648, without immediate retaliation by Penda; Anna was to be Penda's next victim. Cuthred received a large domain of 3,000 'hides' on the Berkshire downs, logically as a 'pay-off' for accepting Cenwalh's return. On Bishop Birinus' death in 650 Cenwalh invited in a Frank, Agilbert, as the second bishop of the West Saxons, but grew frustrated with his failure to learn to speak English and duly set up a second, Saxon bishop called Wine, *c.* 660 as the first bishop of Winchester, his see comprising the south of the kingdom. Wine's new see reflected the rise in importance of the south of Wessex and of Winchester itself, possibly Cenwalh's main residence as Mercia threatened the Thames valley. Agilbert, angry at the appointment, left for Francia. The

Chronicle, however, inaccurately dates Wine's episcopate as only lasting to *c.* 663, whereas in fact he consecrated St Chad as bishop of Mercia in 665.

The date of the loss of the upper Thames valley is unclear, but may be connected to Wine's appointment in Winchester, *c.* 660. Within a year or two Wine also had fallen out with Cenwalh, and he left to acquire the bishopric of London; the vacant see of Winchester was eventually filled in 670 by Leutherius, nephew of Agilbert. In the meantime, Cenwalh had won a major victory over the British of Dumnonia at Penselwood near Wincanton in 658 and chased them as far as the River Parrett; this seems to have marked the conquest of Somerset and brought his kingdom to the Bristol Channel. A second battle at 'Posent's byrg', possibly Posbury in Devon, followed in 661, and Exeter and all of east-central Devon was probably taken over. St Boniface, son of new Saxon immigrants, was born at Crediton in the early 660s, but the scattered nature of mid to late seventh-century Saxon archaeological sites across Devon and the amount of British nomenclature suggests a substantial British presence, not mass slaughter. Cenwalh established the West Saxon state west of Selwood, a region soon to be in need of its own bishop, and the balance of power in the south-west shifted permanently against Dumnonia.

Cenwalh had no such success against Mercia, whether or not he hoped to use the extra resources of his western annexations for military efforts. In 652, he fought either against the Mercians or the British at Bradford-on-Avon, and in 661 Penda's son Wulfhere raided south at, or from, 'Ashdown' (probably the Berkshire Downs) into Hampshire. Wulfhere was able to hand over lordship of the Isle of Wight (settled by Jutes) to his godson Aethelwalh of the South Saxons. Wulfhere established the independence from Wessex of the 'Meonware' of the Meon valley. He was clearly building up Sussex as a rival power to Wessex in south-central England under his aegis, and it is not known how much authority Cenwalh was able to recover in this area. He certainly lost control of the upper Thames valley permanently, and from now on West Saxon power was centred in Hampshire.

He died in 672/4, probably in his fifties, and left a serious power vacuum. According to Bede, the sub-kings divided up Wessex between them and there was no central ruler for a decade; royal authority seems to have been granted initially (and uniquely) to Seaxburh, Cenwalh's widow and possibly the wife he had acquired in *c.* 644. She was later replaced by Aescwine, probably Cenwalh's first cousin.

ESSEX

SAEWARD (616 (?) – 620s) One of the three sons of King Saebert, who returned to paganism on their accession. Bishop Mellitus of London refused to allow them into St Paul's, presumably for attending pagan as well as

Christian religious services (to placate both Christian and pagan subjects?). He was expelled, and the kingdom reverted to paganism. It is not known which brother died when, but by the mid-620s Sigebert the Little, son of one of them, was king.

SEAXBALD (616 (?) – 620s) Brother and co-ruler of Saeward (q.v.).

SEAXRED (616 (?) – 620s) Brother and co-ruler of Saeward and Seaxbald (q.v.).

SIGEBERT THE LITTLE (620s – *c.* 650) The son of one of the three sons of Saebert – Seaxred, Seaxbald and Saeward. Presumably so-called from his size, he succeeded his father or uncle some time in the 620s and had a long but obscure reign. He died around 650 and was succeeded by a cousin, also Sigebert; his son Sigehere was to reign a decade later and may have been under-age at his death.

SIGEBERT THE GOOD (East Saxons, early 650s (?)) Son of Sigeferth, son of a younger brother of King Saebert. He succeeded his distant cousin Sigebert the Little around 650, and was converted to Christianity on a visit to Northumbria, where he was on good terms with Oswy. Sigebert resumed the conversion of the East Saxons, abandoned in 616 but now directed by Churchmen following the 'Celtic' rite in Northumbria, and brought in the Lindisfarne missionary (St) Cedd. Sigebert showed the practical pitfalls of taking Christian values too literally. His Christian desire to show forgiveness led to annoyance at the number of criminals who were escaping punishment, and a kinsman who had been excommunicated (for an illegal marriage) blamed the king for both occurrences and asassinated him. He was succeeded by his kinsman Swithhelm (possibly the murderer or a close connection), who initially returned to paganism but soon repented.

EAST ANGLIA

EORPWALD (*c.* 625 – 628 (?)) The son and successor of Raedwald, king of the East Angles and *bretwalda*, who succeeded him some time after the restoration of Edwin to Northumbria in 617. Raedwald, the greatest king of his people and its only *bretwalda*, probably extended his power to gain control of Lindsey and the land west of the Fens. Mercia had not yet become the major power in central England, but its ferocious new leader Penda took over power some time in the mid-620s, contemporary with Eorpwald's succession, and this would have posed a serious threat. The military leadership of a coalition of kings implied by the title of *bretwalda* passed to Edwin. This may reflect

Eorpwald's inferior quality as a leader to his father. His father had remained pagan, but he was converted to Christianity by his ally Edwin. Probably as a result of his conversion as stated by Bede, Eorpwald was murdered by a pagan called Ricbert. Ricbert then seized the throne and East Anglia returned to paganism (implying that Eorpwald had attempted to follow Edwin's lead and convert his people too) for three years before Sigebert's accession. The date can only be guessed at by working backwards from later events, but can be set approximately at 625–28.

RICGBERT (Late 620s (?)) The usurper who murdered King Eorpwald, elder son of Raedwald, at an unknown date before *c.* 632. His predecessor had been converted to Christianity under the influence of Edwin of Northumbria. Ricgbert, not known to have been a relative, took the throne; according to Bede the kingdom returned to paganism for three years, which we can assume to be the length of Ricgbert's reign. He does not specifically state that the murderer took the throne, but this is usually assumed. Eorpwald's Christian brother Sigebert was recalled to take the throne back some time around 632.

SIGEBERT (Early to mid-630s) The younger son of Raedwald and brother of Eorpwald, he was exiled in his father's lifetime and sought refuge in Francia. This was probably, but not definitely, due to his becoming a Christian; given his Frankish name, his mother may have been a Frank. He was able to return on the overthrow of a usurper (Ricgbert, his brother's murderer [?]) around 630 and set about the conversion of his people. He had more success than Eorpwald had done, and was sent a Frankish missonary bishop called Felix by Archbishop Honorius of Canterbury who set up his see and monastery at 'Dumnoc' (either Dunmow or the coastal town of Dunwich, later lost to the sea). The date can be approximated from the fact that Felix was bishop for seventeen years and his successor Thomas for five before the consecration of Bertgils/Boniface by Archbishop Honorius (d. September 653); Felix's arrival must have been at least twenty-two years before 653.

Sigebert also founded monastery schools to train the next generation of Christians. After a five-year reign he abdicated to enter a monastery, his kinsman Ecgric succeeding (*c.* 637 [?]). He was recalled by popular demand to lead the national army against the invading Penda of Mercia three years later, either as a saintly talisman who should win divine backing or as a man with more military experience. Refusing to use a sword as he had rejected violence and carrying a staff, he was killed in the East Anglian defeat that followed, along with Ecgric.

EGRIC (ECGRIC) (*c.* 639 – 641 (?)) A kinsman of Sigebert, he succeeded the latter on his abdication some time in the late 630s. He was presumably a Christian like his predecessor, and thus patron of Bishop Felix's conversion of his kingdom. The kingdom was under threat from the expanding overlordship of Penda, pagan king of Mercia, who was probably much Egric's superior in military skill and numbers. When Penda attacked East Anglia in *c.* 641 the people (i.e. the senior thegns in the army?) asked Sigebert to lead their forces, showing a lack of confidence in Egric as well as superstitious hope that the holy ex-king would bring them divine support. He did so, refusing to bear a sword as he had renounced violence; both he and Egric were killed. Their cousin Anna succeeded to the throne.

ANNA (641/2 (?) – 53 (?)) The eldest son of Eni, younger brother of East Anglia's greatest king, Raedwald. In or near 641/2, his cousin Sigebert, who had abdicated to enter a monastery, and their kinsman, the new king Egric, were killed in battle by Penda of Mercia. Anna succeeded, probably already a convert to Christianity under the influence of Sigebert and his new bishop, Felix. Penda did not press his advantage, and Anna was able to survive his attentions for a decade (possibly due to Mercia regarding Wessex as a greater military threat).

Anna continued Sigebert's favour to the Church and founded more schools and monasteries, but was more notable for his quartet of talented and determinedly Christian daughters, who proved major actors in Church patronage in coming decades and were all canonised. Their similar tastes and activities suggest early training at a missionary court by their father. Athelthryth/Etheldreda (St Audrey), the most famous, founded and led Ely nunnery after ending her marriage to Ecgfrith of Northumbria; Seaxburh married Earconbert of Kent, founded Minster-in-Sheppey, and then took over Ely as abbess; Aethelburh became abbess of Faremoutiers-en-Brie in Francia. The tradition of active Christian patronesses was duly inherited by the daughters of those that had children, making Anna's influence by proxy long-lasting through the seventh century.

Anna gave refuge to Cenwalh of the West Saxons when he was driven out of his kingdom by Penda in *c.* 644, persuading him to convert to Christianity. Whether or not his interference in protecting Penda's victim led to Mercian punishment, a second serious Mercian attack followed in *c.* 649; a major monastery was sacked and Anna was temporarily driven into exile. He was soon able to return, probably at the end of the campaigning season as Penda's larger army had to withdraw, but was killed in a third Mercian invasion around 625/3. Penda installed his younger brother Aethelhere as his vassal.

AETHELHERE (653 (?) – 65) The brother of Anna, king of East Anglia *c.* 641–53, younger son of Eni, the brother of King Raedwald. He succeeded Anna when the latter was killed in battle by Penda of Mercia, and was imposed as his vassal king. Nothing is recorded of his short reign, and he is usually written off as Penda's puppet. In 655, Aethelhere was among the thirty 'duces' (a term encompassing both the leaders of vassal states with kingly status and governors of provinces within a larger state) who accompanied Penda on his devastating invasion of Northumbria. This showdown with Penda's only serious surviving rival, Oswy, saw Deira ravaged in the latter's absence, but Oswy caught up Penda's army as it returned and defeated it in a major battle at the River 'Winwaed' (near Leeds?) on Sunday 15 November 655. The recent rain hampered Penda's army's manoevurability in mud and it was cut to pieces; many of the Mercians, among them Aethelhere, were drowned in the swollen river.

Aethelhere's younger brother, Aethelwold, succeeded him. Aethelhere is a possible candidate for the grandiose seventh-century ship-burial found at Sutton Hoo, near an important East Anglian royal manor, as his body was probably never recovered and there was no royal body at the site. Others argue that the sumptuous nature of the burial was hardly fitting for a mere vassal of Mercia.

MERCIA

PENDA (c. 626–655) The greatest of the early Mercian kings and probably the founder of its political unity and military greatness. He was unlucky in receiving a bad press as a pagan from Bede, whose Christian Northumbrian royal heroes were his foes. He was at least as powerful as the presumed *bretwalda* Oswy in 642–55, though he has been omitted from the list of such overlords in Bede's work and in the *Chronicle*. He was the son of Pybba and the grandson of Creoda, the founder of Mercia around the 580s; his predecessor was, however, Ceorl, not in the dynastic records. The 'kingship' in the early seventh century was more properly an over-kingship over many junior rulers and 'peoples', based on geographical districts, whose multiplicity is preserved in the Tribal Hideage. Penda may have been under-age or a minor sub-king when Pybba died and had been superseded by an older rival. Ceorl was reigning around 616–17 when Edwin of Deira took refuge at his court, but Penda first appears in 628 as (probable) victor of a battle over kings Cynegils and Cwichelm of the West Saxons at Cirencester. He need not have been 'over-king' of Mercia by this date, only the local king of the Cotswolds area (presumably annexed by Ceawlin of Wessex after his victory at Deorham in 577 and lost to Mercia since). A claim has been made that he and Pybba may have had estates on the Warwickshire Avon, around Pebworth, and that Penda emerged as a successful war-leader in this area. If so, the extension or confirmation of Mercian control of the Cotswolds would have served to win him adherents and a reputation as a warlord, before or after his assumption of the central kingship of Mercia.

One version of his chronology has Penda die in 655 after a fifty-year reign. This is impossible as Ceorl was the Mercian king in 616/17, though confusion may have arisen if the 'fifty years' was taken from the date of Pybba's death, when Penda assumed a local kingship. The 'A' manuscript of the *Chronicle* has him acceding aged fifty in 626, which is also unlikely given his vigorous campaigning into the 650s and the young age of his sons in 655. Alternatively and more likely, he died at the age of fifty after a thirty-year reign; this would make him a young warlord in the 620s and have him succeeding Ceorl in 625/6. Mercia was weak enough in 626 for Edwin to march across it unhindered to attack Wessex.

Penda was in control of Mercia by October 633 (or possibly 634), when he was the ally of his sister's husband Cadwallon of Gwynedd in a conclusive war with Edwin. Edwin was killed at Hatfield Chase near Doncaster, a site implying a Northumbrian/Mercian war over control of Lindsey. This crushed Northumbria and broke it up temporarily into its constituent parts, with Penda left dominating south of the Trent. Cadwallon was killed by the Bernician heir (St) Oswald a year later. Oswald revived Northumbrian power, but Penda remained unchecked until 642, although Oswald formed an alliance with Wessex and in *c.* 636 seemingly marched unchecked across Mercia to meet Cynegils of Wessex on the upper Thames. Penda's murder of Edwin's son Osfrith in the mid-late 630s was probably aimed at appeasing Oswald, and reassuring him that Mercia would not meddle with Deira. (Bede gives Penda a twenty-two-year reign, with mixed fortunes, from his defeat of Edwin, i.e. autumn 633 to autumn 655.) At some time he seems to have allowed his brother Eowa to become co-ruler, but it is not known if this was voluntarily (to secure a loyal deputy when he was campaigning far afield?), to satisfy the requirements of local custom for several co-rulers, or an imposition by Edwin or Oswald who sought to weaken his power. Nicholas Brooks has even suggested that Penda was temporarily deposed by Oswald – at least as senior ruler of Mercia – in Eowa's favour.

Penda's next major ally was again British – and Christian. This was Cyndylan, prince of Powys, which in the mid-seventh century included the upper Severn valley around Shrewsbury (one candidate for Powys' court of 'Pengwern', possibly the Wrekin). The Welsh *Canu Heledd*, now thought to be ninth-century at the earliest, has Penda and Cyndylan as close allies and the place-name evidence shows the Welsh still present in Shropshire. The complicated picture of Anglian/British relations in the 640s and 650s West Midlands may also include a British principality at Lichfield, ruled by Morfael, and the enigmatic name of Penda's 'son', Merewalh, later ruler of 'Magonsaetan' (Herefordshire and southern Shropshire). Later Welsh literature suggests Penda married Cyndylan's sister Heledd; this may be based on reality. The Welsh lament for Cyndylan attributed (erroneously?) to the contemporary poet Llywarch 'Hen' also implies that Cyndylan fought as an ally of Penda, and the Mercian/Powys alliance may explain why in 642 the next war with Oswald saw the Northumbrians marching into Shropshire. Penda routed them at a place which Bede calls Maserfelth (i.e. Oswestry) on 5 August, killing Oswald, who was apparently dismembered and strung up on a tree in a contemptuous pagan ritual riposte to his Christianity. The one major Mercian loss at the battle was Eowa. The British 'History' by Nennius dates Penda's 'ten-year' rule from the battle of 'Maes Cogwy', i.e. Maserfelth; this refers to his sole rule before he made Peada his co-king in 653.

From 642 to 655, Penda was the main military power in southern England. He was able to raid deep into Northumbria to humiliate Oswald's brother Oswy in c. 644, reaching as far north as Bamburgh, which he set afire (the wind put the flames out in time). This argues for both confidence and impressive logistics, even if his host moved fast and lived off the land and Oswy wisely shirked battle. He had married a sister off to Cenwalh, king of the West Saxons from 643, and when that king repudiated her for another woman in c. 645, Penda invaded Wessex and drove him into exile in East Anglia for three years. Probably in retaliation for East Anglian aid to Cenwalh, Penda then invaded that kingdom around 650 and drove Anna into exile; the latter was able to return, presumably when Penda went home, but was killed in a second Mercian attack around 653. His brother Aethelhere succeeded him as a Mercian vassal.

An uneasy treaty with Northumbria in 653 saw Penda's eldest son Peada, new king of the 'Middle Angles', marry Oswy's daughter Aelfflaed (Elfleda) and Oswy's son Alchfrith, sub-king of Deira, marry Penda's daughter Cyneburh. The peace did not last, though it is uncertain if Peada's conversion to Christianity and importation of Northumbrian missionaries infuriated his father on religious grounds, as treachery to the ancestral faith. Behind Bede's story of his widespread ravaging in Northumbria in the next few years – and refusal of vast amounts of gold to desist – it is evident that he did not feel safe until Oswy was destroyed. Another massive invasion of Northumbria in 655 involved thirty 'duces' including the ruler of the East Angles, plus troops from his Welsh allies, and penetrated as far as Bernicia again. Oswy's nephew Aethelwald of Deira joined the invaders despite Penda having killed his father, Oswald. Oswy avoided battle, but Penda could find enough supplies to avoid a precipitate retreat and eventually the two men came to terms. A treaty was agreed, probably with Oswy's son Egfrith as a hostage, as he was at the Mercian court at the time of the battle which followed, and Penda was returning south when hostilities resumed. Possibly encouraged by heavy rain to intercept the Mercians and prevent Penda getting away with his loot, Oswy attacked Penda at the River Winwaed (near Leeds [?]) on 15 November 655 and secured a crushing victory; Penda and Aethelhere were among the many casualties, with numerous men drowned in the swollen river. Mercia was left at Oswy's mercy, though he retained Peada as his sub-king of the Middle Angles for some months.

Penda was probably around fifty, and had had a remarkable career of success which was minimalised by his Christian detractors. He was unfortunate to be the last successful pagan warlord in England, the arch-foe of Bede's heroes, though his toleration of his eldest son's conversion and his Welsh Christian alliances show that he was not a militant foe of the new faith when this would conflict with political advantage. He laid the foundations for the domination of the southern English by Mercia in the later seventh century and the eighth century, his state only suffering a temporary eclipse in 655–58 and soon recovering under his second son, Wulfhere.

EOWA (? – 642) The brother of Penda of Mercia and son of King Pybba, an obscure figure overshadowed by his ferocious sibling. Their father seems to have been succeeded by Ceorl not his sons, probably due to their being young and inexperienced at the time (*c*. 600 [?]); Penda came to power in the mid-620s but may have been operating as a sub-ruler (in Warwickshire?) and building up his military backing for some years previously. There may have been a formal division of the kingdom; Eowa possibly ruled the north. Alternatively, it has been suggested that he was imposed as co-ruler on Mercia by their overlord Edwin of Northumbria in the late 620s or early 630s, before Mercia and Gwynedd's defeat of his kingdom gave Penda full political/military autonomy in 633/4, to weaken Penda's power. Otherwise, Eowa was imposed as co-king or senior ruler by Oswald in *c*. 634/5. Eowa was killed at the battle of Maserfelth (Oswestry) on 5 August 642, fighting for his brother against Oswald of Northumbria. Penda seems to have ended the co-kingship for some years, though his eldest son Peada was ruling the 'Middle Angles' by 653; Eowa's sons as recorded in the genealogies, Alweo and Osmod, were at most junior sub-kings. Ironically the two greatest kings of Mercia, Aethelbald and Offa, who ruled from 716 to 796, were their (self-proclaimed) descendants.

HWICCE

EANFRITH (Mid-seventh century) The very obscure founding king of the Hwicce, the kingdom of the south-west Midlands (approximately Worcestershire, Gloucestershire and parts of Warwickshire) which emerged in the mid-seventh century. Probably identical with the kingdom of the 'Hecani', apparently centred on Worcester, and with a 'kingdom of the West Mercians', which is only rarely mentioned in documents; its main royal residence by the eighth century appears to have been around Winchcombe. The kingdom was probably more 'multi-ethnic' than allowed for by common assumptions about mass-eviction of Britons. The conquest of Gloucester and Cirencester, the only surviving urban settlements, by Ceawlin of the West Saxons in 577 probably opened the area to settlement; the Germanic element in the Hwicce – or their royal house – may have entered the area as West Saxon 'clients', independently, or as part of the peoples that formed Mercia in the later sixth century. The first recorded local presence of Mercia was Penda's defeat of the West Saxons at Cirencester in 628.

Eanfrith, the first recorded king of the Hwicce, has a Bernician name which probably indicates at least partially Northumbrian parentage. His kin may have fled Bernicia in the early seventh century as opponents of Aethelfrith or Edwin, been independent adventurers, or been installed as local governors by Penda or his son Wulfhere. Eanfrith and his brother and co-ruler Eanhere were apparently trusted allies of Wulfhere, who in *c.* 660/1 arranged for Eanfrith to marry his daughter Eata to the new Mercian ally Aethelwalh of the South Saxons. Eanfrith was probably a Christian, given that the marriage was used to require the bridegroom to convert, but had no known court bishop. He died around 674, and his brother briefly outlived him. Eanhere was succeeded by the brothers Osric, Oswald and Oshere, presumably his or Eanfrith's sons, all named after Bernicians.

NORTHUMBRIA

EDWIN (617 – 633/634) The younger son of Aelle of Deira and brother of King Aethelric, he was forced into exile when the latter was killed and Deira overrun by Aethelfrith of Bernicia *c.* 604. Probably born in around 585, as he was forty-eight at his time of death, he spent over a decade in exile at the (Christian) court of the kings of Gwynedd and was regarded as dangerous enough by Aethelfrith for the latter to demand, unsuccessfully, that he be expelled. At this time he must have got to know his future arch-enemy Cadwallon, son of Gwynedd's pacific King Cadfan. Around 615 Aethelfrith marched into Cheshire to attack the princes of north Wales, probably with the threat that they would use Edwin as one of the causes of the war, and heavily defeated them at the battle of Chester. Selyf ap Cynan, king of Powys, was killed and Aethelfrith advanced Northumbria's control as far as the Irish Sea, but Edwin escaped and took refuge with Northumbria's southern neighbour, King Ceorl of Mercia. He married Ceorl's daughter Cwenburh, possibly as part of an alliance against Penda that would entail Edwin being restored to Deira as a Mercian ally, but Ceorl does not seem to have had the nerve to attack Aethelfrith as within a year or two Edwin had moved on to the court of Raedwald, king of the East Angles.

He achieved the support he needed from Raedwald, the most powerful military force in southern England who was to be regarded as *bretwalda* (military/political overlord) following Aethelbert of Kent's death in 616/17. Probably contending with Aethelfrith over control of Lindsey, Raedwald invaded Northumbria on Edwin's behalf in 617 (?) and killed Aethelfrith in battle on the River Idle. The power of the dynasty of Bernicia was broken, and Edwin was restored to power in York. He was also able to continue the union of Bernicia and Deira created by Aethelfrith, this time based in Deira, as Aethelfrith's three sons fled into exile in Dal Riada.

Inheriting his late rival's powerful new kingdom from the Forth to the Trent, Edwin continued its expansion. Little is known of his campaigns and Raedwald, his ally, seems to have been left unchallenged as senior military power south of the Trent. Edwin's own role as *bretwalda* in southern, as well as northern, England probably only commenced with Raedwald's death *c.* 622/5. But he proved as strong a war-leader as Aethelfrith against the British kingdoms to his west, probably aided by his experience of their methods of fighting in his exile among them. He reduced Rheged, Bernicia's arch-rival, to vassalage, and conquered the Pennine kingdom of Elmet as well as other minor British principalities. He may have ruled a multi-cultural realm as military overlord rather than evicting the British en masse. He marched into Gwynedd, where Cadfan (d. *c.* 625) does not seem to have been at all as warlike as his successor Cadwallon and the kingdom's military power had been weakened by losses at Chester. Early in Cadwallon's reign he overran the coast as far as Caernarfon, and apparently *c.* 629 (according to Welsh annals) besieged him on the island of Priestholm. According to Bede, Edwin secured control over Anglesey and the Welsh poem *Moliant Cadwallon* has Cadwallon retreat to Ireland, either in exile or at least to gather recruits. Cadwallon was able to return, but this was the first Anglian penetration into North Wales. Remarkably for this era, Edwin was also able to create a fleet (presumably based in the Dee or Mersey estuaries), as Bede says he subdued the Isle of Man – the first example of Anglian thalassocracy. The Northumbrian domination of the Irish Sea (based on earlier naval achievements by Rheged or Gwynedd, and using their skills?) shows Edwin's flexibility and ambitions. In the North, he pressed the British of Strathclyde back and annexed any of Lothian which had escaped Aethelfrith, probably including Edinburgh (Din Eidyn) whose British kingly line now lapsed. Bede's list of *bretwaldas* has Edwin as overlord of all the English and Britons, though it is unlikely that the distant British in southern Wales or Dumnonia submitted except as a nominal precaution.

It was Edwin's adoption of Christianity under the aegis of the Roman mission in Kent which gave him his greatest distinction and made him a different sort of ruler from Aethelfrith, a model for future Christian warlords according to Bede's approving picture. He was the first major warlord and the first northern king to convert, though Bede may have deliberately ignored the influence of the British Church on his conversion. According to Welsh versions of events he was baptised in exile before 627 by Rhun, the exiled king of Rheged now turned bishop, at the court of Gwynedd. If so, he may have let his adherence lapse on his return to Northumbria rather than alienate his pagan warriors, who Aethelfrith had turned on the British monks at Chester. But around 625 Edwin formed an alliance with Eadbald of Kent, who had returned to paganism on his accession but subsequently been baptised, and married the latter's sister, Aethelburh, as his second wife. The Kentish missionary Paulinus accompanied her entourage to Northumbria. Edwin was not converted at once, but according to Bede he was impressed by two pieces of good fortune in 626 – he escaped death, though not injury, in an attack by an assassin sent by King Cwichelm of the West Saxons and on the same day his wife had a daughter, Eanfleda. He promised to convert to Christianity if he achieved victory in his subsequent campaign to punish Wessex, which proved to be the case. In politico-military terms, Cwichelm's risky action indicates that Edwin's recent victories and overwhelming military dominance of the North already made him seem a threat to Wessex, separated from a border with Northumbria by Mercia. The campaign saw Edwin defeating the West Saxons and killing a number of their kings, though Cwichelm and his senior ruler Cynegils escaped; it was Northumbria's first incursion into southern England and testifies to its military reach.

Following the campaign, Edwin was formally baptised as a Christian by Paulinus, at Easter 627 (or possibly 628 – Bede says it was in the twelfth year of his reign). Mass-baptisms of Bernicians in the river near the main royal residence, Yeavering, followed. Paulinus now became the first bishop of Northumbria, based at York, and Edwin backed his claims to archiepiscopal status and wrote successfully to the Pope for this rank to be granted. In political terms, it made the Church in Northumbria the equal of that in Kent, which was militarily eclipsed, and freed it from any jurisdiction by the Archbishop of Canterbury. Edwin used his personal influence to back the conversion of his people as his exemplar Aethelbert had done in Kent, and according to Bede a formal debate among his leading nobles over their choice of religion followed. If Bede did not dramatise the king's chosen course of action into a good story, Edwin wisely 'stage-managed' the success of a debate among his nobles to win people over rather than peremptorily issuing orders, with less risk of a backlash. The conversion of the leading figures in Northumbria turned out to be permanent. A political dimension should be seen in the fact that, backed by Edwin, it was Paulinus who secured papal permission to consecrate the next Archbishop of Canterbury, Honorius, and Edwin unsuccessfully sought an archiepiscopal pallium for his protégé too. The plan of Pope Gregory for the English Church had envisaged a second archbishopric at York, and Edwin was clearly keen to revive this idea which added to his influence.

Edwin also persuaded the new king of the East Angles, his ex-patron Raedwald's son Eorpwald, to convert to Christianity. This turned out to be a temporary success, as the latter was soon killed. His own nemesis was Cadwallon of Gwynedd, who had been able to return from exile in Ireland and had formed an alliance with the new and vigorous King Penda of Mercia. Whoever held military power in Mercia in 626 had not been able to prevent Edwin marching across their kingdom into Wessex, and probably had to give way and admit vassalage. But now Penda had the military means to rally enough support to back Cadwallon against Edwin; he was pagan, but Cadwallon was Christian (owing adherence to the 'Celtic' Church rites) and religion is unlikely to have played a major role in their attack despite Bede's implications about Edwin's martyrdom. Edwin was defeated and killed at Hatfield Chase near Doncaster on 12 October 633 (or possibly 634), indicating a Mercian-Gwynedd advance on his southern frontier. He was apparently forty-eight. The military power of Northumbria and the unity of the kingdom were temporarily broken, and Cadwallon was able to ravage Deira at will; Edwin's elder son Osfrith (by Cwenburh) had been killed in the battle, his second son Eadfrith was taken prisoner and his widow and younger children and Paulinus fled to exile in Kent. Bernicia was reclaimed by Aethelfrith's eldest son, Eanfrith, and now or within a year Edwin's cousin Osric gained control of Deira.

As it turned out the eclipse of Edwin's direct family was permanent, though his daughter Enfleda was later to marry Eanfrith's brother, King Oswy, and King Ecgfrith (r. 670–85) was thus his grandson. Northumbria was to return to military success – and to proselytising Christian kingship, organised from Iona – under Aethelfrith's younger sons (St) Oswald and Oswy. Edwin was to be regarded as a martyr by a local cult and applauded by Bede, with his relics installed at Whitby. But in political terms, he was as much the heir of the ruthless pagan Aethelfrith as of the Christian patron Aethelbert of Kent.

AETHELBURH (Queen of Northumbria, 626 – 633/34) The daughter of King Aethelbert of Kent and his Frankish wife Bertha. Probably born around 600, she was married to King Edwin of Northumbria by her brother Eadbald in 624/5; the alliance was used to persuade the pagan Edwin to accept a Christian cleric from the Roman mission, Paulinus, as his bride's chaplain. This began the conversion of Northumbria, although Edwin was not immediately converted. He seems to have agreed to baptism after the combined good fortune of escaping a West Saxon assassin, the safe delivery of Aethelburh's daughter Enfleda, and defeating the West Saxons in 626.

When her husband was killed in October 633/4, she, her small children and the bishop all fled back to Kent. A son and a daughter had died in infancy and been buried at York; the two survivors, Enfleda and Uscfrea, and her stepson's young son Yffi, were subsequently sent abroad to be educated in Francia out of fear of Oswald, the new king of Northumbria. As far as is known, Aethelburh herself remained in Kent.

(ST) OSWALD (634/5 – 642) The elder of two sons of Aethelfrith by his second wife Acha, daughter of Aelle of Deira and sister to Edwin. Oswald and his brother Oswy, unlike their half-brother Eanfrith, had a claim to Deira. The family of Aethelfrith had fled into exile on his overthrow in 617, and ended up as suppliants of Dal Riada. Oswald and Oswy were brought up by the monks of Iona, and were converted to Christianity. The monks followed their founder Columba's Irish 'Celtic' rite and practices, such as over the tonsure and when to celebrate Easter, not those of Rome, which had consequences for the development of Christianity in Northumbria. After Edwin was killed by Cadwallon of Gwynedd in 633/4, Eanfrith was able to return to Bernicia while the Welsh devastated Deira; a year later Cadwallon killed Eanfrith and seemed to be intending to destroy the Anglian presence in Northumbria when Oswald intervened. He led an army south from Lothian to the River Tyne to confront Cadwallon, backed by Dal Riada. He surprised and defeated the strategically exposed Welsh warlord at 'Heavenfield' (Hallington [?]), according to Bede after praying to God and planting a cross on the battlefield. Cadwallon was killed, and the military power of Gwynedd finally ended.

Heavenfield restored the legitimate dynasty to Bernicia, and through Oswald's Deiran descent did so in ravaged Deira too. Local particularism required him to install or accept an already extant king, his maternal cousin Osric, as his vassal there, showing that he could not rule as strongly as Edwin had done. Oswald brought in a vigorous missionary bishop from his alma mater of Iona, (St) Aidan, to organise the conversion of those Northumbrians untouched by Edwin's York-centred missionaries or fallen back into paganism in the disasters of 633–4. The Irish/Dal Riadan Church looked more favourably on individualistic hermits than did the Roman Church with their concentration on monasteries observing the Benedictine Rule; Oswald's choice of missionaries thus brought a greater eremitical tradition to Northumbria than was seen in the south (witness St Cuthbert). Iona ecclesiastics followed the Irish practice of basing bishops in monasteries, which they often ruled as abbots, not in urban settlements (there were no towns in Ireland), and Aidan thus served as abbot of his new island monastery, set up on Lindisfarne. Under the influence of Iona, Northumbria also evolved the distinctive non-Roman practice of joint 'double monasteries', a joint male and female community under an abbess (most notably that of St Hild at Streoneshalch/Whitby). Oswald translated for Aidan, who could not speak Anglian at first.

Oswald's responsibility for the distinctive tone of Northumbrian Christianity was decisive. Bede treated him as one of the Christian hero-kings of his book. Bede also reckoned him as fifth *bretwalda*, the leader, if not direct overlord, of (most of) his fellow-kings, but in reality this status is dubious given the survival of Cadwallon's ally Penda. It is likely that an alliance against Penda lay behind Oswald's involvement with Cynegils of Wessex, to whose kingdom he journeyed (traditionally in 635). Oswald married Cynegils' daughter Cyneburh to seal the alliance, and the West Saxon king converted. Oswald was present at Cynegils' baptism by Bishop Birinus, at Dorchester-on-Thames. The site of the ceremony, in the north of Wessex, probably indicates that Oswald travelled overland across Mercia, but he may also have visited Dorset (leaving or arriving by sea?) if the link between him and St Oswald's Bay near Lulworth is authentic. His relations with Kent are likely to have been strained by the presence there of Edwin's exiled heirs, his potential rivals. Edwin's family fled thence to Francia in *c*. 635 for fear of him.

If Oswald ever held military supremacy in southern Britain in the mid- to late 630s, this did not involve or result from a direct clash with Penda. However, in 642 the two powers finally confronted each other and the site of their conflict indicates that Oswald attacked south-west into Shropshire. Whether he was ravaging to bring Penda to battle or seeking to link up with local (British?) allies is unknown; the nearest British kingdom, Powys, was Penda's ally. Oswald was defeated and killed on 5 August at 'Maserfelth', later known as Oswestry ('Oswald's Tree'). The name referred to his fate; Penda dismembered his body, allegedly in a pagan ritual, and hung the pieces up in a tree. A year later Oswy was able to recover the remains; Oswald's head was taken to Lindisfarne and the body buried at Bardney in Lincolnshire. The battle is alternatively called 'Cocboy' in the ninth-century Welsh *Historia Brittonum* and tenth-century *Annales Cambriae*, and 'Maes Cogwy' in the Welsh poem *Canu Heledd* (originally thought to be contemporary, now ninth-century), which refers to its hero King Cyndylan of Powys as the ally of Penda against Northumbria. Oswald was probably aged in his late thirties. His dynasty remained in control of Northumbria, though hard-pressed by Penda for over a decade, and his heroic death for the Christian faith was made the most of by Bede (who enthusiatically detailed the miracles carried out at the site) and other writers as an example to Christian kings. Oswald's niece Osthryth, daughter of Oswy and wife of King Aethelred of Mercia, even appropriated some relics for her new monastery at Bardney in eastern Mercia, amid concern at the propriety of annexing another kingdom's royal saint.

OSWY (642 – 670/1) The third son of Aethelfrith, and his younger son by Acha; Oswald was his full brother. Probably born in 611–12, he fled into exile in Dal Riada with his family after Aethelfrith was killed in 617; he was brought up at the monastery of Iona and convered to Christianity. Either before or after his brother's restoration in 634/5, he took part in campaigning in Ireland and formed a relationship (marriage [?]) with the princess Fina, daughter of High King Colman Rimid (d. 604), by whom he had his son, Aldfrith. He returned to Northumbria with Oswald after Edwin's death at the hands of Cadwallon in 633/4, possibly in the reign of their half-brother Eanfrith in Bernicia (633/4 – 34/5) but certainly when Oswald led a Dal Riadan-backed army to drive out the Welsh in 634/5. He was Oswald's principal supporter, and according to the ninth-century Welsh *Historia Brittonum* married the British princess Rianmelt/Riemmelth, daughter of the (former [?]) king of Rheged, *c*. 636 (?). This was presumably a dynastic alliance to secure the loyalty of her people in Lancashire and Cumbria, former foes but probably a vassal-kingdom with truncated territory by this stage; any remaining male kinsfolk seem to have lost political power and Oswy may have been intended as Oswald's local viceroy. If he was married to Fina he had to repudiate her for this diplomatic alliance, but Rhianmelt either died or was divorced within a decade or so.

In August 642, Oswald was killed by Penda at Oswestry after invading Mercia and Oswy succeeded. Bede names him as next *bretwalda* after Oswald, implying an unbroken line of Northumbrian military/political overlordship, but it is probable that his bias towards the militantly Christian kings of his homeland led him to play down Penda's military dominance south of the Trent in 642–55. Oswy could not maintain his brother's close links with Wessex, whose king was driven out by Penda in 645–48 (?), or intervene to save Anna of East Anglia from destruction *c.* 653. He also had to accept the continuing autonomy of Deira under its own sub-kings, with Osric's son Oswine succeeding him in 634/5; Oswy married their cousin Enfleda, daughter of Edwin, *c.* 644 to bolster their ties and his own claim to Deira (his mother was Edwin's sister). In 651 Oswy invaded Deira and the outnumbered Oswine disbanded his army sooner than fight. He was hunted down and executed, and Deira was handed over to Oswald's son Aelfwald. Unfortunately the plan backfired – Oswine was regarded as a saint by indignant Deirans and became the centre of a cult, Queen Enfleda insisted that her husband build a monastery to atone for killing her cousin and Aelfwald was to desert to Oswy's enemy Penda.

The threat of Mercia continued to loom over Northumbria from 642–55, and Penda had the better of most encounters. He was able to ravage Deira after his victory at Oswestry and in *c.* 644 he raided into Bernicia – a long march from the border – to attempt to sack the dynastic centre, Bamburgh, in an evident attempt to humiliate Oswy; a change in the wind-direction put the fire out in time. The two powers eventually agreed an alliance in or around 653 with a double marriage, whereby Oswy and Enfleda's son Alchfrith married Penda's daughter Cyneburh, and her brother Peada, new sub-king of the 'Middle Angles', married Oswy's daughter Aelfleda (Elfleda). This led to an influx of missionaries from Northumbria into Peada's territory to convert him and his people. Oswy may also have been involved in the election of his late half-brother Eanfrith's son, Talorcan, as king of the Picts *c.* 653, which probably brought a possibility of Pictish aid against Penda and a secure northern border. In 655 Penda felt threatened enough to resume the offensive, with a huge army including thirty 'duces'. Oswy relied on geography for defence and avoided battle, retreating far into Bernicia, and with winter approaching Penda accepted a treaty with Oswy's son Ecgfrith as his hostage. During his return march across Deira, Oswy was emboldened to attack him, possibly by heavy rain bogging down the Mercians. In the battle of the River 'Winwaed', probably near Leeds, on 15 November 655, Oswy won a complete victory and Penda and many of his men, including King Aethelhere of East Anglia, were cut down or drowned in the river.

Oswy was now the most powerful military leader in England, and could more fairly be called *bretwalda* (if this title was formally used). He was able to break Mercia up temporarily, repaying the compliment of his enemies' breaking up Northumbria in 633/4 by annexing Mercia's northern territories (probably as far as the Trent). Peada, his son-in-law and vassal, remained as king of the 'Middle Angles' until he was assassinated in obscure circumstances in spring 656. Oswy may have connived at this to remove a rival, and from Bede's account he kept Mercia kingless for three years (i.e. until autumn 658 [?]) when Penda's younger son Wulfhere, who he had been trying to hunt down, was used as the focus of a Mercian revolt by disgruntled nobles. His ruthless policy of eliminating rivals failed in Mercia as it had done in Deira (now ruled by the loyal Alchfrith) in 651, and Wulfhere was able to operate as senior warlord of the southern English without further interference from Oswy.

The main problem of his later years was the difference in practices observed by the two 'wings' of the Church in Northumbria, those taking their lead from Rome and those following the Irish Church and Iona. Oswy's queen, Enfleda, brought up in the Roman practices by her father's bishop, Paulinus, celebrated Easter at a different date from him and the Iona-trained clerics at court (led by Bishop Colman, an Irishman). The Roman practices were also followed by Alchfrith, and his appointment of a local, but Rome-trained, candidate, (St) Wilfred, to take over the Deiran bishopric from Oswy's nominee Eata led to the zealous Wilfred imposing Roman practices across Deira. Personal rivalries, especially involving the quarrelsome Wilfred, and disputes over office were added to the problems over matters such as Easter and the correct form of monastic tonsure, and in 664 Oswy summoned a religious council at Whitby/Streoneshalch to reach a definitive solution. His kinswoman, Abbess (St) Hild, acted as hostess, Oswy presided and representatives were summoned from Canterbury and Iona to put their rival cases. The ultimate decision lay with Oswy; although the proceedings and outcome may have been distorted by the pro-Rome victors to stress their inevitability, it is probable that Bede's account preserves the essentials of what happened. The supposedly winning argument that the Roman case was that backed by St Peter the Apostle, who had been given the keys of Heaven by Christ, was an expression of the reasoning that the Papacy was a powerful ally, major foreign kingdoms like that of the Franks were its supporters, and its remote 'rival' Iona was backed only by Dal Riada and the northern Irish kingdoms. In choosing the Roman case, Oswy was allying himself with a powerful international institution and most of Europe. As a result of his choice a number of personnel who would not accept it, led by Bishop Colman, left his kingdom; Rome's principal spokesman at the synod, Wilfred, won royal favour and in 669 succeeded (St) Chad, Colman's successor, to become bishop of all Northumbria.

Oswy died on 15 February 670, aged fifty-eight according to Bede. (The date may be 671, for which arguement see the entry on Ecgfrith.) His elder surviving son Ecgfrith succeeded him, having ruled Deira as sub-king since Alchfrith's death *c*. 664, and his widow Enfleda retired to the nunnery at Whitby. Probably inferior to Oswald in his power and influence within England except during 655–8, and at times miscalculatingly brutal, Oswy made decisions affecting his people's future for centuries. It was the lack of his realism which was to destroy his equally ruthless son Ecgfrith and the nation's northern dominions in 685.

ENFLEDA (Queen of Northumbria, *c*. 644–670) The daughter of Edwin of Nothumbria and Aethelburh of Kent, she was born in 626. On the day she was born her father survived an assassination attempt by a West Saxon agent, which he took for a good omen of divine favour indicating that he should convert to Christianity. As a result she was baptised at Easter 626. She fled with her mother and siblings to Kent on Edwin's death in battle in October 633/4, and was subsequently sent to be educated overseas in Francia for fear of an attack by her dynasty's enemy Oswald, the new king of Northumbria. She ended up marrying Oswald's brother and successor Oswy, early in his reign (*c*. 644), in a renewed Kent alliance probably centred on her father's cousin Oswine, the Northumbrian sub-king of Deira and Oswy's reluctant ally. Marrying her gave Oswy, himself the son of a Deiran princess, an added claim for himself and his sons by her to rule Deira; he already had a son (Alchfrith) by an earlier wife, Riemmelth of Rheged, who had died or was now divorced.

Enfleda gave Oswy two more sons, Ecgfrith and Elfwine; the death of Alchfrith, who ruled Deira, made Ecgfrith sub-king of Deira and heir to Northumbria. As Enfleda followed the 'Roman' practices of the Church of Canterbury, brought to Northumbria by her mother's chaplain Paulinus, and Oswy followed the rival 'Celtic' practices he had learnt on Iona, the king and queen celebrated Easter on different dates. This was a major inducement to sort out the problem of two rival rites in Northumbria, and was one of the reasons for the decisive Synod of Whitby in 664 – where the Roman rites used by Enfleda triumphed. She had long been a patron of the leading pro-Rome advocate who won the day at the synod, Wilfred; she arranged for him to enter the monastic life and later helped with introductory letters to her kinsman Eorcenbert of Kent on his decisive journey to Rome as a young man. After Oswy died in February 680 she retired into the monastic life. She died in 704, aged seventy-eight. Her elder son Ecgfrith succeeded to Northumbria; her second son Elfwine succeeded him in Deira in 679, and was killed in battle against Mercia in 679. Her daughter Elfflaed was dedicated as a nun in infancy in thanks for Oswy's victory at Winwead in 655 and became abbess of Gilling.

BERNICIA

EANFRITH (633/4 – 634/5) The eldest son of Aethelfrith of Northumbria, by his first – Celtic – wife, Bebba. The latter may have had had a dynastic connection to one of the minor kingdoms of the North Britons assimilated into Aethelfrith's expanding kingdom; Eanfrith was probably born in the mid-590s.

When Aethelfrith was killed by Raedwald of the East Angles in 616/17, Eanfrith and his half-brothers had to flee north. He seems to have sought refuge with the Picts; if he had not already married a Pictish princess, he now did so. His unnamed wife was the daughter of Gwid/Uuid, a noble who had fought against the Angles at Catraeth c. 595, niece of Cinioch, king of the Picts (r. 621–31), and sister of kings Gartnait (r. 631–5) and Talorcan (r. 641–53). Claims to the over-kingship of the Picts seem to have been on numerous occasions by female descent; Eanfrith's son Talorcan was to become king of the Picts in 653. When Aethelfrith's supplanter Edwin was killed by Cadwallon of Gwyned in 633/4, Eanfrith returned home. He made a successful claim on Bernicia, the northern half of his father's kingdom. Any attempt to claim Deira too would have rested on force rather than hereditary right. Eanfrith was a pagan, like his father and in contrast to his half-brothers – due to the lesser impetus for conversion by the Church on the Pictish kingdom than on his half-brothers' Dal Riadan hosts? Deira was taken over by Edwin's cousin Osric, and was where the war with Cadwallon now centred. Eanfrith remained in control of Bernicia for a year before a breach with Cadwallon, who was able to invade after killing Osric. Eanfrith sued for peace, probably short of troops, but was killed as he arrived to meet Cadwallon. His half-brother Oswald was able to rally enough men in Lothian with help from Dal Riada to defeat and kill Cadwallon; Eanfrith's family were excluded from power in Northumbria thereafter.

DEIRA

OSRIC (633/4 – 634/5) The son of Aelfric, younger brother of Edwin and son of King Aelle. After the death in battle of Edwin and his elder son Osferth against Cadwallon of Gwynedd in October 633 (or 634) the unity of Northumbria collapsed, and Cadwallon ravaged at will across Deira in what may have been a genocidal attempt to evict the Anglian population. Edwin's younger children fled with his widow and Bishop Paulinus to Kent, and Osric (probably the only adult male of the Deiran royal house available) took over the kingdom. Bernicia was reclaimed by Eanfrith, eldest son of King Aethelfrith. It is not known if Cadwallon set up or grudgingly tolerated Osric, who had been baptised under Edwin but reverted to paganism in 633/4, possibly to satisfy disgruntled local Deiran thegns who felt that the Christian God had deserted them and that the recent disaster was their old gods' punishment on them. By summer 634/5 Osric was able to rally the forces of Deira and attack Cadwallon, but his initial success in trapping him at a fortress was brief. The superior Gwynedd army broke out, and Osric was killed in the resulting battle. The ravaging of Deira resumed unchecked until Oswald, Eanfrith's brother, drove out the invaders and reincorporated it into Northumbria. Oswald had to accept Osric's son Oswine as his sub-king there, which shows the loyalty of the ruling class to the late king as well as to Edwin.

OSWINE (634/5 – 651) The son of Osric, who succeeded him when he was killed in Cadwallon's attack on Deira. Although Deira's army had been defeated by the invading Welsh and the ravaged kingdom was thus at a disadvantage, its nobles were clearly able to require their rescuer King Oswald of Bernicia to accept Oswine rather than annex the weakened kingdom. The division of Northumbria into two thus continued, doubtless against Oswald's original intentions, and he respected his presumably loyal new junior ally's rights. Presumably Oswine aided Oswald against Cadwallon, his father's killer, in the unsuccessful campaign of 642 into Powys, where Oswald was killed. The more ruthless Oswy was not so content to let Deiran autonomy survive.

Oswine was praised for his piety and humility by Bede, and was apparently much loved by his people. He was a friend and supporter of Bishop Aidan, the evangelizer of Northumbria, who is said to have feared for his safety, presumably with Oswy's intentions in mind. Possibly to forestall any attempted Deiran alliance with Mercia, Oswy attacked Deira in an unprovoked war in August 651. Heavily outnumbered and probably accepting that resistance would give the inevitable victor an excuse for bloodshed, Oswine disbanded his army near Catterick in northern Yorkshire. He and his attendant took refuge with a local landowner, Hunwold, who betrayed him to Oswy; Oswine was then arrested and executed at Gilling on 20 August. Aidan's death a few days later may have been hastened by shock at the killing. Deira was annexed and was given to Oswy's nephew Aethelwald, who ironically went on to betray him when Penda invaded in 655; local resentment at the murder of Oswine led to him becoming the focus of a popular cult as a saint and martyr. Oswy was unable to prevent Oswine becoming the first Anglo-Saxon 'king and martyr', with a monastery being set up at the site of his martyrdom in implicit rebuke to Bernician aggression.

AETHELWALD (651–655) The son of King Oswald of Northumbria, adult by the early 650s and possibly born before his father's return from Dal Riada in 634. He may have been his son by Cwenburh of Wessex, who Oswald married in 635 (?). He claimed the kingdom of Deira after (St) Oswine was killed by Oswy in August 651. The latter's overthrow of the dynasty of Deira was intended to secure greater control of the kingdom, and it is not clear if Oswy installed his nephew as his sub-ruler or if Oswy originally intended annexation and Aethelwald forestalled him. As Oswald had been related to the old Deiran royal house via his mother Acha, Aethelwald had a hereditary claim. A patron of monasticism like his father, he invited St Cedd to set up a monastery at Lastingham and take on missionary work. But his relations with his uncle Oswy deteriorated, and in 655 Aethelwald joined Penda of Mercia in his large-scale invasion. The Mercian army, backed by the Deirans, ravaged north, apparently without a major battle with the probably outnumbered Oswy, and eventually an agreement was reached whereby Penda withdrew. As his army reached the River Winwaed, possibly near Leeds, Oswy attacked them on 15 November 655 and inflicted a heavy defeat in which Penda and several of his sub-kings were killed. Bede says that Aethelwald withdrew from the battlefield; his rule came to an end with this defeat. If Aethelwald was not killed, Oswy presumably deposed him and he fled into exile.

LINDSEY

CAEDBAD (Early seventh century (?)) The king of Lindsey in the early to mid-seventh century; according to the royal geneaology, son of Coedgils and grandson of the dynastic founder Creoda/Critta. If the latter was the same as the later sixth-century Mercian dynast Creoda, with Lindsey ruled by a junior line of their Icelingas dynasty, he would have been a cousin of Penda. His British name (Catuboduos) suggests a degree of inter-marriage between the royal house of Lindsey and surviving, or neighbouring, British nobility. The kingdom, despite its easterly situation in England and closeness to the early-settled Humber, retained a British name based on the main town of 'Lindum' (Lincoln). At the time, overlordship of the lands between Trent, Humber and the Wash was disputed between three large Anglian kingdoms – Northumbria, Mercia, and in the 610s and 620s East Anglia – and Caedbad and his immediate succesors would have had to perform an uneasy balancing-act between the current leading 'power' and its challengers. Lindsey may have been converted (from Northumbria) in Caedbad's reign, if this was the later 620s. But the role of its kings in the conversion is unrecorded; they did not feature in local hagiographies or as founders of bishoprics and minsters.

4

c. 655 to *c.* 690

KENT

EGBERT (664 – 673/4) The son and successor of Eorcenbert; his mother was Seaxburh, daughter of Anna of the East Angles. Born in his father's reign, he was under twenty-four when the latter died on 14 July 664 and his mother retired to her nunnery at Minster in Sheppey. He had no hesitation in securing his throne quickly from genealogically senior rivals, the sons of his father's predeceasing elder brother, who were swiftly executed. Their unjust deaths led to them becoming the centre of a local cult, and he paid off their sister Eafa's demands for compensation by granting land to found a second religious house at Minster. As religious patron, perhaps to rebuild his reputation, he founded a church at Reculver and granted the foundation charter of Chertsey Abbey in Surrey. The latter shows that his authority was seen as extending into Surrey, at least by agreement of Wulfhere of Mercia who was married to his sister, Eormenhild. Archbishop Deusdedit of Canterbury had died on the same day as Eorcenbert and Egbert consulted Oswy of Northumrbia about his successor; their initial choice died. The man appointed by the Pope in 669, the Cilician Theodore of Tarsus, was unfamiliar with English affairs and probably relied on Egbert as well as his clerics for advice as first. Egbert died young on 4 July 673 (or possibly 674), aged probably about thirty, leaving two young sons, Eadric and Wihtred; his death plunged Kent into prolonged political crisis as Egbert's mother, his brother Hlothere (Lothar) and his brother-in-law Wulfhere contended for control of the kingdom.

HLOTHERE (CHLOTAR) (673/4 – 685/6) The younger son of Eorcenbert and brother of Egbert; his name (the Frankish 'Chlotar' or 'Lothar') is unique for an English king and indicates cross-Channel cultural influence. His mother was Seaxburh of East Anglia. He was probably, at most, thirty when Egbert died on 4 July 673, leaving two young sons (Eadric and Wihtred), and he assumed the leadership of an 'anti-Mercian' faction of nobles resisting the claims to regency by his sister's husband, Wulfhere of Mercia. The latter won out at first as the dominant military power in southern England, though Hlothere may have become titular co-ruler; within a year or so he had assumed authority and was challenging Mercia. The Kentish nobles seem to have backed Hlothere to preserve more independence, and a military confrontation was resolved with an agreement leaving Hlothere in control as king. Eadric was at most titular co-ruler until he came of age. Wulfhere's death and Hlothere's assertion of control over lands west of the Medway in 674/5 led to an invasion of Kent by the new Mercian king, Aethelred, in 676, and Rochester and its new cathedral were brutally sacked. Possibly regretting the bloodshed as he was to prove a peaceful and pious king and later became a monk, Aethelred came to terms and Hlothere continued as king.

Closely allied with the Church under the vigorous new (Cilician) Archbishop Theodore, who seems to have relied on him for secular partnership, Hlothere was a major patron of church-building and a just ruler, re-issuing and updating King Aethelbert's law-code at the end of his reign. The decade of his unchallenged government was a time of peace in contrast to what followed. It was Eadric, restless for rule, who did not remain content with appearing in documents from *c.* 679 as co-ruler, and who raised an army against him early in 685. Hlothere was defeated in battle, wounded and deposed and died on 6 February 685, probably aged a little over forty. (D. P. Kirby suggests an alternative date of 686.) Bede gives Hlothere a reign of eleven years and seven months. Eadric seized the throne only to fall victim to Caedwalla of Wessex a year later.

EADRIC (673/9 – 685) The elder son of Egbert, who died on 4 July 673 (or possibly 674). He and his brother Wihtred were backed by their grandmother and guardian, Seaxburh, and also had the backing of their father's sister Eormenhild and her husband Wulfhere of Mercia. The latter, the most powerful ruler in southern England, demanded the right to rule in the boys' minority but was opposed by Egbert's brother Hlothere (Lothar) with an anti- Mercian faction.

Wulfhere seems to have won out by threat of force and Eadric was nominally king, with Seaxburh as regent under Wulfhere's overlordship, but within a year Hlothere (possibly co-ruler) had usurped authority. Preoccupied, Mercia did not retaliate as Wulfhere was dying in 674/5, and Eadric remained at most king in name only until his majority with Hlothere in power. Eadric (now in his late teens?) started to witness charters as co-king from 679 and seems to have exerted increasing authority. The period of co-rule ended when in February 685, Eadric, using an army of South Saxons which may suggest limited support at home, invaded Hlothere's lands and defeated him. Hlothere was either killed or driven into exile, and Eadric ruled as sole king but aroused criticism as hot-headed and violent. If he had been able to claim any sort of authority among his South Saxon backers, kingless since 684/5, this soon ended and in 686 Caedwalla of Wessex invaded Kent. On 31 August he defeated Eadric in battle, and took over Kent for his brother Mul. Eadric was either killed or fled; Wihtred was restored in 691.

MUL (686 – 687 (?)) The brother of Caedwalla of the West Saxons, installed in Kent after the defeat of Eadric in August 686. Mul would have had difficulties as ruler in any case, lacking local connections and being the first king of Kent from outside the dynasty of Aesc; within months the people of Kent rose against him. He faced revolt in Canterbury, and fled to a building in the precincts of the cathedral – probably taken by surprise and unable to escape on horseback. The insurgents set it afire, and he was burnt to death. Caedwalla ravaged Kent in retaliation, but was unable to subdue it; its rule passed to King Sigehere of Essex as the injured Caedwalla had to withdraw to Wessex and abdicate.

SWAEFRED (Kent, 688/9 – 692 (?); East Saxons (?), 693 – 707 (?)) The son of the holy King Saebbi, he was probably involved with his father's more aggressive co-ruler Sigehere in taking over West Kent after the West Saxon invader Caedwalla's abdication in 688. He then succeeded Sigehere as king of the area, and extended this to all Kent in the military vacuum while Caedwalla's successor Ine was securing Wessex.

This second foreign-imposed king of Kent was at least from a close ally, unlike the recent Wessex puppet Mul, and he avoided the latter's violent end which suggests that he was more acceptable. Backed by his brother Sigeheard, Saebbi's co-king, he retained West Kent when the superseded legitimate heir Wihtred took over the east with Church support in 691. Within a couple of years he was expelled or left voluntarily; if he was 'Swaefheard' he became joint king of Essex with Sigeheard in 693.

OSWINE (688/9 – 690 (?)) Known due to a charter of January 690, where he grants an estate in Thanet to his kinswoman, Abbess Aebbe of Minster. He was in his second regnal year, so he succeeded before January 689; he presumably took over part of (eastern [?]) Kent in the vacuum after Caedwalla's decline in health, possibly as an opponent of the rival East Saxon claimants. He was probably descended from Eormenred, brother of King Eorconbert, and took advantage of his geographical location in the east to survive any West Saxon attempts to remove him in 688/9. Swaefherd initially joined him to witness a grant in 689, suggesting a temporary alliance against the West Saxons that broke down after Caedwalla's abdication. By 692 he had been superseded by Wihtred.

SUSSEX

AETHELWALH (South Saxons, <660 – 684/5) King by 660, and ally of Wulfhere of Mercia, who had stood godfather to him at his baptism. He is the first recorded king of the South Saxons since Aelle; the kingship may have lapsed after the military requirements of early battles with the local British. Mercia was pressing southwards against the South Saxons' rivals, the West Saxons, attacking the latter's king, Cenwalh. The South Saxons were still pagan, but Wulfhere was an enthusiastic Christian and married to a Christian Kentish princess; Aethewalh's baptism probably occurred while on a mission to Mercia, as part of the terms of alliance. His wife was Eata, daughter of Wulfhere's client-king Eanfrith of Hwicce. The Mercian invasion of eastern Wessex in 661 led to Wulfhere detaching the Isle of Wight and the territory of the 'Meonware' in eastern Hampshire from Wessex and making Aethelwalh their new overlord, to weaken Wessex and build up South Saxon power.

Around 680 the exiled bishop of York, (St) Wilfred, crossed Aethelwalh's western lands on his travels and decided to take on the task of conversion. Arrangements were made with Aethelwalh, and he granted Wilfred land in Selsey for his new monastery and church. Wilfred thus became the first bishop of Sussex. The king was killed in 684/5 in an incursion into Sussex by the displaced West Saxon 'atheling' Caedwalla, whose father had been killed in Wulfhere's invasion and whose lands may have formed part of the territory Wulfhere had given to Aethelwalh. The disaster ended the temporary resurgence of the South Saxon kingdom. Caedwalla was driven out of Sussex by the king's ealdormen Andhun and Berthun, and turned his attention to taking over the West Saxon kingdom before attacking Sussex again.

WESSEX

SEAXBURH (c. 672/3 – 673/4) The first (and only) regnant queen of an Anglo-Saxon kingdom, and the only female ruler except for Aethelfleda of Mercia. Some regnal lists of Wessex leave her out of the reckoning. The widow of King Cenwalh of the West Saxons, and probably the second wife who he married, c. 644 after divorcing a Mercian princess, she was apparently chosen as ruler on his death between 672 and 674. They were presumably childless, or an under-age son was too young to succeed and soon died. Bede records that the kingship lapsed for ten years after Cenwalh's death; the regnal lists are at odds with this but it may be that central power and war-leadership lapsed. Seaxburh either died or retired after a year (?) and was succeeded by Aescwine, possibly as a man was needed to lead the armies.

AESCWINE (674 (?) – 676 (?)) An obscure prince who succeeded either Cenwalh or, more likely, the latter's widow Seaxburh. The date is unclear, and if Seaxburh ruled for a year after Cenwalh's death it was probably around 674 or 675. He was son of Cenfus (*fl.* 660), who is recorded as claiming the kingship and from charters ruled in northern Wessex; Cenfus was son of Cuthgils, brother of Cynegils and son of King Ceolwulf. The ninth-century *Chronicon ex Chronicis*, citing West Saxon records, even has Cenfus as king of all Wessex for two years after Seaxburh, and then Aescwine ruling for three years and Centwine for seven. But Aescwine's Mercian campaign (see below) is dateable as preceding King Wulfhere's death in 674/5, so it is impossible that Centwine (d. 685) only succeeded Aescwine in 677/8; Aescwine was definitely ruling in 674/5, though possibly with his father Cenfus as co-ruler.

According to Bede, the kingship lapsed on Cenwalh's death and the kingdom was ruled by sub-kings for a decade; the extensive genealogy and the multiplicity of men claiming royal status indicates that there was a number of 'kings' ruling jointly, probably each in possession of a hereditary region centred on patrilineal estates. Failure to find an agreed candidate on Cenwalh's death demonstrated and prolonged this weakness, though Bede may have played up the decentralisation to make the restoration of royal power by Caedwalla more dramatic.

Aescwine, apparently able to win acceptance from his peers unlike his father, may have been chosen as king in a military crisis – Queen Seaxburh could not lead in war. If there was a crisis the likeliest challenger would have been Mercia, and Aescwine's probable family estates in northern Wiltshire may indicate that he had experience of fighting Mercia. He is recorded as fighting Wulfhere of Mercia successfully in 674/5, at an unidentified 'Beda's Head', and this campaign may have been the cause of his election. He is said to have reigned for only two years; his early death thus prevented any subsequent success in restoring a strong kingship, which had to wait for another six to nine years.

CENTWINE (West Saxons, 676 (?) – 685) The second of the kings of the West Saxons during what Bede describes as a ten-year vacancy in the central kingship following the death of king Cenwalh (672/4). The *Chronicle* continues to record kings, as does the royal genealogy; it is possible that the reference means that the end of the direct line of Cenwalh (and a vacancy for a war-leader during the rule of Cenwalh's widow Seaxburh?) weakened the kingship and strengthened the many junior local dynasts of royal blood, sub-kings based in inherited areas of power.

Traditionally, Centwine succeeded Aescwine after a two-year reign; the uncertain date of Cenwalh's death and whether or not Seaxburh reigned for a year means that this can only be approximated at 676. He was supposedly Cenwalh's brother, the (younger) son of Cynegils as stated in the *Chronicle* annal for 676 – but in that case why did he not succeed the childless Cenwalh? The annal also calls Cynegils' father Ceolwulf son of Cutha, not Ceol as stated elsewhere – but it is only a theory that there were two men called Cynegils, one the son of Ceol and one the son of Ceolwulf, and so Centwine must be Cenwalh's cousin, not brother. The 'ten years' reference to the lapse in central power has also been interpreted as meaning that the restoration of (central?) royal power in Wessex took place in Centwine's reign, around 682/3, not after 685 under Caedwalla as implied by Bede. Caedwalla, an exile under Centwine and probably using his attack on Sussex in 684/5 to gather loot and supporters for a revolt, was dynastically close to the later West Saxon dynasty and a patron of Christianity, so both the later ninth-century writers of the *Chronicle* and Church historians had reason to minimalise Centwine's achievement. Indeed, Centwine banned the exiled Northumbrian Bishop (St) Wilfred, later a friend of Centwine's enemy Caedwalla, from Wessex at the behest of his own queen, Eangyth, sister of the wife of Ecgfrith of Northumbria.

The *Chronicle* records that Centwine won a major victory over the British of Dumnonia in 682 and 'chased them as far as the sea'. Wessex had overrun Somerset after Cenwalh's victory at Penselwood in 658 and was in possession of the Exeter area by *c.* 660, so it is most likely that the battle took place somewhere in northern or western Devon and the pursuit led Centwine as far as northern Cornwall – or a victory in the south near Okehampton led to pursuit down the Tamar to the sea in eastern Cornwall. Success as a war-leader may have been the cause or the result of Centwine reasserting his control over his sub-kings. Centwine was thus an underrated monarch, reduced to obscurity by his early death or (more likely) abdication in 685. Any heirs who he left were quickly displaced by Caedwalla. A son of Centwine's, Oshere, is supposed to have lived to the 720s and a daughter, Eadburh, was an abbess.

CAEDWALLA (West Saxons, 685–688) The creator of an extended West Saxon kingdom south of the Thames, later achieved permanently by Egbert. He was allegedly the son of Cenbert, son of Ceadda (Chad?), son of Cutha/Cuthwine, the superseded son of *bretwalda* Ceawlin. If this version, in the 'A' manuscript of the *Chronicle*, is accurate his usurpation saw the return to power of Ceawlin's own descendants, kept out of the kingship by his brothers' families since his overthrow in 591/2; but this genealogy may have been fabricated to add to the dynastic legitimacy of Caedwalla and his cousin and successor Ine. His British name is the same as that of the Gwynedd warlord Cadwallon (killed 633/4), and suggests a forgotten degree of royal inter-marriage with the Britons within or neighbouring Wessex. Possibly Caedwalla's father or grandfather may have lived in a region of Wessex with a substantial British survival (Dorset?) or in exile.

The kingship of Wessex seems to have been shared by a multitude of athelings through the seventh century, possibly with hereditary patrimonies under one 'over-king', and the latter to have lapsed for some years after Cenwalh's death in 674 (?). The restoration of central power under a dynamic warrior-king is variously ascribed to Caedwalla and to his predecessor Centwine; the latter achieved the first major military success for decades and may have been eclipsed because it was Caedwalla's near-relatives who commissioned the *Chronicle*. Cenberht seems to have died or been killed in Wulfhere's Mercian invasion around 661. Caedwalla, probably born in the late 650s to 661/2, was already a renowned young warrior with a warband but not yet king when he first appears in the records in 684/5; Bede calls him an exile and he may have lost his father's lands to the sub-kingdom of the Meonware (the Meon valley) used by Wulfhere to threaten Wessex. Caedwalla invaded Sussex and killed its king, Aethelwalh; he was a pagan but may already have been acquainted with the exiled Bishop Wilfred of York, recently installed at Selsey to convert the South Saxons, who appears to have been on good terms with him. But conquest was prevented by the 'duces' Berthun and Adhun, who drove Caedwalla out.

Caedwalla became king when Centwine retired to a monastery in 685, probably as the best-supported candidate with a successful warband. His accession may have been disputed, as Bede only gives him two years as king and he abdicated in 688. He was regarded as the restorer of the kingdom's power; there remained a multitude of rival princes with a claim to the throne but until the 720s the king was not troubled by serious revolt. Caedwalla commenced a systematic conquest of his neighbours. In 686 Arwald, the last king of the Jutish lands on Wight, supposedly descended from Cerdic's nephew, was killed and his lands annexed; these may have included the Jutish 'Ytene' (the New Forest area) on the mainland. The royal house was exterminated, with two young princes escaping to the mainland but being caught and executed; at Wilfred's request, Caedwalla allowed them to convert to Christianity first. Caedwalla enforced baptism on the pagan Wight Jutes, regarding himself as a Christian missionary warrior in the tradition of his kingdom's former overlord St Oswald under Wilfred's Northumbrian influence.

In 686 Caedwalla moved back into Sussex to kill Berthun, evict Andhun and take over the kingdom. He continued his march into Kent, an implicit challenge to Mercia; King Eadric was defeated and possibly killed in battle (August 686 [?]). The conqueror now imposed his own brother Mul as the new king, but this first imposition of a non-native was resisted and in 687 a revolt in Canterbury saw Mul forced to take refuge in a church building which was then burnt. Caedwalla invaded Kent in retaliation, but despite a victory was unable to secure control – possibly due to a serious wound incurred in this or the Wight campaign. Late in 688 he abdicated in order to journey to Rome as a pilgrim, probably crippled and thus useless as a military commander. His resignation and choice of destination were to be emulated by later kings throughout England; his cousin Ine succeeded him.

On arrival in Rome he was baptised (as 'Peter') by Pope Sergius at Easter 689 and died shortly afterwards. Bede ascribes his death to a sudden illness, not his wounds; he may not have believed himself dying when he set out for Rome, though this was assumed later. According to Bede his tomb recorded his age at thirty. Commended by Bede for his enthusiastic Christianity despite his massacres, he was the first militarily powerful West Saxon ruler to threaten his neighbours since Ceawlin.

ESSEX

SWITHHELM (650s – 663) The son of King Seaxbald, one of the joint rulers from 616 (?) to the 620s, he succeeded the murdered King Sigebert the Good in the 650s. The account of the regicide in Bede makes it unclear if he was the assassin, a royal cousin excommunicated for an illegal marriage (by Canon law, not local custom), perhaps to a cousin, and denied royal support. The new king, possibly merely the accidental beneficiary, was baptised by Bishop Cedd at the East Anglian court at Rendlesham and backed the completion of the kingdom's conversion. His shadowy co-ruler was his brother Swithfrith. He died in 663, when his cousins Sigehere and Saebbi succeeded.

SAEBBI (663 (?) – 693) The son of Sexred, one of the three sons of King Sledda who ruled as co-kings from 616. In around 663 he and his cousin Sigehere succeeded their distant relative Swithhelm. He was the more religious of the two and concentrated on endowing the Church; the political narrative of their reign centred on Sigehere. Living a holy life of austerity like a monk and being referred to by Bede as more like a cleric than a king, he was a leading patron of St Paul's cathedral in London. From 688 (?) he was the sole king, but seems to have avoided Sigehere's recent intervention in the affairs of Kent where a native prince, Wihtred, now returned. He died in 693 after a long illness, probably in his sixties, Bede recorded. He was buried in St Paul's, and later stories of the miracles at and involving his tomb led to his becoming a popular local saint.

SIGEHERE (663–688) The most vigorous of the East Saxon rulers of the seventh century, as far as the meagre records make out. The son of Sigebert the Little, he became co-ruler with his cousin Saebbi on the death of Swithhelm in 663 and returned to paganism in the crisis of the plague of 664. Wulfhere of Mercia, his powerful western neighbour, had to send Bishop Jaruman to reconvert him; Sigehere also formed a close alliance with Mercia, marrying Wulfhere's niece (St) Osyth, daughter of Frithuwold of Surrey. Late in his reign he backed Caedwalla of Wessex in his Kentish adventure of 686–8, but when the warlord abdicated in 688 and Kent remained in revolt, Sigehere intervened himself. This first East Saxon interference in its ex-overlord's affairs showed how the balance of power had changed temporarily, with Wessex and Mercia otherwise engaged. Sigehere assumed authority in West Kent, only to die soon afterwards; either he or Saebbi's son Sigeheard arranged for the latter's brother Swaefred to succeed him in Kent. Sigehere's death left Saebbi, assisted by Sigeheard, ruling Essex.

EAST ANGLIA

AETHELWALD/AETHELWOLD (655 – 663/4 (?)) The younger brother of kings Anna and Aethelhere of East Anglia, he succeeded the latter on his death in battle at Winwaed on 15 November 655. The disaster temporarily destroyed the power of East Anglia's Mercian overlords. Aethelwald, a Christian like Anna and possibly Aethelhere, benefited from this greater freedom of action. He seems to have asserted a degree of influence over his neighbours in Essex and used it for the benefit of the Church, inducing King Swithhelm to accept baptism. The reunification and reassertion of Mercia under Wulfhere from 658 may not have been an immediate threat. Aethelwald died in 663/4 and was succeeded by his nephew Ealdwulf.

EALDWULF (664 (?) – 713) The son of Aethelric, brother of kings Anna, Aethelhere and Aethelwold who ruled East Anglia in succession from *c.* 641 to 663/4. He was in his seventeenth year as ruler at the time of the Synod of Hatfield in 680. He was probably quite young when he succeeded, given his lengthy reign of fifty years, which is the longest recorded for Anglo-Saxon history. His mother, Hereswith, was great-niece of Edwin of Northumbria, her family having fled thence in 632/3. East Anglia was prosperous enough for the introduction of coinage in the later seventh century and presumably kept up its trading-links with the Continent. He appears to have died around 713, when he was probably at least in his sixties, and was succeeded by his son Alfwold.

MERCIA

PEADA (*c.* 653–656) Eldest son and heir of Penda, appointed by him as sub-ruler of the 'Middle Angles' around 653. This gave him rule of the south-east of his father's large kingdom, probably encompassing Buckinghamshire, Bedfordshire, Northamptonshire and the upper Thames valley; it is possible that this was one of the traditional geographical and/or ethnic sub-divisions of Mercia, which had many separate 'peoples' under one over-king. Regarded with praise by Bede, he was soon married to Aelflaed/Elfleda, the daughter of his father's rival Oswy of Northumbria, in a failed diplomatic rapprochement. His sister Cyneburh married Oswy's son Alchfrith, sub-ruler of Deira. Peada was persuaded to abandon his father's paganism, admit Northumbrian missionaries including (Saints) Chad and his brother Cedd, and convert. The conversion may have been planned by the devout Oswy, though it is not certain that Penda's paganism means that he violently opposed the initiative and believed that Oswy was endeavouring to subvert his son.

Peada remained loyal to his father and may have participated in his failed invasion of Northumbria in 655. When Penda was killed at the River Winwaed in November, Mercia was at Oswy's mercy; he confirmed Peada as king of the Middle Angles (as his vassal) but left the main kingship vacant. Oswy and Peada jointly founded a monastery at Medehamstede (Peterborough) in the Fenland. Only five months later, at Easter 656, Peada was assassinated in obscure circumstances. His wife was implicated, and if so may have been acting on her father's orders. All of Mercia was left kingless, but in 658 (?) Peada's younger brother Wulfhere was to be used by the local nobility as the focus for that successful revolt which Oswy probably feared in 656.

WULFHERE (658 – 674/5) The second of three sons of the great warlord Penda, he and his brothers were left at the mercy of Oswy of Northumbria when he killed their father at the River Winwaed in November 655. Oswy allowed Wulfhere's elder brother Peada to retain the kingdom of the 'Middle Angles', where the younger boys presumably fled, but all Mercia was annexed on Peada's murder at Easter 656. Oswy sought out Wulfhere to kill him, but he was hidden by loyal thegns and re-emerged three years after the Winwaed disaster (i.e. autumn 658) to lead a national Mercian rebellion. Oswy's governors were driven out and Wulfhere restored the independence of Mercia, which Oswy had to accept. For all practical purposes Wulfhere was as dominant in southern England after *c*. 660 as Aethelbert, Raedwald and Penda had been, with clear military primacy over Wessex. Raiding south to, or from, 'Ashdown' (the Berkshire downs) in 661, he was able to hand over parts of eastern Hampshire to his ally Aethelwalh of Sussex and to compel the kings of Wight to transfer their allegiance from Wessex to Sussex. Several West Saxon sub-kings seem to have been killed, with King Cenwalh humiliated by the loss of territory, and Wulfhere was clearly aiming to build up Sussex at Wessex's expense. He also formed an early alliance with Earconbert of Kent, whose daughter Eormenhilda he married, and was overlord of Essex by *c*. 663. He was able to install the ex-bishop Wine of Wessex in the see of London in *c*. 670.

His local control was probably exercised by his brother-in-law Frithuwold, who appears as his sub-king of Surrey by 674 and seems to have been Mercian. Wulfhere may have been converted to Christianity at Peada's Christian court, which had been converted from Northumbria; his choice as the first bishop of newly-Christian Mercia in *c*. 658 was the Northumbrian Trumhere. His own religious links were mainly with Canterbury. Either he or Penda installed loyal dynasties of long-lasting sub-kings in their south-western territories – the possibly Northumbrian line of Eanfrith and Eanhere in Hwicce and the possibly half-Welsh line of Merewalh (his half-brother?) in Magonsaetan. Both kingdoms duly received bishoprics, controlled from Mercia's ally Canterbury. He also assisted the new, Anatolian-born Archbishop Theodore of Canterbury in summoning the first synod of all the bishops in England at Hertford, within Mercia, in 672.

In 673, Wulfhere was confident enough of his influence in Kent to demand the regency for the under-age new king, Eadric, Eormenhilda's nephew. This had to be conceded initially, but within a couple of years locals rallied round Wulfhere's rival Hlothere, the late King Eadric's brother. Kentish troops may have been needed to assist his invasion of Northumbria in 674, a first direct challenge to Mercia's one-time conquerors arising from a confrontation over control of Lindsey. Ecgfrith, who had once been a hostage at Penda's court, defeated the invasion and a revolt in Kent on Hlothere's behalf followed.

Wulfhere died unexpectedly before he could retaliate, late in 674 or early in 675; if Bede is correct that he reigned for seventeen (full) years, as opposed to ruling into his seventeenth year, it may have been later in 675. He was probably in his mid-thirties. His brother Aethelred succeeded him. As powerful a king in southern England as his father, though usually unwilling to confront Northumbria, he had as much right as Oswy to be accounted senior ruler south of the Humber.

AETHELRED (674/5 – 704) The younger brother of Wulfhere of Mercia, and third son of Penda. He was probably born around 640. Their father Penda's death at the hands of Oswy of Northumbria at the Battle of Winwaed in November 655 temporarily destroyed Mercian power and reduced Aethelred's eldest brother Peada to vassal-king of the surviving part of the kingdom, the 'Middle Angles', until his violent death in 656. Peada's recent conversion to Christianity on marriage to Oswy's daughter Elfleda had led to the dispatch of missionaries from Northumbria; Aethelred may have been among their converts, or else converted in Wulfhere's reign after the latter restored Mercian independence in 658. Unlike Wulfhere, he was known for his piety; he married Elfleda's younger sister Osthryth, who assisted his support for the Church.

Aethelred succeeded Wulfhere late in 674 or early in 675, and proved as vigorous a ruler. Kent had recently revolted against Wulfhere, with the latter's under-age ruler Eadric being supplanted by his uncle Hlothere. In 676, Aethelred struck back and sent an army into Kent to ravage and regain disputed territory; his army's brutal sack of Rochester and burning of its new cathedral sent Bishop Puttoc fleeing into exile. But once Aethelhere had reasserted authority he was able to come to an agreement with Hlothere which kept the latter in possession of his throne, and Puttoc was compensated by being made the first bishop of the see which Archbishop Theodore created for Aethelred's western border provinces at Hereford by agreement with the king.

A patron of the Church, Aethelred continued the conversion by (St) Chad's missionaries (begun under Wulfhere). The royal couple's most notable monastic foundation was at Bardney in Lincolnshire, where Osthryth installed the relics of her uncle St Oswald, appropriating his cult for her husband's kingdom. Aethelhere's relations with Northumbria remained uneasy, though the main thrust of his brother-in-law Ecgfrith's expansion was luckily northwards. The two states continued to clash over Lindsey and in 679 Aethelred defeated a Northumbrian army, killing his wife's other brother Elfwine, sub-king of Deira; this brought retaliation from Ecgfrith and the danger of blood-feud, which Aethelred's ally Archbishop Theodore halted with his mediation.

From Ecgfrith's death in battle in 685, Aethelred was the most powerful king among the English, though Bede does not rank him as a *bretwalda*. He refrained from intervening in the turbulence in Kent in 686–88 and did not challenge the military ascendancy of Caedwalla of Wessex south of the Thames; after Caedwalla's abdication he intervened to back a prince of the Kentish dynasty, Oswine, on condition that he accepted Mercian overlordship. The latter was murdered within three years; Aethelred had no reason to challenge the eventual victor Wihtred, relative and candidate of his brother Wulfhere's Kentish widow Eormenhild. His wife Osthryth retired into the nunnery at Bardney at some date before 697, when she was murdered by a group of Mercian nobles (apparently in a blood-feud over her involvement in her sister's husband Peada's killing in 656). Aethelred may have married again; he was, however, drawn to the monastic life and in 704 he abdicated to take over as abbot of Bardney. His brother Wulfhere's son Coenred succeeded rather than his own son and in 706 Aethelred was able to require the new king to come to Bardney to be admonished. The *Anglo-Saxon Chronicle*'s length for his reign is given as twenty-nine years.

Aethelred died in 716, probably in his early to mid-seventies. He was not the first Mercian king to convert and back the Church, but he was the first to take on Christian activities personally as part of his duties of kingship and have close relations with the Church leadership.

SURREY

FRITHUWOLD (670s) The only recorded king of Surrey, as known from charters of 673–5. At the time he was the sub-king there for its overlord Wulfhere of Mercia, whose sister Wilburh was his wife. Surrey ('South Region', probably of Essex) had been settled back in the later fifth or early sixth century from the archaeological record, and may have existed as a kingdom – a vassal of the East Saxons and later of Kent. However, Frithuwold is unlikely to have had a hereditary claim except via female descent, as land-grants for south-east Mercia in the seventh century show that a family with alliterative names similar to his held estates in Buckinghamshire and the similarly-named (early eighth-century) Saint Frideswide had royal relatives ruling around Oxford. Frithuric, possibly his father or brother, granted land at Breedon-on-the-Hill in Leicestershire to a monastery in *c*. 675/90. If the family dominated that area they were probably of 'Middle Angle' blood and/or allegiance, sub-kings of Penda in the 640s to 655.

Penda's second son Wulfhere had recently restored Mercian rule over the south-east Midlands from *c*. 658, and Frithuwold was probably his nominee to rule the middle Thames valley. He granted Chertsey Abbey an important charter in 673/5. His daughter, (Saint) Osyth, whose strong religious interests may have been inherited from him, married Sigehere, king of the East Saxons from *c*. 663 and another protégé of Wulfhere; their son was the saintly Offa who abdicated to journey to Rome. Frithugyth, who married King Aethelheard of Wessex (a Mercian ally from *c*. 726), may have been Frithuwold's younger daughter or granddaughter. Another daughter may have been Saint Osgyth of Aylesbury, who a twelfth-century *Life* called the daughter of a King 'Fredeswald' and Wulfhere's sister; if this late document preserves any genuine details, its heroine was brought up at Quarrendon in Buckinghamshire, possibly another family estate. The strong family connections in the middle Thames region – north of the river – may indicate that Frithuwold's territorial base was here, within Mercian territory, not in Surrey. The Surrey kingship was duly suppressed by Mercia under the centralizing early eighth-century rulers and disappears from history.

HWICCE

OSHERE, OSRIC and OSWALD (*c*. 675 – 690s) The three brothers and co-rulers who succeeded to Hwicce on the death of King Eanhere around 675. Nothing is known about them except as witnesses to charters, and they were all clients of their Mercian overlord, King Aethelred. They were Church patrons – Oshere established minsters at Riple, Inkberrow and Withington; Osric founded monasteries at Gloucester and Bath; and Oswald founded the abbey of Pershore in 699. Apparently Osric died first in around 685, when he vanishes from charters; Oswald lasted until *c*. 690 and Oshere for another decade or so. Aethelbert and Aethelwaerd, even more obscure, succeeded Oshere and ruled in the 700s, followed by Osred in the 730s.

MAGONSAETAN

MEREWALH (650s (?) – 685) The first known king of this obscure minor kingdom of Mercia, a vassal of its powerful neighbour. His name means 'noble

Welshman', which adds to the controversy over the origins and nature of this supposedly West Anglian kingdom where there is very little evidence of Germanic settlement in the seventh century. The name 'Magonsaetan' appears to be geographical, as with other local 'peoples' of Mercia, and refers either to 'Magnis' – the principal Roman town of northern Herefordshire, now Kenchester near Hereford – or to the nearby village of Marden. If it was the former, it may have originated in the local territory legally and economically dependant on Magnis after the end of Roman rule, and been British rather than Anglian in origin. The kingdom comprised Herefordshire and Shropshire, and was dependant on Mercia whether or not a 'ruling class' or dynasty of Anglian origin moved in to take over a small British kingdom. The military power of its northern/north-western neighbour in the 640s and 650s, Powys, under Cyndylan, suggests that it came under Mercian influence only after his death.

Merewalh was recorded in the genealogies as a son of Penda, which begs the question of why that Angle gave his son a Welsh name? This cannot be written off as subsequent propaganda to link his dynasty to their patrons, as in charters they refer to themselves as the kin of Penda's dynasty and their Kentish relatives. The kingdom may have emerged as a dependency of the wide-ruling Penda, whether or not ethnically mainly British, and Merewalh may have been his son by a British wife. One logical suggestion is that his mother was Cyndylan's sister Heledd, known to later (twelfth-century) literary legend as Penda's British wife, and that he was an ally of both kingdoms which fought together against Northumbria in the 640s and early 650s. He seems to have been pagan in his youth as he was converted in 660 (?), which suggests an origin at Penda's court not as a British prince. He married Eafa, a kinswoman of his Mercian overlord Wulfhere's Kentish wife Eormenhilda, around this time, and had two sons, Merchelm and Mildfrith, by her and a third, Merefin (the Welsh 'Merfyn'?), by a later marriage. He had three daughters who all entered the Church – Mildburh, abbess of Much Wenlock; Mildryth, who succeeded her mother as abbess of Minster-in-Thanet, and Mildgyth. The close Christian links with Kent were extended when, in 679, Puttoc, refugee bishop of Rochester, whose cathedral had been sacked by the Mercians in 676, arrived as the first bishop of Magonsaetan, based at Hereford. Merewalh died in 685, and was buried at the Mercian royal centre of Repton; Merchelm succeeded him and Eafa returned home as abbess of Minster-in-Thanet, dying in 698.

MERECHELM (685 – *c.* 700 (?)) The elder son and successor of King Merewalh; his name means 'helmet of the Mercians', suggesting his intended role as a protector/ally to his people's overlords. He succeeded to the throne in 685, and vanishes from the records around 700; his brother Mildfrith succeeded him.

NORTHUMBRIA

ECGFRITH (Sub-king of Deira, c. 664 – 670/1; Northumbria, 670/1 – 685)
The elder son of King Oswy of Northumbria by his second (or third) wife Enfleda, daughter of Edwin; he thus had a hereditary claim to both Deira and Bernicia. Born in 644/5, he was ten when he was taken hostage by Penda of Mercia in the latter's final invasion of Northumbria and sent to his wife's court. Around 664 he succeeded his half-brother Alchfrith as sub-king of Deira, and remained in that role until his succession to the main kingdom on 15 February 670. In 660 he had married the formidable (Saint) Etheldreda (Audrey), daughter of Anna of East Anglia, who was about twelve years older than him, in his father's alliance with that kingdom. His religious-minded wife's alleged vow to retain her virginity contributed mostly to the failure of his marriage. Ecgfrith's brother Aelfwine took over in Deira in 670. His probable date of accession was 15 February 670, when Bede states that Oswy died; but both Bede and the Northumbrian regnal list state that Ecgfrith was in his fifteenth, not sixteenth regnal year when he died in May 685, so it may be that he acceded in February 671.

He pursued a particularly aggressive policy towards the Picts, aiming to extend his borders as far north as possible; in 672 he killed their king in battle and was supposedly able to cross a river dryshod on the bodies of the fallen. Annexation of Fife followed, and in 681 he was able to set up an Anglian bishopric at Abercorn. Around 675 he defeated the new ruler of Mercia, Aethelred, who subsequently married his sister Osthryth in a treaty which retained Northumbrian predominance as the greatest military power among the Anglo-Saxon kingdoms. He made a new marital alliance with Kent, marrying Eormenburh, the cousin of King Ecgbert. But in 679 a second clash with Mercia on the River Trent, probably over control of Lindsey, saw an unexpected Northumbrian defeat. Ecgfrith's brother Aelfwine of Deira was killed, and this led to a blood-feud between the king and his brother-in-law Aethelred until Archbishop Theodore of Canterbury restored peace and Aethelred paid appropriate compensation.

As part of his expansive policies, Ecgfrith had been driving British inhabitants out of Rheged, west of the Pennines, and bringing in Angles. Exiles fled to eastern Ireland and launched raids across the Irish Sea, and in retaliation Ecgfrith raided across the Irish Sea to the Leinster kingdom of Brega in 684. His naval power thus outmatched even Edwin's, but his military risk-taking was to cost him his life. Early in 685 he launched another massive invasion of the Pictish kingdom, pressing north of the Tay into Angus. No known Pictish foe had marched this far north since the Romans. His victory would have permanently altered the balance of power in the island. The time of year was unusual, suggesting a surprise attack. But he was defeated and killed at the battle of Nechtansmere in Angus by King Briude/Bridei mac Beli on

20 February 685, a blow which ended Northumbria's northward expansion and led to the loss of all lands north of the Firth of Forth. The Picts sent his body for burial at the abbey of Iona, their own royal burial-site, a mark of respect for a formidable foe as well as reflecting his ancestors' connections with the site. His widow retired to Carlisle Abbey as a nun, and his surviving half-brother Aldfrith was able to return home to claim the throne.

ALDFRITH (685–705) The eldest son of Oswy; his mother was the Irish princess Fina who Oswy had met while in exile during the reign of Edwin (617 – 33/4). He was probably born after Oswy and his elder brother Oswald returned to Northumbria, but he was to be passed over in favour of Oswy's younger children and there seems to have been a question mark over the legitimacy of the marriage (if indeed it occurred). Aldfrith was to be regarded as illegitimate. Aldfrith may well have returned to Ireland with his mother (perhaps on Oswy's marriage to Rhianmelt) as he accepted his exclusion from the throne, kept away and devoted himself to Christian study – first in Ireland, later in southern England at Canterbury and Malmesbury. By the time of his unexpected elevation as king in 685, he was writing poetry and riddles.

The death of his half-brother Ecgfrith in battle at Nechtansmere in May 685 left Northumbria kingless and Alfdrith the last male of the dynasty. The middle-aged scholar was chosen as king with the backing of his half-sister Elfleda despite his lack of experience. The late king's conquests north of the Forth were abandoned to the resurgent Picts, but otherwise the kingdom survived the disaster intact and Aldfrith returned Irish hostages taken in the 684 invasion. His reign proved peaceful apart from a campaign against the Picts in 698. As Aldfrith had been trained in both the Irish 'Celtic' and Roman southern English religious traditions, he was well placed to continue the rapprochement between the two rites in the kingdom. Wilfred, exiled leader of the most uncompromising form of Roman triumphalism, was recalled at Aldfrith's accession and given the bishopric of Deira (Ripon/York) in 686 with Ecgfrith's nominee being evicted, and in 687 he succeeded the saintly Cuthbert as bishop of Lindisfarne to control the Churches of both Deira and Bernicia. But he proved too unpopular, particularly for his aggressive promotion of Roman customs; in 691 he was exiled again.

The reign of Alfdrith saw the height of the artistic creations of Northumbrian Christianity with a fusion of both Roman and Celtic artistic traditions – most notably in the Lindisfarne Gospels. Aldfrith seems to have commissioned this work, and his background in scholarship and wide experience of travel and study made him a suitable patron for this and other contemporary works. A rare example of a seventh-century scholar-king who participated in, as well as supporting, cultural endeavour; his poetic interests have led to speculation that he also commissioned the epic *Beowulf*. He married Cuthburh, sister of King Ine of Wessex, and had at least one son; she retired from court to found her own nunnery at Barking before his death and later founded Wimborne Minster. Given his age and their interests, the marriage was probably a diplomatic arrangement to produce heirs.

Aldfrith died at Driffield near Leeds on 14 December 704, apparently after a lengthy decline. He was probably in his mid-sixties. He left under-age heirs; an ambitious thegn called Eadwulf usurped the throne from the elder, Osred, but was quickly removed in his favour after two months. In retrospect, Aldfrith's reign seemed a golden age of culture and political stability; the kingdom of Northumbria entered a period of turbulence in 705 which permanently affected its strength, though not its unity.

CUTHBURH (Queen of Northumbria, *c.* 692 – 703 (?)) The sister of King Ine of the West Saxons, and daughter of Cenred. She was married early in her brother's reign (*c.* 692 [?]) to his childless ally, King Aldfrith of Northumbria, who was at least in his late forties and was the last male of his dynasty. Children were thus essential to prevent dynastic disputes on his death, and she gave him at least one son, Osred, probably born around 695. Aldfrith's other 'son', Osric, may have been her second son or really the son of the likenamed King Alchfrith, his half-brother. She put the religious life above her duties as queen, where she could expect to play a prominent role as mother of an under-age reigning son if her husband did not live long, and seems to have returned to Wessex before Aldfrith died in 705. There she became the founding abbess of Wimborne Minster, a religious house associated with the royal family, where King Aethelred I was buried in 871.

DEIRA

ALCHFRITH (or EALHFRITH) (655 (?) – 664 (?)) The son of Oswy of Northmbria by his first wife, British princess Rhianmelt/Rhiammelth of Rheged. The apparent extinction of the male line of this kingdom – by this time a vassal of Northumbria – may indicate that the marriage, *c.* 635, was designed by Oswy's brother Oswald to tie Rheged to his kingdom and Rhianmelt was intended to transmit the loyalty of her people to their new lords. Alchfrith appears to have been Oswy's heir in the 650s. He was adult enough to fight with his father against Penda of Mercia at Winwaed in November 655. The current sub-king of Deira, Oswald's son Aethelwald, had deserted to Penda and was either killed or expelled from Deira; Oswy installed Alchfrith as the new king. Alchfrith was married to Cyneburh, Penda's daughter, probably before 655. He helped to persuade his wife's brother Peada to convert to Christianity before Winwaed.

In Oswy's role as overlord of a truncated Mercia, Alchfrith was a crucial link to Peada (soon killed) as sub-ruler of what remained. Relations between

Oswy and Alchfrith, who was remembered as strong-headed, worsened as Alchfrith took decisive loyalties in the controversy between the use of the Roman and 'Celtic' customs in the Northumbrian Church. In 658, Alchfrith welcomed the Rome-trained Northumbrian cleric (Saint) Wilfred back to Deira as bishop at Ripon after his recommendation by King Cenwalh of the West Saxons, expelling Oswy's nominee Eata, who followed the 'Celtic' practices. In 664, Oswy summoned a synod at Streoneshalh (Whitby) to make a decisive ruling. This was in Rome's favour, and Alchfrith's ally Wilfred was accepted as the new Bishop of York.

Alchfrith seems to have died in, or soon after, 664. While Wilfred was in Rome to collect his pallium of office, Oswy, as overlord of Deira, appointed his own nominee, (Saint) Chad to replace him. Alchfrith's reaction is unknown. Such a challenge to his authority might have been expected to cause him to revolt, but if he did react adversely his death prevented any confrontation. It is possible that the embarrassment of a conflict between father and son, two vigorous patrons of the Church, was covered up; more likely Alchfrith died suddenly, soon after Wilfred left for Rome. The plague of 664/5 is the likeliest cause of Alchfrith's death; he could not have been much over thirty.

5

c. 690 to 756

KENT

WIHTRED (691–725) Younger son of Egbert (d. 673) and brother of Eadric (d. 686 [?]), he was titular co-ruler with his brother under their grandmother Seaxburh's regency in 673–4. Their maternal uncle, Wulfhere of Mercia, and their paternal uncle, Hlothere (Lothar), both sought to take over Kent, the latter with eventual success, and Eadric alone emerged as co-ruler after c. 679 and removed his uncle in 685. Eadric's defeat by Caedwalla of Wessex in August 686 led to the removal of the native dynasty and struggles for control between Wessex, Mercia and Essex, but in 691 Wihtred returned from exile with Church backing. (He was in his sixth regnal year in April 697 according to a land-grant, so he claimed power some time after April 691.) Probably overthrowing the Mercian (?) nominee Oswine, while both Mercia and Wessex were preoccupied, he seems to have ruled only East Kent (with the Church centre, Canterbury) until the Essex claimant Swaefred lost the west in c. 692. According to Bede, both Wihtred and Swaefred were kings when the new archbishop, Beorhtwald, was elected in April 692.

Thereafter he ruled as sole king, restoring an era of peace and stability after a decade of chaos, and had enough military strength for Ine of Wessex to abandon his claims and negotiate a finalised frontier in the 690s. Wihtred, a strict adminstrator relying on Church support, updated the Kentish law-code, and advised Ine on legal matters ahead of the issuing of the Kentish-influenced first West Saxon law-code. He exempted the Church from taxation in 708, an innovation taken up later by other kings and linking the Church's financial prosperity (and resulting prestige and power) to royal patronage. He died on 23 April 725, probably in his early sixties at most given his father's and elder brother's ages.

He was succeeded by three sons as co-rulers, which suggests that he put family unity above the political need for one strong king despite the dynastic feuds of the 680s.

EADBERT (I) (725 – 762 (?)) One of the three sons of Wihtred, who succeeded him on 23 April 725 with his brothers Aethelbert (II) and Ealric. The latter soon vanishes from records. The charter evidence would imply that he was junior to Aethelbert, who retired in *c.* 748 but returned for a few years, and there was probably a geographical division of the kingdom with Eadbert ruling west of the Medway. After Aethelbert's retirement Eadbert may have moved to East Kent, the senior portion, and associated his son Eardwulf as co-ruler. The latter predeceased him. Eadbert lived to the early 760s (possibly 762). Presumably he was a loyal client of Mercia; he attended Offa's court in London in 748. He was probably at least in his mid-fifties, and was the last king of the line of Aesc. He was buried at Reculver rather, than as usual for Kentish kings, at Canterbury. He was succeeded briefly by Eanmund/Ealhmund and then by Sigered. Events were to show that the stability and prosperity of Kent ended with Eadbert.

AETHELBERT II and EALRIC Co-rulers with Eadbert, and his younger brothers. Aethelbert appears to vanish from the charters around 748 and appear a few years later, possibly due to temporary retirement. Both preceded Eadbert.

SUSSEX

NOTHELM (NUNNA) (*fl.* 690s – *c.* 725) An obscure king of the South Saxons, who came to power at a time when the kingdom had been twice invaded and overrun by Wessex in recent years and was a restive West Saxon client-state. Kent had revolted successfully and now came under the influence of Essex and later Mercia, but the new West Saxon king, Ine, prevailed in Sussex as he was delineating the new Kent-Sussex border (as overlord of Sussex) with the new Kentish king, Wihtred, in the mid-690s. Nothelm witnesses charters as the local king from this period on into the eighth century, and was clearly Ine's nominee and vassal. His reign is obscure but appears to have been peaceful, with Ine a strong leader who would not have tolerated resistance; in 710, Nothelm is found serving in his army with South Saxon troops in the successful invasion of north-west Devon. Nothelm apparently ruled with a colleague, Wattus, by *c.* 714 and the location of their charter-grants makes it probable that if they divided the kingdom into East and West Sussex, Wattus ruled the former. Nothelm's position may have been weakened when Ine suffered a decline in power in the early 720s; in 722–5 a rebel West Saxon atheling, Ealdbert, was at large in Sussex resisting Ine's attacks. The rebel received local support and it took Ine three years to defeat him. It is not known if Nothelm was still alive at this point, if the rebellion led to or followed his death, or if he backed Ine or the rebels; it is only a guess that as Ine's client he may have been expelled.

WATTUS (Early eighth century) Attested in charters as Nunna/Nothelm's co-ruler after *c*. 700; possibly of East Sussex.

ATHELSTAN (720s) An obscure client king established by Ine of the West Saxons, from the evidence of charters ruling in the 720s. The location of his grants makes it apparent that he reigned in East Sussex, probably as junior to the senior ruler Nothelm and in succession to Wattus. His reign coincides with Ine's invasion of Sussex in 722 to deal with a refugee West Saxon prince, Ealdbert, and the resulting three-year war testifies to the amount of resistance. Which side Athelstan took is unknown, but West Saxon overlordship probably ended with Ine's death in 726; his successors were weaker rulers overshadowed by Mercia.

WESSEX

INE (688–726) Kinsman and successor of Caedwalla; according to the later genealogies used in the 688 entry of the *Anglo-Saxon Chronicle* he was the son of Cenred, grandson of Ceolwald and great-grandson of Cuthwulf, a brother of Caedwalla's grandfather. Cuthwulf was son of Cuthwine, son of Ceawlin – a man who only appears in the *Chronicle* as Ceawlin's co-commander at Deorham in 577 (?). Ine was thus of Ceawlin's direct line, superseded in 592, and he had a brother (Ingeld) and a sister Cuthburh, wife of King Aldfrith of Northumbria and later founding abbess of Wimborne Minster. The later West Saxon dynasty from 802 claimed decent from Ingeld, Ine's brother, so it is possible that this genealogy was created or 'improved' to add to their legitimacy in the ninth century. It can only be a guess that Cuthwine, if he was really Ceawlin's son, had predeceased him or had been expelled with him in 592 and his family had thus lost their place in the succession for nearly a century; this may have been what Ine and his supporters wanted people to believe, but in any case it seems that Ine was able to restore stability to the kingdom.

His predecessor, a dynamic young warlord, had annexed Sussex and Kent in 685–8, but chose to abdicate due to injuries and went on pilgrimage to Rome where he died at Easter 689; Ine was probably his nominee as a close kinsman. He inherited a strong army, and possibly also a degree of centralization (for military co-ordination?) forced by his two predecessors. Kent came temporarily under East Saxon influence without any known attempt by Ine to keep it, though the kingdom had to pay compensation for the murder of Ine's kinsman Mul, Caedwalla's brother and puppet-king. A new king of the South Saxons (Nothelm) emerged in the early 690s, apparently as Ine's client after several years of West Saxon action against rebels; Ine, probably hampered by unrecorded rival athelings disputing his accession, resorted to indirect rule.

Ine's main achievement was the establishment of a West Saxon law-code, based on that of Aethelbert of Kent but the first for a Saxon, rather than Jutish, kingdom. Work on it began soon after his accession and was completed in 694; it served to strengthen the king's position by making him guarantor of law and order on behalf of God, enabled his officials to interfere in local legal process and granted him a share of fines to build up his revenue. He seems to have consulted the new king of Kent, Wihtred, about the code, and the two kingdoms established a finalised border which ended decades of conflict. The code also served to regularise the position of the surviving British population within Wessex, which place-names show to have been substantial in Devon; however, they remained legally inferior to the Saxons. Like Aethelbert and his own predecessor Caedwalla, Ine worked in tandem with the Church, but unlike Caedwalla he evidently grasped the importance of law and administration. The subsequent increase of royal power went in tandem with the eclipse of the power of local sub-kings, and Ine was almost certainly the initiator (and certainly the main beneficiary) of the creation of a 'county' system of government. Wessex was divided into shires, regulated geographical units under a royally-appointed ealdorman; civil strife over the throne was to resume, but the position of the king was strengthened via his kingdom-wide system of officials. It also appears that Ine stimulated trade and royal revenue in his domains by the creation and promotion of the new trading-settlement of Hamwic, at the mouth of the Itchen in Hampshire – a Wessex version of Continental trading towns like Quentovic.

For the first time a separate bishopric was created for the western part of the kingdom, west of Selwood, in 705. (Saint) Aldhelm was the first bishop. Ine's father's lands may have lain in Dorset. Dumnonia (Cornwall) may have regained some territory in the Exmoor area in the decades after the Saxon victory of 682 and Ine may have decided to counter this. A battle at Langport in Somerset, which was well within the county and more likely to indicate a Dumnonian offensive than a Saxon advance, in 710 ended with Ine's victory and the death of King Gereint. Nunna participated, bringing South Saxon aid to his overlord, and it was logically around this time that Ine fortified Taunton. He was able to advance as far as the Tamar, where a defeat in 722 halted his advance; if he ever penetrated Cornwall this ended his success, but he had secured all of Devon. His decades of strong rule seem to have ended in renewed civil strife, probably due to him being childless; the *Chronicle* saw fit to note his brother Ingeld's (his obvious successor) death in 718. In 721 he killed an atheling called Cynewulf and exiled another called Ealdbert; the latter must have started a rebellion or returned with a warband, as in 722 Ine's queen, Aethelburh, besieged him in, and sacked, Taunton. The absence of the king may indicate that he was ill, or that he was militarily preoccupied elsewhere. Ealdbert escaped into Sussex, where he had enough local backing to stage a three-year war before Ine killed him.

In 726 Ine abdicated to journey to Rome as a pilgrim, as Caedwalla had done. He had ruled for thirty-eight years, the longest reign in West Saxon history, and must have been in his sixties. He left no obvious successor, and the victor of a succession dispute was his wife's brother Aethelheard, who had Mercian backing. Ine died in Rome in 728, having given the temporary success and unity of Wessex under Caedwalla a permanent administrative and legal framework. Lacking an heir, he failed where his presumed relative Egbert was to succeed a century later.

AETHELHEARD (726–740) Aethelheard succeeded the childless King Ine of Wessex (his brother-in-law according to one charter) on his abdication to travel to Rome in 726. The West Saxon kingdom had been riven with struggles over the throne towards the end of the 38-year reign of the childless Ine, with his queen Aethelburh successfully besieging a pretender called Ealdbert in Taunton in 722; if Aethelheard was her brother, she probably backed his candidacy. He was in a weak position, lacking dynastic legitimacy – in contrast to his rival in 726, Oswald. A decisive military intervention was made by Aethelbald of Mercia in Aethelheard's favour. The latter then probably became his vassal, a return to the weaker role of Wessex vis-à-vis Mercia in the 660s.

The Mercian name of Aethelheard's wife, Frithugyth, suggests links with Mercian sub-king Frithuwold of Surrey and with Saint Frideswide of Oxford. Oswald survived until 730, possibly still resisting. Being a Mercian ally did not preserve Wessex from aggression by Aethelbald, who invaded Aethelheard's western territories in 733 to take Somerton and apparently annex northern Somerset; later Berkshire and northern Wiltshire were also overrun. Aethelheard was also required to assist his patron against the Welsh of Powys; in 737 his wife Frithugyth journeyed to Rome, possibly to add to his declining prestige by a pilgrimage in place of a king who did not dare to leave his insecure kingdom. He died in 740 and was succeeded by his kinsman Cuthred, his brother according to the much later Simeon of Durham. His capabilities as a ruler were clearly constrained by his weak position.

CUTHRED (740–756) The successor of Aethelheard as king of the West Saxons in 740. According to the later eleventh-century historian Simeon of Durham, he was his brother, which would make him also the brother of Ine's queen, Aethelburh, and so probably already adult in the 720s.

Unlike his predecessor, he seems to have been willing to challenge Aethelheard's patron Aethelbald of Mercia, unless the latter's opposition forced the conflict of 740/1 on him. He was successful enough to retain his throne, possibly by accepting continuing Mercian overlordship, as in 743 the two rulers were fighting in alliance against the Welsh. As far as can be ascertained his reign was mostly without domestic challenge apart from an 'arrogant ealdorman' who he defeated in 752, though the violent death of Atheling Cynric (his son?) in 748 may have had political reasons.

Henry of Huntingdon expands the minimal reference to it in the *Chronicle* to an account of his promise as a war-leader and his death in a mutiny. Cuthred's relationship with Mercia was marked by a second war in 752, when Cuthred fought Aethelbald at 'Beorgford', possibly Burford in Oxfordshire. He was compelled to have Aethelbald as co-witness for land-grants to Glastonbury Abbey. Cuthred died in 756, apparently heirless; Sigebert succeeded. The death of Cynric possibly resulted in a return of instability, to Wessex's detriment and Mercia's benefit.

SIGEBERT (756–757) Elected to succeed Cuthred in 756, from his name it seems he had East Anglian or Frankish connections. Of unknown lineage, he evidently aroused antagonism and within a year he was driven out by a revolt in favour of Cynewulf; Henry of Huntingdon calls him a tyrant. He must have retained some support, as he was allowed to retain Hampshire (his home county?) in the agreement that followed. But he does not seem to have remained content, as he soon quarrelled with his chief supporter, Ealdorman Cumbra, and murdered him. He was driven into the Weald, where he was murdered by a herdsman; evidently the demeaning circumstances were remembered into the following century as part of the famous story of blood-feud between his family and Cynewulf which ended in slaughter thirty years later. His brother Cyneheard duly murdered Cynewulf in 786, evidently sharing Sigebert's vengeful and turbulent nature.

ESSEX

SWAEFHERD (693–707 (?)) Possibly the same person as Swaefred (q.v.); if not, he was the co-ruler with Sigeheard in Essex from the death of Saebbi in 693. The longest-surviving of these two co-rulers died in 707 when Offa succeeded; which it was is unknown.

SIGEHEARD (East Saxons, <693 – 700s) The son of King Saebbi, he was ruling the western parts of his father's lands (Middlesex) before the latter died in 693, according to charters. Given his father's age, devoutness and ill health, he was probably effectively ruler of Essex for several years before then. When he succeeded to Essex itself, his brother Swaefred, ex-king of Kent, became his co-ruler; it is possible that he had been the principal backer of the latter's brief takeover of Kent in 689/90. He died some time in or before 707, when his distant cousin Offa became ruler.

OFFA (707–709) Son of King Sigehere (d. 688) and his wife (Saint) Osyth, daughter of Frithuwold of Surrey and the Mercian princess Wilburh. He was a 'golden youth', born late in his father's reign and was barely twenty when he succeeded his father's cousin Sigeheard; according to his admirer Bede he was good-looking and extremely popular. Inheriting his saintly mother's passion for the holy life, he abdicated within two years in 709, travelling to Rome as a pilgrim in the manner of Caedwalla of Wessex and persuading his cousin Ceonred of Mercia to join him. They then became monks. Bede made the most of his virtues and the inspiring example which he set, and he was the first Anglo-Saxon king to abdicate in his youth while in good health. It is possible that there were political struggles among the nobility and the extended East Saxon royal family, encouraging his departure. His cousin Saelred succeeded him.

SWAEBERT (709–738) Co-ruler with Saelred after the abdication of King Offa in 709; from his name, probably a close relative (son?) of Swaefred or Swaefheard (the same person?) of Essex and Kent. He appears to have died in 738.

SAELRED (709–746) A distant relative of the saintly young King Offa, who succeeded on his abdication in 709. Saelred ruled with an even more obscure co-king, Swabert, until 738, and was presumably a loyal vassal-king of Mercia as no clashes are recorded. He was killed in 746, but the *Chronicle* does not record if this was by assassination or in battle (against Mercia or East Anglia?). A cousin, Swithred, succeeded him.

SWITHRED (746–759) Probably a dynastic connection of kings Swithhelm (d. 663) or Swaefred/Swaefheard, he was the son of Sigemund. Swithred succeeded King Saelred, who died violently in 746. It is unknown if this was a coup or if he was chosen as Saelred's son Sigeric was under-age. The only event of note in his reign seems to have been the loss of London, principal town of the realm, to Mercian administrative control. He died in 759, when Sigeric succeeded him.

EAST ANGLIA

ALFWALD (713 (?) – 749 (?)) The son of Ealdwulf, who he succeeded as king of East Anglia in or near 713. His father had reigned for around fifty years, so he was probably already in his thirties or forties. Little is known of his reign, during which East Anglia appears to have remained at peace as a junior ally of Mercia without the tension and border-wars which marked the latter's relationship with its other large southern neighbour, Wessex. He was the dedicatee chosen by Felix, author of the hagiography of the Fenland saint Guthlac of Crowland, and may thus have commissioned the book as an act of piety. He sent a supportive letter to Saint Boniface, working to convert the

Frisians close across the North Sea from his kingdom. Alfwald died around 749 after a reign of thirty-six years, probably elderly and it seems without heirs. Beonna eventually emerged as sole ruler.

BEONNA (749 (?) – early 760s) The successor of Alfwald, probably in or near 749. The latter is the last known ruler to have been a member of the ancient royal house, the Wuffingas, and Beonna's name would suggest an east Mercian origin. He and his co-rulers, Hun and Alberht, were probably in a weak political position lacking dynastic legitimacy; the appointment or election of three men may have been a resolution to rival claims or a move by East Anglia's powerful neighbour Aethelbald of Mercia to keep the kingdom weak. Beonna soon emerged as sole ruler, and the increased silver content of his coinage suggests a time of agricultural and mercantile prosperity. The fact that he was able to issue a new coinage, and the growth of a new East Anglian trading-centre at Ipswich, argue for an assertion of the kingdom's trading potential independent of Mercia in the first years of Offa's reign (after 756). Boenna seems to have survived into the 760s, but the absence of later coinage may obscure a longer reign. The next king, Aethelred, had a dissimilar name and was probably not related.

MERCIA

CEONRED (704–709) The son of Wulfhere of Mercia, presumably by his only recorded wife, Eormenhild of Kent. Probably born in the early to mid-660s, he was a child when his father died in 674/5 and his uncle Aethelred took the throne; he succeeded the latter in 704. The 'E' version of the *Chronicle* uniquely gives his accession at 702, two years before his father abdicated; he was possibly made co-ruler then. Not much is recorded of his reign, except for continuing conflict with the Welsh and the continuing influence of his uncle (now abbot of Bardney), who in 706 summoned him to promise to keep good relations with (Saint) Wilfred. He seems to have shared his uncle's (and his mother's family's) ecclesiastical interests; in 709 he abdicated the throne to accompany his saintly friend Offa, the young king of the East Saxons, to go on pilgrimage to Rome. Coenred's cousin Ceolred succeeded him, and proved a much more controversial ruler.

CEOLRED (709–716) The son of Aethelred of Mercia, probably by his unknown second wife, not his first wife Osthryth, and so born in the 690s. He was superseded by his older cousin Coenred when his father abdicated in 704, but succeeded Coenred when the latter abdicated to travel to Rome as a pilgrim in 709. Possibly still in his teens, he was remembered as a rash, extravagant and debaucherous ruler, though his reputation may have suffered on account of the contrast with his virtuous father and cousin. Ceolred felt threatened by his cousin Aethelbald, who had to flee into exile in the Fenland and hide at Crowland Abbey. Other victims of his tyranny are probable from his later reputation. He fought against Ine of the West Saxons at Adam's Grave in northern Wiltshire in 715, but otherwise his reign seems to have been peaceful – though possibly marked by tension with his nobles and the Church.

He died suddenly at a banquet in 716, allegedly being struck by a fit of madness, which the Church regarded as divine punishment for his immoral life; it may have been epilepsy, alcoholic excess or poison administered by his enemies. He was already being denounced in his lifetime by the religious community at Much Wenlock, where a vision was recounted alleging that the angels had abandoned him because of his wickedness; the monastery's connections with the royal house of Magonsaetan may be significant here. Saint Boniface returned to the attack decades later, suggesting a long-term grudge. Ceolred was buried at Lichfield, and may have been succeeded briefly by an unknown Ceolwald (from the alliterative names probably his brother) before his distant cousin Aethelbald returned home to take the throne. He was the last of the main line of the Icelingas dynasty.

AETHELBALD (716–757) The son of Alweo, son of Penda's brother and co-ruler, Eowa (*fl.* 640s). He was thus second cousin of Penda's grandson Coenred (abdicated 709); when the latter set off for Rome, Aethelbald was seen as a threat by his successor Ceolred and was driven into exile. He took refuge in the Fenland with the hermit Saint Guthlac at Crowland, but returned on the harsh Ceolred's sudden death at a banquet in 716. Aethelbald was chosen as the new king, but it is unclear if he was selected as the closest lineal heir or his allies staged a coup.

A strong ruler, Aethelbald wielded the same authority over his neighbours as his cousins Wulfhere and Aethelred had done from *c.* 660 to 704. Continuing Mercian military supremacy south of the Humber, he had influence over the smaller East Saxon and East Anglian kingdoms with useful mercantile access to London. He may have backed Aethelheard as king of the West Saxons on Ine's death in 726, and was able to gain control of Berkshire in 730; in 733 he led a successful incursion into Somerset. There was sporadic renewed conflict with Aethelheard's successor Cuthred, who joined Aethelbald's campaigns against the Welsh as his junior ally, but late in the latter's reign was able to win a rare victory over him at Beorhford (Burford?). Cuthred had to accept Aethelbald as his overlord, witnessing charters to Glastonbury. The main military activity of Aethelbald's reign was against Powys. Despite his military power, Aethelbald could not achieve a decisive victory, and it was probably the constant insecurity from raids that led to the construction of Wat's Dyke late in his reign as the first known Mercian fixed defensive frontier. It is not known if Aethelbald was consciously using a Roman military model. Notably, he was the first ruler to use the title of *Rex Gens Anglorum*, 'King of the English', in his charters from 746. He had only short-term successes against his northern rival, Eadbert of Northumbria, taking advantage of his absence on a Pictish campaign to sack York in 750.

The ecclesiastical records present Aethelbald as a formidable, predatory and unscrupulous ruler, nominally Christian but disrespectful of the Church and utilising it for his secular purposes. He was capable of using Church money for governance and requiring monks to work on secular building-projects, and was admonished by Saint Boniface for violence and ungodliness. He never married or provided an heir, a surprising omission for an otherwise methodical ruler. Aethelbald's alleged promiscuity and lust for nuns may have been played up by his critics to emphasise his wickedness. Aethelbald was murdered by men of his own bodyguard at Seckington in 757 after an impressive forty-one-year reign, probably in his early sixties. As with his own succession, a coup may have been to blame; his replacement Beornred was from outside the main dynastic line.

BEORNRED (757) The beneficiary of the murder of the childless Mercian king, Aethelbald, in 757, and possibly involved in the mutiny of the royal bodyguard which led to the killing. He had no known connection to the Mercian royal house, though he was probably a senior noble or ealdorman to have any backing in a succession struggle. His name suggests a family link to Beornwulf and Beorhtwulf, kings in the early to mid-ninth century, and thus membership of a powerful family. He was driven out of Mercia later in 757 by Aethelbald's cousin Offa the Great and vanishes from history.

MAGONSAETAN

MILDFRITH (Early eighth century) Third king of Magonsaetan, son of King Merewalh and the Kentish princess Eata. He succeeded his brother Merchelm around 700, but only appears in charters until *c.* 706. The kingdom had no recorded rulers after him and was apparently absorbed into Mercia, possibly when he died without children. The Welsh raiding that led to the eventual building of Offa's Dyke along the western frontier of Magonsaetan in the mid-eighth century would have made it logical for Mercia to take over the defence of this small kingdom to protect it. Possibly the last rulers of Magonsaetan lacked the resources in manpower to mount an adequate defence – or was this used as an excuse by a predatory Mercia?

NORTHUMBRIA

EADWULF (704–705) The usurping ruler of Northumbria on the death of the elderly Aldfrith in December 704. The latter's son Osred appears to have been under-age, and it may be that nobles impatient for an adult war-leader and/or opponents of Aldfrith's dynasty backed his coup. His dynastic credentials are unknown, although there is a theory that he was the unknown king whose brother was Mol/Mul, father of the future King Aethelwold (acceded 759). His usurpation commenced the instability which was to plague Northumbia in the eighth century. He was unable to secure adequate support, most notably from the Church under Bishop Wilfred; he was overthrown within two months by forces led by Beorhtfrith, sub-king of Lothian, backed by Wilfred (probably in February 705).

OSRED I (705–11) The elder son of Aldfrith by Cwenburh, sister of Ine of Wessex. Born in 695/6, his young age at his father's death in December 704 led to the first of many usurpations of the throne. The usurper Eadwulf was deposed within two months by Beortferth, sub-king of Lothian, backed by (Saint) Wilfred. The two served as effective regents in the government, with Wilfred, restored to the see of Hexham, backed by the new king's aunt (Saint) Elfleda, abbess of Whitby, as the boy's spiritual director. Wilfred and (Saint) John of Beverley, new bishop of York, governed the Church and Beortferth controlled civil and military affairs, but the former died in 710, the other either died or soon retired, being last heard of in 711, and the adolescent king proved a determined and wayward personality. Bede referred to him as a young Josiah, i.e. an enthusiastic purger of immorality, but most testimony is critical. He was later accused of abducting and raping nuns and preying on women, and in the ninth century Aethelwulf accused him of killing his nobles or driving them into monasteries. Many nobles were executed or exiled, possibly after trouble over his sexual depredations, though he proved a brave leader in battle against the Picts. He was killed in Lothian in 716, probably in a revolt led by Coenred, a distant kinsman, aged around twenty. Notably, his brother Osric was not the rebels' first choice to succeed him; legitimacy was not a paramount issue.

CENRED (COENRED) (716–718) A distant kinsman of the royal house of Northumbria, the son of Cuthwine and allegedly descended from Ocg, younger son of the founder, Ida. He was a leading participant in the successful revolt of 716 against the murderous young King Osred, and was chosen as the new king on its success. The late ruler's younger brother Osric may well have been too young to be a serious candidate, and the experienced Cenred a better choice. The murder was probably greeted with relief by the nobles, but Cenred was still the first king chosen from outside the direct royal family; he was possibly oppressive like his predecessor. If he sought to deter rebellion by pre-emptive killings this seems to have failed, as his own death in 718 was apparently violent. Osric succeeded him.

OSRIC (718–729) The second son of Aldfrith to rule Northumbria, and probably, but not certainly, his younger son by Cwenburh of Wessex. If so he was born around 696/8, and was probably seen as too young to be chosen as king when Aldfrith's tyrannical son Osred was murdered in 716. Within two years Coenred was dead, most likely by violence, and Osric was installed on the throne as the last legitimate male of the main line of Bernicia. (It has been suggested that he was the son of Alchfrith, Aldfrith's half-brother who died in *c.* 664, and if this is accurate he would have been substantially older but had a weaker claim to be king in 716.) Nothing is recorded of his reign, a good sign given the recent turbulence and the endemic wars with Northumbria's Pictish neighbours. The cycle of revolts and rival claims to the throne was to resume after Osric's death, and the most significant aspect of his kingship was probably his lack of a clear heirs. He died in 729, possibly aged a little over thirty, and was succeeded by Coenred's brother Ceolwulf.

CEOLWULF (729–737) Son of Cuthwine and younger brother of Cenred, the usurper who overthrew Osred in 716. Allegedly descended from Ocg, a younger son of Ida, he would have derived his main support as a dynastic claimant from his brother's success; he was chosen king on the death, in 729, of Osred's brother, Osric. The main line of Northumbria was now extinct. Known as 'Eochaid' in the Irish annals and possibly educated in Ireland after his brother's overthrow, he was remembered as learned and a devout son of the Church; he was the dedicatee of Bede's *Ecclesiastical History* in 731 and clearly took an interest in its comprehensive narrative of the Christian evangelization of the English and the stories of their most Christian kings. It is probable that he saw Bede's Christian kings, generous patrons of the Church, as his own inspiration; he seems to have given major grants of land to the Church, which were resented by secular lords thus deprived of potential estates. Around 731 there were a number of attacks on Churchmen, probably by local landowners, and some conspirators seized Ceolwulf, deposed him and forcibly tonsured him as a monk; this may have seemed an apt fate for him. But he was restored within a few months. In 735 the bishopric of York was raised to an archbishopric, confirming the intentions of the Papal mission to England in 597, which had been halted by the eviction of Paulinus in 633/4. The Church in the north of England thus had equal status with that of Canterbury in the south; the first archbishop was Ceolwulf's distant kinsman Egbert and his ecclesiastical connections may indicate that he had been lobbying Rome to carry this out. He abdicated to enter the Church as a monk in 737, probably of his own volition this time, and going to the principal Northumbrian religious (and artistic) centre at Lindisfarne, to which he gave generous gifts. His kinsman Eadbert, the archbishop's brother, succeeded him; he appears to have lived as a monk until 764 and thus probably reached his seventies.

EADBERT (737–758) Eadbert's accession in the second half of 737 followed the abdication of Ceolwulf to become a monk. His father is given as Eata, great-great-grandson of a younger brother of the later sixth-century rulers Theodric and Aethelric. Given the obscurity of this line, the pedigree may have been invented to establish his legitimacy. The decisive connection may have been that he was brother to Ecgbert, the first Archbishop of York (735). He was a distant cousin to his predecessor. He was probably chosen as a competent warrior as a contrast to his predecessor, capable of dealing with the combined threats of Mercia and the Pictish kingdom; both had powerful rulers at this time, Aethelbald and Oengus/Angus. From a ninth-century reference to the January 753 solar eclipse occurring in his fifteenth year, his formal accession must have been early in 738, indicating a disputed election.

Much of his reign was engaged in warfare against neighbouring states. In 740 Aethelbald invaded and sacked York; Eadbert was eventually able to drive him out, but only after substantial damage had been done. During this campaign Eadbert executed a potential rival called Eanwine, son of Eadwulf who had briefly held the throne in 704–5; the rebel may have been colluding with the Mercians or seeking to take advantage of the invasion. In 750 another claimant to the throne, Offa, allegedly a son of King Aldfrith and so from the main royal line, was defeated and forced to flee to Lindisfarne monastery. Rather than offend the Church by breaking into sanctuary, Eadbert starved him out; the bishop of Hexham, possibly the rebel's ally, was imprisoned. The fact that Eadbert's brother was the chief bishop of Northumbria was probably crucial in his keeping the adherence of the Church although the violation of sanctuary, too great an outrage to ignore, brought a temporary estrangement.

Eadbert had more success against the Pictish kingdom. When Angus was captured by Strathclyde in 750, the latter became the main threat; by 752 Eadbert had annexed the lands of Kyle from King Dumnugual. In 756, Eadbert combined with Angus to invade Strathclyde and besiege the principal royal residence, Dumbarton. The resulting treaty made Strathclyde a vassal of Northumbria – its most favourable northern frontier since the disaster of 685. The credit for this undoubtably goes to Eadbert, the most successful royal commander since Ecgfrith. The following year, 758, he abdicated like his predecessor and retired to the abbey of York. His son Oswulf succeeded, but was murdered within a year and instability returned to the kingdom. Eadbert made no attempt to return to power, which may suggest that he was physically incapable or lacked support; he died in 768.

6

756 to 796

KENT

SIGERED (762 – 4 (?)) Cited in a charter of 762 as witness to a grant of land to the bishop of Rochester; as the location is in western Kent and his name is East Saxon, he may have been an East Saxon noble. His appearance follows the death of co-king Aethelbert II of Kent, and he may have been installed as a compliant co-king by Essex's overlord Offa of Mercia to rule with Aethelbert II's brother Eadbert. By 764 another charter has him recorded as king of 'half Kent', and the other half is in the control of his new co-ruler, Eanmund/Ealhmund. He then disappears from history, possibly removed by his patron Offa or dying.

EALHMUND or EANMUND (762–4 and *c*. 784–5) Possibly the eponymous father of Egbert, king of the West Saxons from 802; one source says that the latter's father had been a king of Kent. If the two are the same, then Ealhmund of Kent was the descendant of Ingild, a brother of Ine of Wessex. His appearing as a ruler of Kent would suggest a dynastic link to their royal family, possibly in the female line, which Egbert would later have used to justify his annexation of that kingdom to Wessex.

Assuming the ninth-century pedigree of the West Saxon royal house in the *Chronicle* to be accurate, Ealhmund was the son of Eafa, son of Eoppa, son of Ingeld. He took over Kent on the extinction of the direct royal line in 762, possibly reigning simultaneously with Sigered (assuming that he and King 'Eanmund' are the same man). The nobles' choice of him may have reflected a desire to ally with Wessex against the power of Mercia. His accession was evidently displeasing to Offa, who invaded Kent in 764 and seems to have deposed Ealhmund. He fled into exile, but was able to return to the throne on the death of Egbert around 784. If Ealhmund named his son Egbert, probably born in the 770s or early 780s, after the current Kentish king, this may suggest a family link or political alliance with him. He was soon either evicted or killed by Offa in another Mercian invasion, probably in 785.

HEABERHT (764 – ?) One of the client kings who Offa of Mercia installed in Kent after his invasion of 764, displacing Sigered. He appears on the first known silver pennies minted in Canterbury in the late 760s, following Frankish models and indicating a degree of commercial prosperity for his kingdom. He is not recorded after 771, and was probably dead before his colleague Egbert's subsequent revolt in 776; logically his death ended an ameliorating factor between Offa and Egbert.

EGBERT (760s – before 784) A problematic ruler, who appears in Kent as co-ruler to King Heaberht in 764/5 and survived for over a decade and a half. It is sometimes supposed that his accession reflected a local backlash against Kent's unwelcome overlord Offa, who witnesses a land-grant in Kent on his own authority at Canterbury with Heaberht in attendance (the first such example of direct Mercian power) in 764. The episode does not recur until the 780s. Egbert may have been named after the prestigious Kentish king of that name of the 660s, and been a descendant; he may also have been the eponymous ancestor (maternal grandfather?) of King Egbert of Wessex, who derived his claim to Kent from him. In that case, King Ealhmund may have been his son-in-law.

Egbert and Heaberht witness a charter in the late 760s without reference to Offa, which may suggest the temporary lapse of Mercian pressure. Egbert appears on his own coinage in Kent through the 770s, and in 776 was probably involved in the problematic battle which the Kentish army fought with Offa at Otford. This first known example of a military clash between the hopelessly-outnumbered Kentishmen and the all-powerful eighth-century Mercians evidently represented some sort of defiance of Offa and an attempt by him to punish it – and there is no indication in the brief mention of it in the *Chronicle* that Offa won (as might have been expected). Possibly Offa was over-confident and lacked troops, or could not follow up any victory; it is a reasonable assumption but no more that, as Sir Frank Stenton suggested, Egbert successfully led a 'nationalist' defiance of Mercia. In any case, good relations were soon restored. A generous patron of the Church of Canterbury and on good terms with its clerics (which may have been aided by their dislike of Offa's desire for a Mercian archbishopric), Egbert was still king in 779, but Ealhmund had been restored by 784. Significantly, once Offa had restored his authority over Canterbury in the mid-780s, he cancelled a number of Egbert's grants to the local church as being given without proper (i.e. his?) authority. Henry of Huntingdon, allegedly based on earlier sources, gives Egbert a reign of twenty-four years – probably slightly too long.

SUSSEX

OSMUND (*fl.* 760s) An obscure vassal-king of Mercia who ruled Sussex from the late 750s, or possibly earlier, to around 772. His relationship to earlier rulers like Athelstan is unknown, and he may have ruled with a fellow-king, Ealdwulf; possibly Offa kept Sussex divided to minimise the risk of revolt. Offa seems to have suppressed the title of king in 772 and reduced the native rulers to 'duces' (governors), possibly on Osmund's death. He was probably a close relative (father?) of the next recorded rulers, 'duces' Oswald and Oslac.

OSWALD (770s) Oswald was, with the equally obscure Oslac, sub-ruler of Sussex under Offa of Mercia from around 772. They were probably sons of the previous recorded king, Osmund. As far as Mercian records were concerned, they were no longer entitled to the rank of king and were referred to as 'duces', governors. They ruled in tandem with Ealdwulf, who probably held authority in East Sussex while they ruled the west.

WESSEX

CYNEWULF (757–86) King from 757 to 786. Of unknown lineage but with a name that suggests connections to the seventh-century West Saxon rulers, Cynewulf was the beneficiary and possibly the leader of the coup of 757 when senior West Saxon nobles deposed the new king, Sigebert, for unspecified misrule. The ex-king was allowed to keep lands in Hampshire, possibly as one of the sub-rulers who are usually referred to as 'comites' (counts, as in Francia – royal officials of noble rank) rather than 'kings' in eighth-century documents. Sigebert was later driven out after quarrelling with his ealdorman and killed in exile; the fact that the ex-king temporarily retained some lands and power indicates Cynewulf's weakness in a disputed accession.

Cynewulf appears to have been generous in grants to his 'comites' (unless the number of grants for his reign merely reflects their survival), and retained power for twenty-nine years, the longest reign since Ine's. Cynewulf made only one challenge to the overwhelming power of his neighbour Offa of Mercia, whose court he attended in 772. Too strong to suffer the fate of the deposed client kings of Kent or the executed Aethelbert of East Anglia, Cynewulf came off worst in his one recorded clash with Offa at Bensington/Benson in Oxfordshire in 779 without dire consequences. Unlike direct Mercian clients he did not have Offa as witness of his charters, retained unambiguous royal rank and probably regarded himself as less of a client than an ally. His longevity in a century of disputed political power speaks for itself, but in 786 he was trapped while visiting his mistress' estate at Merton (thought to have been near Winchester) and killed by his predecessor's brother Cyneheard, who he was about to exile. The story was recorded in detail in Alfred's time, probably at the latter's insistence as an inspiring example of heroic conduct for his embattled people – Cynewulf's men refused to surrender to his attacker, even when the king had fallen, and he had to kill them all. This devotion was a Germanic warrior-ideal, but Cynewulf clearly inspired loyalty from his bodyguard.

BEORHTRIC (786–802) Of unknown origin, Beorhtric was elected as king of the West Saxons in 786 on the murder of Cynewulf in a blood-feud by the brother of his own predecessor, Sigebert. He continued his predecessors' Mercian alliance, and in 789 married Offa's daughter Eadburh. Offa clearly looked on him favourably and assisted him by forcing his rival Egbert (who probably had more of a dynastic claim to Wessex and may have challenged him in 786) into exile in Francia. If this was in 798/9, as one source indicates, it may hint that Beorhtric only faced a serious threat when Egbert reached adulthood; alternatively the latter may have been a threat since 786 and Beorhtric, Offa's nominee, exiled him in 788/9.

In 789 the first Scandinavian descent on Wessex took place, when a party of shipborne Vikings landed in Dorset and killed a royal official who was attempting to force them to report to Dorchester. Tension with Mercia seems to have followed Offa's death in 796, with Beorhtric encouraging the failed revolt against Mercia in Kent; a treaty with the new Mercian king, Coenwulf in *c.* 799, following the crushing of Kent, seems to have put Beorhtric as the junior party. He was poisoned at Wareham in 802, seemingly by his wife Eadburh, when he accidentally drank a cup of wine she had prepared for an enemy. The reputation of the murderous queen, who then fled to the Frankish court, may well have been exaggerated in retrospect by Beorthric's successor Egbert; by the time the *Chronicle* and Asser's life of Alfred were compiled she was regarded as a murderous termagent unchecked by her husband.

EADBURH One of the two daughters of Offa and Cynethryth of Mercia, Eadburh was married off to Beorhtric of the West Saxons in 789. It is difficult to separate fact from fiction in her story, as by the later ninth century she was the subject of lurid tales recounted by Asser. Political bias is probable. She was supposed to have been the main power behind Beorhtric's throne, active in politics and assertive in defending her interests: quite likely from a daughter of the formidable Offa. It is possible that she was to assist her father by keeping the West Saxon monarchy from challenging Mercia when the latter was harshly suppressing the independence of Kent.

Whether Eadburh routinely resorted to poisoning her enemies, as alleged, is more dubious. Her position weakened following the deaths of her father and brother in 796; the new king, Coenwulf, was no close kin. She is supposed to have accidentally killed her husband at Wareham in 802, when he drank a potion intended for one of her enemies. Following this her husband's exiled rival Egbert was elected king, probably by an anti-Mercian faction, and she fled to the court of Offa's ally, Charlemagne. According to the *Life of Alfred*, he offered her a choice of marrying either him or his son, probably his heir, the younger Charles. (Their comparative ages were about sixty and twenty-seven in 802.) She chose the son, a practical preference for the candidate who should have lived longer (in fact the young Charles predeceased his father). In retaliation the Emperor told her that if she had chosen him he would have given her to his son as a reward; due to showing her ambition, she would have neither of them and was banished. The story shows signs of being a morality tale. Eadburh is supposed to have left Francia and died in poverty years later at Pavia in northern Italy, where her tomb was shown to passing English pilgrims. Possibly King Alfred had seen it himself on his Italian visits in 853 and 854/5. The legend that she had resorted to prostitution is equally dubious. Her unpleasant reputation and misuse of her role as queen is supposed to have led to a West Saxon law banning the use of the title for the king's wife, who now became known as the 'Lady'. This tradition was challenged by Egbert's son Aethelwulf in 856.

ESSEX

SIGERIC (759–98) The longest-ruling, but one of the most obscure, of his dynasty. The son and successor of Saelred, who died violently in 746, he succeeded his distant cousin Swithred in 759 and was presumably regarded as a loyal governor by his overlord, Offa of Mercia. He abdicated in 798 to go on pilgrimage to Rome, probably in his sixties, and was succeeded by his son Sigered.

EAST ANGLIA

AETHELRED (770s (?) – 80s) One of the most obscure rulers, only known through his saintly son's greater fame. He succeeded the equally obscure Beonna, at an unknown date in the 760s or even 770s. The current power of Mercia under Offa would make it probable that East Anglia was his vassal state at this time, though its kings avoided the declining status into 'ducal' rank that afflicted smaller kingdoms within Mercia (Hwicce) or allied to it (Sussex), or the constant warfare which marked Mercian struggles with Kent. Logically, Aethelred was at least acceptable to Offa, who may have been a relative; his name may indicate that he was called after the holy King Aethelred of Mercia. At some date prior to 794 he was succeeded by his son Aethelbert. The fact that in 794 the latter was seeking a (first?) bride, Offa's daughter, can be interpreted as making him reasonably young – in which case he would have been born in the 760s or 770s and his father been at least twenty years older.

(SAINT) AETHELBERT (? – 794) The ruler of East Anglia after his father Aethelred; the date of accession is unknown. Very little is known about him, except that he had the unusual distinction of being executed by his overlord Offa the Great of Mercia in 794. The subsequent hagiography of him states that he acceded to the throne aged fourteen and was a relative of Offa, who was at least the backer if not the installer of his line. The place of his death was apparently the royal Mercian manor of Sutton Walls near Hereford; he was buried nearby at Marden, presumably as Offa did not want his body returning home as an object of anti-Mercian veneration. The St Albans version of his life puts the blame on Offa's queen, Cynethryth, possibly from desire to exonerate their Mercian patron.

A cult grew up and he was subsequently sanctified as a 'martyr', a result common with other rulers or royal claimants believed to have been unjustly victimised by their superiors, like Oswine of Deira (d. 651). The date of death may have been the date on which he was commemorated, 20 March.

Later his body was moved to Hereford, the nearby see, where a shrine was built at the cathedral with him as its patron saint. The cult does not imply any notable degree of holiness on the part of the recipient. A legend recorded in the twelfth century stated that Aethelbert had journeyed to Mercia to negotiate a marriage alliance with Offa, aiming for the latter's daughter Alfthryth; it is possible that Offa, capable of ravaging insurgent Kent and imposing his own puppets on allied kingdoms, suspected Aethelbert of plotting to end East Anglia's vassal status and of inspecting Mercian defences for use in case of war. The execution would have been intended as a warning to vassals of what awaited would-be traitors. It is possible that Offa sent his troops into and annexed East Anglia in 794, as the next king, Eadwald, is not known to have been established there before 798.

MERCIA

OFFA THE GREAT (757–96) The most powerful ruler of Mercia and the overlord of southern England for most of his reign, he was able to claim to be 'King of the English' and showed ruthless use of his superior resources in pursuing his control over his vassals. But surprisingly little detail is known of his thirty-nine-year reign (the second longest in Mercian history), though its peacefulness implies political stability and effective control over his nobles. He was presumably of royal blood; if the genealogies were not altered to improve his claim, he was a cousin of King Aethelbald and descended from Eowa, brother and co-ruler of Penda. His father was Thingfrith, son of Eanwulf;

the latter was presumably the eponymous grantee of estates at Henbury and Westbury in the lands of the Hwicce by Aethelbald and founder of the Worcestershire monastery at Bredon. He seized power soon after the murder of Aethelbald (whose belligerency seems to have been his own political model) in 757, overthrowing the 'usurper' Beornred.

His first twenty years in power are largely blank, with a hiatus in the *Chronicle* records, but any struggle over the succession made no impact outside Mercia and his predecessor's vassal kings (Essex, Kent, Sussex, and East Anglia) were presumably quickly acquiescent. The creation of a new Mercian coinage in the 760s, based on current Frankish models, suggests awareness of the latest useful royal initiatives on the Continent.

The sheer preponderance of Mercian military power over its smaller neighbours, and its useful central position in England, acted to assist the smooth continuance of its domination. However, a recorded Welsh victory near Hereford in 760 was an illustration of the problem Mercia faced from raiding across its open western border, with attackers able to melt away into the mountains and evade punitive royal armies. The new king's response was to mobilise his resources to build the famous Offa's Dyke, from the Wye north to Flintshire, a permanent obstacle to raiders which held up swift movement into and out of Mercia and was presumably well-patrolled. It skilfully made use of natural features to make it more difficult to cross and was to mark the permanent Anglo-Welsh border, though the abandonment of earlier settlements beyond it was a defeat. The date and process of the creation of the Dyke, ascribed to Offa by later tradition following Alfred's biographer Asser (a south Welsh cleric), is obscure; it served to end endless 'hit-and-run' Welsh raids and show that the king could protect his subjects and monitor travellers. Given the earlier building of Wat's Dyke to the north, Offa may not even have originated the strategy of building dykes (inspired by the Roman walls in Northumbria, but adapted to the Anglian lack of skill in handling stone?), or have extended an earlier local defence-dyke and renamed it after himself. It would also have served as a link for customs posts, making all traders pass through controlled points and pay their taxes to the king. Offa was recorded in Welsh sources as campaigning against the south Welsh in 777/8 and 783/4, and may have been on campaign during the visit of the papal legate in 786 as the latter visited 'Britain', i.e. the Welsh lands.

Offa was effective at projecting his image as the most powerful ruler in all England and acting as a local equivalent of his overseas counterpart, Charlemagne, as seen by his extensive coinage. A new gold coin (*'mancus'*) was famously based on Arabic coins, showing it was needed for trade with their lands, and used Arabic lettering. His terminology as 'King of the English' followed that of his predecessor. Alfred of Wessex referred to him as a law-giver, though none survive. Before his reign, local sub-rulers within Mercia had slowly lost their rank and autonomy, as seen by the terminology used for them by the centrally-controlled charters; now he extended this centralisation outside the kingdom. Sussex's sub-kings were reduced to the rank of ealdormen or 'duces' in 772. The most perennial problem was Kent, although he was aided here by the extinction of the royal line around 762, which enabled him to play on factionalism and back local allies. In 764 he invaded Kent, whose king, Sigered, disappears from the records thereafter. He is recorded as visiting Canterbury, where he witnessed a grant of land to the church of Rochester as the overlord of the Kentish king. He imposed one king, Ealhmund or Eanmund (a West Saxon prince?), and around 764/5 he installed two new rulers, Heahbert and Egbert, possibly dividing the kingdom so they could counter each other's power. After Heahbert's death, local resistance increased and/or Egbert became more restive; in 776 there was a revolt and Offa was driven to invade Kent. The resulting battle at Otford may have been a defeat for him despite his overwhelming preponderance of resources, as the rebel king survived for most of another decade. Only with Egbert's death in *c.* 784 was Offa able to intervene; Ealhmund was restored, probably as his client, and on his death or eviction, within a couple of years, Offa abolished the kingship and assumed direct control. This lasted until his death, but the speed and success of revolt then suggests that it was only fear that kept local nobility loyal. The future rebel Eadbert Praen was probably the ex-priest 'Odberht' who Offa unsuccessfully tried to persuade Charlemagne to extradite from Francia; instead the Frankish king sent the refugee, and other political exiles, to Rome in *c.* 795 to secure papal support as Offa dispatched Archbishop Aethelheard to Pope Leo for an order to have them repatriated. Evidently Charlemagne found Offa's enemies a useful political resource.

Offa had more military success against King Cynewulf of Wessex, who he defeated at Bensington in 779, although in the 770s Cynewulf was able to grant land in the middle Thames valley at Cookham without reference to Offa, which suggests reassertion of West Saxon power close to London (at the time of Kentish resistance to Offa under Egbert?). Offa may have been involved in the election of his later protégé Beorhtric in 786 and certainly had more influence over him than over his predecessor; he was able to claim that Beorhtric was his vassal. Possibly the end of Egbert's rule in Kent and Offa's assertion of direct rule there in *c.* 785/6 forced Wessex into greater dependence on him.

In the mid-780s he turned his attention to the archbishopric of Canterbury, which was based in hostile Kent and had fraught relations with him under its incumbent, Jaenbeorht. Offa's solution was the unprecedented idea of creating his own new archbishopric for Mercia, under his direct control. In 786 papal legates visited England to check on observation of canon law and hold an ecclesiastical council, and the following year Pope Hadrian raised the Mercian bishop Hygeboerht to be the first (and only) Archbishop of Lichfield. This was furiously opposed by Canterbury and it contradicted the sixth-century papal plan for English sees, but Offa had enough influence at Rome to block complaints for his lifetime. Allegations were later made that Jaenberht, the alienated Archbishop of Canterbury, had plotted to admit Frankish troops to Kent if Charlemagne and Offa went to war over their marriage-alliance crisis. But Aethelheard, the next archbishop – from Lindsey, within Mercia, so probably a Mercian client – was on good terms with Offa and received grants of Mercian land. The new archbishopric of Lichfield incorporated the East Anglian bishoprics of Domnoc and Elmham, suggesting a Mercian move to incorporate the sub-kingdom's Church into Mercia and diminish any interference there by Canterbury.

Offa's ambitions and pretensions were also demonstrated in 787 by his new archbishop's coronation of his son Ecgfrith as co-ruler of Mercia. The heir had been named after the last powerful king of Northumbria, and crowning him in his father's lifetime was unprecedented, but secured his succession in a state without its direct royal line since 716. Arguably, it removed the element of election of a king by the nobles in favour of papal-sanctioned 'divine right', with resistance implying blasphemy. It followed the practices of the Byzantine Empire and Francia in crowning sons as co-rulers; Offa was looking to Continental monarchies, not Mercian tradition. Possibly his queen, Cynethryth, a Frank (?), influenced him. But his ambitions overreached themselves in *c.* 789 when his alliance with Charlemagne faltered; he had arranged to marry a daughter to Charlemagne's heir, but when he endeavoured to pressurise his ally to marry his daughter to Ecgfrith in return Charlemagne refused and cut off trade. Offa regarded himself as the equal of Charlemagne; the latter did not. As seen above, Charlemagne then sheltered some of Offa's refugee enemies in Francia in the early 790s; by 799 the future West Saxon nemesis of Mercian power, Egbert, was to join them but it is unclear if Offa or Coenwulf exiled him. Offa's apparent murders of potential rivals of Ecgfrith were lamented as a disaster for Mercia by the Northumbrian scholar Alcuin in Francia; possibly this aided stability in 796–823 by diminishing the potential for rebellion, but then meant that once the royal house of Penda and Eowa was removed in 823 there were no 'legitimate' claimants to hand.

Offa's autocracy may have become more blatant with age, if the story of the unprecedented execution of the visiting king of East Anglia (Saint Aethelbert) in 794 is accurate. The seizure and beheading of this vassal-king, at the royal manor of Sutton Walls near Hereford, was the only execution of a king by his fellow sovereign in Anglo-Saxon history, even if legend is correct in specifically blaming the queen rather than Offa. Its shocking nature was shown by the cult that grew up around the victim. Some writers (Mercians trying to exonerate Offa?) were to blame Cwenthryth for it; it seems to have followed Aethelbert's arrival to negotiate a marriage to Offa's daughter. Possibly the visitor was believed to be spying out Mercian defences in anticipation of a coming war, and Offa regarded this as treason to his lord and intended to show that a vassal-king was no different to any other traitor. Whether he killed his visitor on impulse, or acquiesced in his queen's decision, he seems to have taken the opportunity to suppress the kingship of East Anglia.

In his later years his two daughters were married to the kings of the largest Anglo-Saxon states remaining – more allies than vassals, though in Wessex's case not in the official terminology. Eadburh was married to Beorhtric of Wessex (and allegedly later poisoned him), and in 792 Aelfleda married the insecure King Aethelred 'Moll' of Northumbria, already expelled once and more in need of Offa's military backing than Beorhtric. Offa died on 26 July 796, probably in his sixties as he was adult and able to rally strong backing in 757. Ironically, his son died a few months later and his dynasty collapsed, though rebelling Kent was reoccupied and Mercian military control of the south lasted until 825. A ruthlessly determined ruler with a clear sense of his own worth and vast pretensions, he was able to utilise all the resources at his disposal and become the first Anglian ruler to operate as a near equal to his Frankish counterparts. He sought to follow Continental models as much as Mercian ones. But his harsh treatment of vassals was frequently counterproductive, with rivals intimidated and punished rather than won over. He relied on naked power rather than any concept of Christian kingship, and his blatant brutality sowed the seeds of Mercia's collapse after 825.

CYNETHRYTH (Queen of Mercia, *fl.* 770s – 796) The wife of Offa the Great, she was the first woman to be portrayed on English coinage. This innovation suggests her exalted concept of her role, and her ambition is also apparent from her plan to marry her daughter off to Charlemagne's eldest legitimate son Charles (presumed next king of the Franks) and her son Ecgfrith to his daughter in *c.* 789. She thus regarded the Mercian monarchs as equals to the greatest sovereign of the age; he did not and turned the idea down. According to a later life of the executed (Saint) King Aethelbert of East Anglia, the visiting monarch's shocking murder at Sutton Walls, Herefordshire, in 794 was Cynethryth's doing not Offa's. The incident may have arisen from another abortive marriage-plan involving Cynethryth's daughter, though she may have been blamed by someone seeking to exonerate her husband. One of her daughters, Eadburh of Wessex, was allegedly a serial killer. For all her dynastic efforts, the successive deaths of Offa and Ecgfrith in 796 extinguished the dynasty.

ECGFRITH (796) The son of Offa the Great and Cynethryth; probably named after the eponymous king of Northumbria as a suitably powerful warrior-king. He was crowned as nominal co-ruler by the first and only Archbishop of Lichfield, Hygeberht, in 787. The unprecedented crowning of an heir in his father's lifetime was foreign to English ideas, and followed current Byzantine practice to secure a smooth succession. This reflected the grandiose pretensions of the eighth-century Mercian monarchy. Little is known about Ecgfrith, who was issuing charters in his father's lifetime but never received any territory to rule even nominally. Later stories made him out to be as ruthless and arrogant as his father, who killed several potential rival heirs for his benefit. Offa's hopes were dashed, as when Ecgfrith succeeded him on 26 July 796 he only reigned for 141 days. His age is unknown, and there is no indication if his death was natural or violent. The latter is less likely. A distant kinsman, Coenwulf, succeeded him.

HWICCE

EANBERHT, UHTRED, EALDRED Brothers; sub-rulers of the Hwicce under Offa in the 760s, and referred to in his charters as 'reguli', i.e. not of full royal rank, and 'duci', i.e. royal 'ealdormen'. This may have been the view of their Mercian overlords rather than of the Hwiccans themselves. They vanish from history, with Ealdred last attested in a charter of 779. They were presumably suppressed by Offa and replaced by his own officials, 'down-grading' their lands to normal counties within Mercia. The principal local landowners at the main Hwiccan royal estate of Winchcombe in the mid- to late eighth century were apparently Offa's distant cousins, the kin of his son's successor Coenwulf, so it may have been confiscated from the old royal family.

LINDSEY

ALDFRITH (*c.* 785–95) Aldfrith, son of Eata son of Eanfrith; apparently the last king of Lindsey. He is probably the man referred to as a witness in a charter of Offa dated to after 788/9, and is independently testified to by a short royal genealogy which traces his line back to the early seventh-century (?) Critta/Creoda. In that case he was ruling as a Mercian sub-ruler and in attendance at Offa's court, and his nominal rule testifies to a degree of local autonomist feeling which Offa found it safer not to challenge. But the identification of the man in the genealogy with the charter-witness is not certain.

NORTHUMBRIA

OSWULF (758–9) The son and successor of Eadbert, who abdicated in his favour (possibly as too infirm to fight) in 757. The new king was probably in his twenties or early thirties. He was murdered within a year, on 24 July 758, at Market Weighton, perhaps by relatives of a noble of possibly royal blood called Eanwine who his father had executed. Aethewold 'Moll' was elected to succeed him over a week later, suggesting that the murder was an isolated act of vengeance rather than part of a carefully-planned coup by a large faction to remove the new dynasty.

AETHELWOLD 'MOLL' (759–65) Chosen as king of Northumbria by the council on 5 August 759, nearly a fortnight after the murder of his predecessor Oswulf. (The date is definitive, as the battle of Eildon between 6–9 August 761 took place at the start of his third regnal year.) He was of unknown descent and thus not closely related to Oswulf; his second name 'Moll' may indicate descent from the Mul who is recorded as a brother to an unknown king (probably Eadwulf, usurper in 704). If he had any link to the main dynastic line of Ida it was even more remote than that of his predecessor; possibly all the closer candidates were ineligible by youth or lack of support. His short reign was plagued by misfortune, first a plague in 760 and then a revolt by Oswine against whom he fought a three-day battle in the Eildon Hills in August 761. The following year he married Etheldreda, probably the mother of his son Aethelred.

More natural misfortune followed with a severe winter in 763–4 and a resulting famine. Whether or not superstitious Northumbrians feared that the recent disasters implied divine displeasure on their electing a usurper, on 30 October 765 a council deposed Aethelwold. He was forced to enter a monastery, which may indicate residual goodwill towards him in person. Al(ch)red replaced him, but nine years later the latter's deposition was to lead to the installation of Aethelwold's son as king.

ALCHRED (ALRED) (765–74) The son of Eanwine and grandson of Beornholm, a junior branch of the dynasty of Bernicia (perhaps descended from Ida's younger son Edric). The family may have been based in Lothian. On the deposition of Aethelwold 'Moll' on 30 October 765, Alchred was chosen as king; he subsequently married Osgifu, daughter of his predecessor-but-one Oswulf, to strengthen his dynastic position. Closely associated with the Church, he was also a backer of missionary work within pagan territories conquered by the Franks and opened friendly relations with Charlemagne. A mission was sent to Francia in 773, contemporary with disturbances at York which forced a visiting Frisian scholar to flee. From spring 767 Alchred had a relative, Aethelred, as Archbishop of York, but his clerical mainstay turned out to be his nemesis. After a dispute with Aethelbert the latter headed a meeting of the royal council which deposed Alchred at Easter 774. He was exiled to the Pictish royal court; his son Osred had enough support to return to the throne in 788.

AETHELRED 'MOLL' (774–9 and 789–96) The first king of Northumbria to reign twice, a symptom of the growing political instability in his homeland.

He was the son of Aethelwold 'Moll', usurper from (at best) a junior branch of the Bernician royal family; his father's marriage in 762 puts a probable date to his birth, unless he was the son of an earlier marriage. It was probably his age which was the decisive factor in his failure to be chosen when his father was deposed in October 765; Al(ch)red was made king instead. Aethelwold may still have been alive in his enforced monastic retirement when Aethelred was installed on the throne on Alred's deposition at Easter 774. The decisive role was that of Archbishop Aethelbert of York, and the new king may have been his choice as possessing a degree of dynastic legitimacy (or Church backing with his father a monk).

Probably under the control of his council to begin with, Aethelred asserted himself later in the 770s. He warned off potential rebels by making examples of traitors, and in 778 three 'ealdormen' were executed by the royal officials Aethelbald and Heahbert. This drastic action may have emboldened enemies to remove the king before he became a firm ruler, and in spring 779 he was driven out of the kingdom by Elfwald, son of his father's predecessor Oswulf.

Aethelred did not give up his political hopes, and continuing violent coups gave him his chance as his successors proved no more secure. In September 790, he returned to the throne following the deposition of Alred's son Osred II. Aethelred resorted to his earlier determination to strike first and intimidate opposition, though one early would-be victim, 'ealdorman' and later King Eardwulf, escaped his killers. In 791 the sons of Elfwald, evidently in fear of their lives and taking sanctuary in York Minster, were lured out with false promises and drowned; in 792 (or 794) opposition coalesced around Osred, who returned to challenge for the throne, but Aethelred had him hunted down and killed. A fortnight after Osred's killing Aethelred married Aelfleda, the daughter of Offa of Mercia, at Catterick. The marital alliance with the dominant king of the southern English indicates Aethelred's political need of a strong ally – and its timing implied that he needed Offa's backing against Osred. According to the *Chronicle*, fearsome portents and famine preceded the unprecedented sacking of the monastery of Lindisfarne and the shrine of Saint Cuthbert on 8 June (or possibly January) 793 in a seaborne Viking raid. This was a warning of far worse raids to come. The expatriate Northumbrian scholar Alcuin, who had already written to the king urging him to display less vindictiveness and to stop lying to his subjects, wrote from Francia to warn the king that the sack was a sign of God's displeasure with politically unstable and violent Northumbria, declined into un-Christian ways since his youth. By implication Aethelred, with his political killings, bore a share of responsibility for this divine displeasure. Alcuin also criticised the king and his court for immorality and extravagance.

On 19 April 796 Aethelred was murdered by an unknown Ealdred, apparently a partisan of Osbald who now usurped the throne. The latter had no known dynastic legitimacy and only lasted for twenty-seven days, which argued that the coup was not well-prepared or supported. His dynasty never regained the throne, though the assassin was killed by Aethelred's supporter, Ealdorman Torhtmund, in 799 with Alcuin's approval, so he inspired some loyalty. One interpretation would dismiss him as a violent, treacherous and unscrupulous dynast, a symbol of how far the stable Northumbrian monarchy of the later seventh century had fallen, and cite Alcuin's complaining letters in support of this. His breaches of the normal standards of behaviour were legion. But his return to the throne and short-term successes would argue that he did not lack ability or support.

AELFWALD (779–88) The son of Oswulf, murdered in 759, and grandson of King Eadbert. The third of his line to rule and aged at least twenty at his accession, he was chosen as king on the deposition of Aethelred 'Moll' in 779. A degree of feud with the line of Aethelwold and Aethelred 'Moll' is probable given their long-lasting conflict. Probably backed by Archbishop Ethelbert of York and aided by noblemen scared of suffering the same fate as three ealdormen Aethelred had recently killed, he was the protégé of a magnate called Beorn. His backer was soon killed by allies of Aethelred, ealdormen Osbald and Aethelheard, in December 780, and Aelfwald seems to have been a weak ruler who could not control his feuding magnates or halt civil unrest. The retirement of the dominant archbishop, a possible patron of his, in 780 also weakened his power, given the outcome. In 786 the papacy sent a legate, George, to investigate the declining state of the diocese of York, probably at the request of its clergy and/or the king, who could not keep order themselves; his backing was duly forthcoming in a decree reaffirming the sanctity of kingship and legitimacy of the current dynasty (both evidently under question). George went on to Mercia, accompanied by the expatriate Northumbrian scholar Alcuin, a York-trained cleric now in Charlemagne's service in Francia.

But if Aelfwald had hoped that the Pope's intervention would shore up his authority, it was only a temporary solution. It is possible that the alienation of land to the Church and to secular lords by kings seeking support in the repeated dynastic strife of the eighth century had weakened the royal ability to act as the fount of land and patronage to an extent that no king could outmatch his most powerful and truculent subjects. Drastic action only led to charges of tyranny and revolt, as seen by Aelfwald's predecessors' fates. In September 788 he was assassinated by a former supporter called Sigca, a senior thegn present at the 786 legatine Church council at 'Scythlecester', probably Chesters-on-the-Wall, near the Tyne. He was buried at Hexham, aged around thirty; it is possible that his frequent residence in the Bernician part of his realm, and cult there, indicates local family links. A cult grew up around him, with claims that a divine light had been seen shining at the site of his killing, similar to Saint Oswald; his links to the Church may have led to posthumous eccelesiastical veneration and criticism of his less generous successors.

Alcuin linked the decline of Northumbrian morals to the time of this coup, implying that he was more virtuous than his successors; another reading, however, would also imply that the 'rot' had set in during his reign. His sons Oelf and Oelfwine took sanctuary in York; the king was replaced by Osred II, son of ex-king Al(ch)red and representative of the third rival line contending the throne.

OSRED (II) (788–90) The son of ex-king Al(ch)red, probably by his marriage to King Oswulf's daughter Osgifu in 768. As such he was the personification of a potential alliance between two of the three feuding rival lines of mid-eighth-century kings, those of Alchred and Eadbert, and could have served as an agent of stability had the endemic feuds of the nobles been stifled by a strong, well-resourced ruler. Probably around eighteen when King Aelfwald (his uncle if he was Osgifu's son) was assassinated on 23 September 788, he only reigned for two years. In September 790 he was overthrown; Aelfwald's predecessor, Aethelred 'Moll' was recalled. He fled to the Isle of Man. In 792 he returned to challenge Aethelred, who was arousing aristocratic opposition with (pre-emptive?) executions of senior nobles, but was defeated and was killed on 14 September. He was buried at Tynemouth priory, which would indicate that the revolt had centred on Bernicia.

7

796 to 860

KENT

EADBERT PRAEN (796–8) Possibly a dynastic connection of the extinct (762) male line of the royal house. He was in priestly orders by 796, possibly enforced by Offa to invalidate him for the throne. His exile in Francia may have been ordered by Offa, or undertaken in order to avoid execution. He may have been the 'Odberht', an ex-priest, whose extradition from Francia was unsuccessfully demanded by Offa in *c.* 795; Charlemagne sent this man and other exiles to the new Pope Leo in Rome to ensure that the latter did not listen to requests from the visiting Archbishop of Canterbury, Aethelheard, to have them sent home. Renouncing his priestly vows and returning from Francia on Offa's death in 796, he led rebellion in Kent. Pro-Mercian Archbishop Aethelheard of Canterbury fled sooner than consecrate him king and was deposed, leading to a rift with the Church despite its opposition to Offa's new archbishopric of Lichfield. Eadbert attempted to negotiate with Pope Leo to recognise his actions, but was roundly condemned as an apostate.

Mercia was temporarily distracted but Eadbert was not able to call on the help of any of its rivals. Having secured the backing of the Pope, the new Mercian king, Coenwulf, invaded Kent in 798 and the weight of Mercian military force proved decisive. Eadbert was captured and blinded and had his hands cut off, but was imprisoned rather than being killed. Coenwulf, who had installed Cuthred as the new king, felt secure enough to release Eadbert around 805. He seems to have ended his life as a monk, possibly at Winchcombe in south-western Mercia.

CUTHRED (798–807) The brother of Coenwulf (and Ceolwulf) of Mercia, installed by the former as his vassal-king of Kent on the defeat of anti-Mercian rebel Eadbert Praen in 798. This marked a return to full Mercian domination, through proxies rather than by outright annexation as practiced by Offa. Cuthred evidently relied on his brother's military power and the inevitability of drastic retaliation in case of revolt to stay on his throne. He died in 807, upon which Coenwulf assumed the kingship.

BALDRED (c. 825–7) Of unknown dynastic links if any, Baldred was probably a local noble in Kent, which was forcibly incorporated into Mercia from c. 807 under Coenwulf. The death of this vigorous warlord in 821 and the deposition of his brother Ceolwulf in 823 gave Kent opportunity to resume its resistance to Mercian rule, and Baldred was elected as king of Kent around 823, probably on Ceolwulf's overthrow. He was expelled or killed by Mercia's enemy Egbert of Wessex after that ruler defeated Beornwulf at Ellandun in 825. Wessex now took control of Kent and installed its own nominees, its junior princes, as sub-kings.

AETHELWULF (825–39) See under WESSEX, to which he succeeded in 839.

ATHELSTAN (839 – 51/5) The king who succeeded to Kent (with Essex), a sub-kingdom of Wessex, on the death of Egbert of Wessex in July 839 (?). The sub-kingdom had been made an appanage of the West Saxon royal house when Egbert conquered it from Mercia in 825, being given to his son and heir Aethelwulf; now the latter succeeded to Wessex and Kent was handed to another relative. What is unclear is who Athelstan was – the phraseology in the *Chronicle* entry could mean that he was either the son of Egbert, i.e. Aethelwulf's younger brother, or the latter's son. If the second scenario is correct, he would have been Aethelwulf's eldest son and heir and was probably already in his teens – though this leaves a massive age-difference between Athelstan, born c. 820–5, and Aethelwulf's youngest son Alfred, born 848/9. In this case, he was probably the son of a first, unrecorded wife of Aethelwulf's, not Osburh. It is more probable that he was Aethelwulf's younger brother, regarded as a capable sub-king with his brother's eldest son Aethelbald still a boy.

It is possible, though less likely, that this Athelstan had already had experience of ruling in East Anglia as Egbert's nominee since c. 825, forming part of a network of West Saxon athelings governing south-east England. He seems to have ruled without incident until a Viking naval assault on Kent in 850. Athelstan and his ealdorman Ealhere met the attackers at sea off Sandwich and defeated them, a rare example of an English naval victory over usually more numerous and skilled Scandinavian seamen. Seven ships were captured, but the fact that the enemy was able to winter on Thanet or Sheppey suggests that the West Saxons could not follow up their victory. A massive invasion up the Thames by around 300 ships followed, and Athelstan was absent from the resulting campaign; it was his brother or nephew Aethelbald who was Aethelwulf's lieutenant at Aclea. Even if Athelstan was otherwise engaged rather than ill or dead, he died before Aethelwulf set out for Rome in 855, leaving Aethelbald's next brother Aethelbert as king of Kent.

WESSEX

EGBERT (802–39) The founder of West Saxon greatness, and of the largely uninterrupted line of monarchs descended from him which still rules over his kingdom 1,200 years later. He was from one of a number of rival lines of contenders competing for the throne, with his chances slim as a youth as his branch had not held power since Ine. His descendants claimed that his father Ealhmund was the great-grandson of Ine's brother Ingeld; this may have been invented to bolster his legitimacy but pride in lineages among contemporary nobles and the memorisation of genealogies would make it risky for invention to escape unnoticed. Ealhmund is a problematic figure: was he the man who ruled twice as king of Kent in the early 760s and early 780s, presumably with the approval of their overlord Offa? If he did so, Egbert may have been born and raised in Kent and named after the eighth-century King Egbert, or his seventh-century namesake and predecessor. It would be logical, but remains unproven, that Ealhmund married a Kentish princess (or had a Kentish mother) and that it was this which eased Egbert's ability to hold Kent after 825 in contrast to all previous foreign rulers.

One story has it that Egbert was a contender for the throne of Wessex on the murder of Cynewulf in 786 and was passed over in favour of Beorhtric. If so, he is likely to have been at least in his mid-teens, born *c.* 770–2; if this is inaccurate he may have been born as late as 778–80. He was exiled, probably to Offa's court, as after Offa married his daughter to Beorhtric the latter requested that Egbert was exiled to Francia. Alternatively, if the *Chronicle*'s version is correct – that Egbert was in Francia for three years – the arrangement was made with Offa's successor Coenwulf in their treaty of 799. Offa may have kept Egbert at his court as a candidate to impose on Wessex in case of war with Beorhtric. Egbert had experience of the greatest Christian realm of the era, Charlemagne's Frankish empire, and married a Frank called Redburga; she is said to have been his host's daughter, sister or niece but she is not recorded in Frankish records so she was possibly one of Charles' numerous illegitimate offspring. (A sister is unlikely, Charles' father having died in 768. His only brother died in 771.) Egbert was able to return to Wessex on the accidental poisoning of Beorhtric by his homicidal wife Eadburh in 802; the written records of Egbert's descendants indicate that they did all they could to blacken the reputations of both. Egbert may have agreed that his wife should avoid queenly status as a gesture to nobles alienated by the influence of Beorhtric's queen; this seems to have been what his grandson Alfred told Bishop Asser. Egbert was thus wiser than his son was to be in 856.

The first two decades of Egbert's reign are remarkably devoid of incident, and it is clear that he avoided provoking trouble with Wessex's powerful neighbour, Mercia, under Coenwulf. Wessex seems to have been stable as in Cynewulf's long reign, and later events imply that Egbert built up a strong army ready to challenge his neighbours on opportunity and may have allied with the vigorous new Archbishop of Canterbury, Wulfred, in the early 820s, enabling his Kentish adventure to have Church support. The absence of political challenges from outside Egbert's family may imply that he was the West Saxon king who finally ended the multiplicity of landed athelings able to raise support, putting each shire in charge of a chosen ealdorman with exclusive loyalty to him. Rival contenders within the extensive Cerdicing dynasty may have been deprived of lands or kept under strict supervision. But the absence of records may mean that he was lucky in the dying out of other princely lines.

The only known warfare early in his reign was a battle on his accession between Ealdorman Weohstan of Wiltshire and the invading ealdorman of the Hwicce; the West Saxons won though both commanders were killed. In 815 Egbert invaded and subjugated Cornwall, achieving the completion of the long conquest of the south-west which had remained unfinished since Ine's major victories. The British enemy, numerically and militarily inferior, had been left alone for most of the eighth century; Egbert apparently ravaged the land and suppressed their kings, but faced a revolt in 825, which he suppressed. Mercia was now weakening after the death of Coenwulf in 821 and several quick successions; during the revolt Beornwulf, possibly its instigator, invaded Wessex to take advantage of Egbert's preoccupation but Egbert was able to march back and intercept the invaders. Egbert won the crucial battle of Ellandun (near Marlborough in Wiltshire), and defeated the Mercians so completely that they were unable to interfere in his subsequent campaigns. Military leadership in southern England passed to Egbert, and the Mercians' losses of 825–7 against the East Angles completed their eclipse. Egbert sent an army under his son Aethelwulf into Kent, and the Mercian puppet-king Baldred was evicted and Aethelwulf installed as the new king; if Egbert was of royal Kentish blood and/or his father had reigned in Kent, the connection would have made the new arrangement more acceptable than the previous Mercian vassalage and there were no recorded revolts in the next thirty years. Surrey and Sussex were finally annexed, meaning that Egbert had completed Caedwalla's abortive creation of an extended West Saxon kingdom south of the Thames, and Essex too was overrun.

The domination of the south-east was completed as the king of the East Angles successfully appealed to Egbert for aid to throw off Mercian rule, and he became a West Saxon ally and (temporarily?) a vassal. It is probable that this man was Athelstan, the king named in mid-late 820s coinage, and possible, from his name, that he was of West Saxon blood – even that he was the Athelstan who succeeded to Kent in 839. In this case, he was either Egbert's younger son or grandson and a group of Cerdicing family members was set up to rule Egbert's vassal-kingdoms. More certainly, Egbert was able to take advantage of the Mercian defeats against the East Angles and in 829 he invaded Mercia itself, evicting the new king, Wiglaf. Mercia submitted and Egbert marched his army as far north as Dore in the Peak District, where the Northumbrian king, Eanred, came to terms (which Wessex if not Northumbria interpreted as vassalage); Roger of Wendover later wrote that he campaigned in Northumbria itself. He issued coinage in London as king of the Mercians.

In 830, Egbert led his troops into Powys to devastate the lands of Cyngen ap Cadell, the hereditary foe of Mercia; the war was probably intended to unite Mercian nobles under his command and show that their new king knew how to protect their kingdom. Egbert was now recognised as the *bretwalda*, implying supreme military leadership and a degree of political overlordship over other English kings, and was the first West Saxon to achieve this since Ceawlin. But either before or after this campaign, Wiglaf was able to return to power in Mercia in 830. Egbert did not invade Mercia again and had no obvious distractions, so it was probably by his agreement to head off possible revolt after he had taken his army home; it was impractical to unite Wessex and Mercia, whether or not he had seriously contemplated this during the recent interregnum. The degree of Egbert's control, as opposed to nominal leadership, beyond the Thames after 830 is debateable; he lost control of London. Indeed, in the 830s his own kingdom was to be the scene of increasingly serious Viking raids with Sheppey being plundered in 835 and Egbert himself suffering his only recorded defeat in a battle against raiders at Carhampton, Devon (or possibly Charmouth) in 836. In 838 the Scandinavians formed an alliance with the Cornishmen, and the latter threw off Egbert's authority and marched eastwards to invade the Tamar valley. The revolt may imply that Egbert was failing, but he was able to inflict a crushing defeat on them at Hingston Down near Callington; Cornwall did not revolt again until 926. In 838/9, he also secured agreement with the archbishopric of Canterbury to recognise the kings of Wessex permanently as their overlords, granting estates to them in return.

Egbert died in July 839 (?), aged either in his late fifties or his late sixties. He had recently asked permission from the Frankish emperor, Lewis, to cross his lands en route to Rome, so he was probably forestalled in a plan to follow his predecessor Ine's example. Aethelwulf succeeded to Wessex, and it was probably by the terms of Egbert's will that the sub-kingdom of Kent was kept in being for Athelstan. Egbert had been the most successful king of Wessex to date, replacing Mercia as the main military power in southern England after nearly 200 years and creating the nucleus of what was to become the kingdom of England. He had (briefly?) held supreme authority among the English kings, and even if he was lucky in a long line of powerful heirs he was one of the greatest Anglo-Saxon kings. He was also probably the longest-lived of his dynasty for 250 years; only Edward in 1066 lived to over sixty and Edgar Atheling in 1125 to seventy.

AETHELWULF (Kent, 825–39; West Saxons, 839–58) The father of King Alfred, and son of King Egbert of Wessex. His father, allegedly the descendant of Ine's brother, founded a new line of dynasts when he returned from exile in Francia in 802. Aethelwulf, Egbert's son by the Frankish Redburga (supposedly a daughter of Charlemagne, but if so probably illegitimate), was born in the early 800s – possibly before his father's return to Wessex. He was adult by the time that Egbert defeated the Mercians in 825 and moved to annex Mercia's rebellious vassal Kent and ally with East Anglia. The West Saxon expansion restored the brief hegemony of Caedwalla south of the Thames in the 680s, and Aethelwulf was appointed to rule the new sub-kingdom of Kent, Sussex and Essex. Egbert's line possibly had royal Kentish blood.

Aethelwulf succeeded his father in Wessex in July 839 (?), and passed on Kent to his relative (brother or eldest son?) Athelstan. He was probably already married to Osburh, daughter of Hampshire official Oslac (of royal Jutish descent), or else to an unknown first wife who died young. His first marriage(s) produced four or five sons, who all reigned as kings though none were long-lived. The first West Saxon king to succeed his father for over a century, he continued stability but, unlike Egbert, did not challenge his neighbours for uncertain pre-eminence. Alliance rather than conquest marked his relations with the eclipsed Mercia, though it seems that Aethelwulf expanded his frontier north to annex Berkshire in the 840s (retaining a Mercian, his namesake, as ealdorman). The co-operation between the two kingdoms led to a marital alliance with Burghred, who married Aethelwulf's daughter Ethelswith at Easter 853; a joint expedition by both against Powys followed, a success which led to their last king, Cyngen, fleeing to Rome.

Scandinavian raids continued through Aethelwulf's reign, with Ealdorman Wulfheard defeating an attack on Southampton in 840, but the raiders defeating the Dorset levies at Portland in 840 and Aethelwulf himself at Carhampton in 843. In 848, the forces of Somerset and Dorset won a victory over a fleet at the mouth of the Parrett, and in 850 Aethelwulf's junior king, Athelstan, won a naval encounter off Sandwich – suggesting that Wessex had already invested in a competently-trained fleet before the better-known naval initiatives of Alfred. The Vikings wintered on Thanet or Sheppey, and in 851 a force of around 300 ships – probably the largest army to raid England so far – moved into the Thames valley via London. The Mercians were defeated, but when the attackers moved south into Wessex Aethelwulf and his son

Aethelbald won a decisive victory at Aclea (probably Ockley in Surrey, on the Roman road from London to Chichester). The *Chronicle* calls this the largest slaughter of the Scandinavians until the present (the 880s), implying a greater victory than any of Aethelred's and Alfred's in the 870s, but it did not prevent another attack on Kent in 853; the raiders then wintered off the coast.

Aethelwulf had already sent his youngest son Alfred to Rome in 853, and in 855 he followed in person. First he dedicated a tenth of his lands to God, handing them over to the Church – enhancing his Christian reputation and seeking divine favour against the Vikings. The alienation of this land from secular beneficiaries may have disaffected personnel who looked to the king for grants, and bolstered the opposition which crystallised around Aethelbald in 856. The *Chronicle* denies that Aethelwulf had any intention of abdication in naming new co-rulers; he could not leave his people leaderless and appointed his experienced son Aethelbald to rule the western shires and the next, Aethelbert, to rule Kent. Having spent a year in Rome as a guest of Pope Benedict, showing that this was more than a brief visit, he journeyed back via the court of Charles the Bald in Francia and married Charles' daughter Judith (Verberie, 1 October 856). Aethelwulf was over fifty and Judith about fourteen, and the alliance probably complemented a military agreement against raiders. Despite the prestige of alliance with the Carolingians, the danger of more sons to claim the throne may have seemed a threat to his elder sons. The question arises of whether granting Judith the title of queen (unused since the infamies of Eadburh around 800 [?]) was taken as giving her potential sons rights to the throne.

Aethelbald, backed by the bishop of Sherborne and ealdorman of Somerset, refused to allow Aethelwulf back into his kingdom; Aethelbald may have had reason to think his father had broken an agreement. Aethelwulf was unable to muster enough support to invade the west when Aethelbert backed him and gave him admittance to the east; he had to accept a reduced role as co-king of Kent for the rest of his life. He died soon afterwards, on 13 January 858, probably at Steyning (West Sussex) where he was buried, aged around fifty-five to sixty. He left his personal property to his younger sons, with the proviso that it should remain as one unit within the family and be duly inherited by the survivor (in the event, Alfred). Aethelbald and Aethelbert maintained the division of the kingdom, and the former married his young stepmother; later Alfred had his father reburied at Winchester. Eclipsed in his reputation by Egbert and Alfred and a failure compared to both, Aethelwulf's humiliating loss of his kingdom and lack of support in 856–57 show his political failings. He abandoned using his military power to enforce submission across England as Egbert had done and chose alliance with Mercia not war, thus avoiding the backlash his father had faced in 830. Yet he had won the first serious victory over a massive Scandinavian attack in 851, created a viable fleet and, within his limits, served as a model for his younger sons' successes.

OSBURH (Queen/'Lady' of Wessex, 839 (?) – 53/6 (?)) The mother of Alfred the Great, and wife of Aethelwulf. It is not known if she was mother of all his sons, with some historians doubting that she could have given birth to sons so disparate in age from Aethelbald (adult by 851, so presumably born *c.* 830/5) to Alfred (born 847/9). She may thus have been a second wife. Her father was Oslac, a Hampshire noble and royal butler, who claimed descent from the royal Jutish line of Wight. According to Asser, who probably had the story from Alfred, she valued learning and once set her (two youngest?) sons a challenge of memorising the most from a book. She must have died before October 856, when Aethelwulf interrupted his return journey from Rome to marry the much younger Frankish princess Judith as his second wife. She was later revered as a saint, and her lineage was probably used by her publicity-conscious youngest son Alfred to stress his Jutish descent (which was highlighted in the *Anglo-Saxon Chronicle*) and so acceptability as a ruler in Kent as well as Wessex.

AETHELBALD (West Saxons (west kingdom), 855–60) The eldest surviving son of Aethelwulf of Wessex, born some time in the early to mid-830s. Given Aethelbald's age, it has been suggested that his mother was not Osburh, mother of his youngest brothers, who was still having children around fifteen years later, but an unrecorded first wife of Aethelwulf. He was witnessing charters in the 840s, and in 851 was old enough to fight at his side in the battle of Aclea, possibly Ockley in Surrey. The West Saxon army cornered and inflicted a rare defeat on a strong force of Vikings which had sailed up the Thames and had already defeated the Mercian army. When Aethelwulf decided to make a pilgrimage to Rome in 855, Aethelbald was left in control of the larger western part of the kingdom, from Hampshire to Cornwall, with his younger brother Aethelbert ruling the remaining, eastern shires.

When in 856 Aethelwulf endeavoured to return to his kingdom with a new, Frankish wife, Charles the Bald's daughter Judith, Aethelbald refused him admission. His principal supporters were Bishop Ealhstan of Sherborne, a fighting cleric who had commanded armies, and the ealdorman of Somerset. The crisis was minimised in the *Chronicle*, but later sources present it as a bid for power by an undutiful son and his ambitious advisers. It is possible that nobles and Aethelbald utilised discontent at Aethelwulf's grant of a 'tithe' of his property to the Church; Aethelbald promised a more aggressive policy to Viking raids, while Aethelwulf's marriage could provide new heirs to diminish his half-brothers' inheritance. Alternately, Aethelbald may have expected his father to abdicate and feared being superseded on his return. Aethelwulf had to make do with co-rule of Aethelbert's eastern lands, which he had earlier ruled as junior co-ruler to his father Egbert, and civil war was avoided. On Aethelwulf's death, Aethelbald retained his own lands, the greater part of the kingdom, and Aethelbert continued to rule the east. Aethelbald caused controversy in 858 by marrying his young stepmother Judith, aged around sixteen, who was about a decade younger than him. By canon law this amounted to incest, but there was a precedent for his action (again with a Frankish princess) in Eadbald of Kent's marriage in *c.* 617.

Aethelbald had no opportunity to show his mettle against the Vikings again. He died in December 860, probably at or near Sherborne where he was buried; the location would suggest that he favoured residing in the lands west of Selwood where his support had centred in 856. He was probably under thirty; the early deaths in that (and the next few) generations of his family may suggest a hereditary weakness of constitution. Aethelbert succeeded to a reunited kingdom, and Judith returned to her father in Francia; she subsequently ran off with the future Count Baldwin of Flanders.

ESSEX

SIGERED (798 – 825 (?)) The son and successor of Sigeric, who abdicated in 798. A vassal-king of Mercia, his authority was eroded by the restoration of Mercian power over his rebellious neighbours in Kent by Coenwulf and a century-and-a-half of being overshadowed by Mercia turned to outright emasculation of the dynasty. Around 811, Coenwulf reduced Sigered's rank in Mercian-controlled charters to 'dux', i.e. governor not king. Essex now followed Sussex and Hwicce in becoming a Mercian province; Sigered continued as a loyal vassal. In 825, Essex joined Kent and East Anglia in revolt after Mercia's crushing defeat by Egbert of Wessex at Ellandun, and Sigered disappears from the records as Wessex took control. He may have been killed or expelled as a Mercian loyalist.

SIGERIC II (830s (?)) Recorded as a ruler of the kingdom in the early-mid 840s; possibly a Mercian client installed after the reassumption of independence by King Wiglaf in 830, and so hostile to Wessex.

EAST ANGLIA

EADWALD (*fl.* 798) The first known king of the East Angles after Offa's execution of (Saint) Aethelbert in 794; his reign seems to have followed an interregnum when Offa presumably ruled the kingdom via governors without a king. His first (known) coins are dated 798, and it is probable that he benefited from the temporary eclipse of Mercia on the deaths of Offa and his son Ecgfrith to lead a revolt. His name may suggest a family link with the royal line of the seventh and early eighth centuries. The briefness of his coinage suggests reasserted Mercian control. Eadwald and/or his unknown successors appear to have been Mercian governors, using Mercian coinage, until the revolt in 825.

ATHELSTAN (Mid-820s – *c*. 837) East Anglian history in the early ninth century is largely blank, and no rulers are recorded between Eadwald in *c*. 800 and Athelstan, who was reigning around 825. The strong overlordship of Mercian kings Coenwulf and Ceolwulf from 796 to 823 meant that no new ruler could succeed except with their permission. Possibly the absence of royal coinage from East Anglia in these years indicates a requirement to use Mercian coins and refusal to grant royal rank to their governors of the kingdom, whether of royal blood or not.

Athelstan was probably the unnamed king who turned to Wessex for aid in throwing off Mercian control in 825, taking advantage of Egbert's defeat of Mercia at Ellandun. Beornwulf of Mercia invaded in retaliation but was killed, thus saving East Anglian independence; it suggests a major degree of determination and competence on the part of the outnumbered East Anglians and their king. The next Mercian king, Ludecan, met a similar fate a year or so later (*c*. 827). The *Chronicle* probably downplayed his role in favour of its own king's ancestor, Egbert.

Athelstan seems to have acquiesced in the overlordship of Egbert, now the greatest military power in southern England and annexer of Kent. East Anglia accepted Wessex as its overlord after 825 or 829. Athelstan disappears from the meagre records after 837, with Aethelweard (from his alliterative name probably close kin) succeeding him. He may have ruled for up to thirty years, albeit as a Mercian governor who happened to hold royal rank until 825. As an Athelstan ruled Kent from *c*. 839, it has been suggested that they were the same man. In this case, Athelstan would have been a younger son or grandson of Egbert, and thus a supporter of the king of Wessex. He would have succeeded Egbert's elder son Aethelwulf, his brother or father, as subking of Kent on Egbert's death.

AETHELWEARD (East Angles, 837 (?) – ?) A king of whom next to nothing is known except that he succeeded Athelstan, vassal and ally of Wessex, as ruler of East Anglia, *c*. 837. Given the similarity of names, he was probably related and may well have been his son; it is speculated that the two were of West Saxon blood. He may have shared his throne in his later years with Beorhtric, who succeeded him around 850.

BEORHTRIC (? – 854 (?)) One of the most obscure East Anglian kings, who succeeded Aethelweard some time in *c*. 850–54 and may have been his co-ruler for an initial period. His name would suggest a Mercian family origin, and possibly a link with its king, Beorhtwulf. Nor is it known if Beorhtric was related to his successor, Edmund, who was crowned at Christmas 854; the latter's hagiography makes no mention of Beorhtric, so if he was Edmund's father or other relative his rule left no impression on folk-memory.

MERCIA

COENWULF (796–821) The successor of Ecgfrith, son of Offa the Great, when that ruler's surprise death in December 796 ended the rule of the junior line of the Icelingas in Mercia. He was allegedly the son of Cuthbert, descendant of Penda's younger brother Cenwalh, but his dynastic claim may have been manufactured to improve his legitimacy. It has been suggested that the interest he and his relatives showed in Winchcombe, the former capital of the kingdom of Hwicce, where he founded a royal church, may indicate a link to local eighth-century Hwiccan aristocrats (related to their former kings?) with similar names such as Cuthbert and Abbess Cuthswith of Inkberrow, Worcestershire. Probably elected as the strongest contender, he earned a reputation as ruthless and unprincipled; Alcuin accused him of usurpation and of setting his wife aside for a successor (possibly after his accession to improve his dynastic position or win noble support). He allowed Pope Leo III to judge the validity of his accession and the deposition of Archbishop Aethelheard of Canterbury by the new, anti-Mercian king, Eadbert Praen. Eadbert had taken advantage of the deaths of Offa and Ecgfrith to revolt against annexation, and Coenwulf attempted to use the flight of the archbishop from Kent to persuade the Pope to relocate the archbishopric permanently to London (i.e. in Mercia). This was refused. But once Coenwulf had papal support to remove the usurper in Kent he invaded to defeat, capture, mutilate and deport Eadbert (798). Coenwulf's brother Cuthred was made the new king, Aethelheard was restored to his see and Kent remained under control for three more decades.

Coenwulf proved as vigorous a ruler as Offa, and was to be remembered for his harsh actions. He seems to have removed or enforced vassalage on East Anglia, whose coinage ceased around 800. In 799, a treaty was concluded with Offa's son-in-law, Beorhtric of Wessex, with the latter as junior partner, and soon Coenwulf was using the title of 'emperor' like his Continental counterpart Charlemagne – probably the first of any of Britain's kings to use the imperial title. There was also a military clash with Northumbria in 801. Gwynedd was raided in 798, which may have resulted in two decades of peace, aided by the mutual antagonism of its rulers, Cynan and Hywel. The paramount ruler of southern Britain from *c.* 800 and effectively as powerful as Offa, Coenwulf was eclipsed by his predecessor in later memory (probably due to the enmity of the West Saxon dynasty and the Church at Canterbury). Cautious with the Church, Coenwulf abandoned Offa's unilateral creation of a new archbishopric at (Mercian) Lichfield to usurp ecclesiastical power from unreliable Canterbury; he endeavoured to create a Mercian archbishopric for

London, but accepted Rome's refusal of this and obediently demoted Lichfield back to a bishopric. But when he took full control of Kent on Cuthred's death in 807, Coenwulf came into conflict over lay appropriation of Church lands with the new archbishop, Wulfred (a Mercian or Middle Saxon), and the latter went to Rome to win papal backing for his claims. Returning in 815 backed by the Pope, Wulfred held a religious council at Chelsea in 816 and reasserted the right of the Church to deprive lay appropriators and denied the earlier papal-approved right of the kings of Mercia to appoint abbots and abbesses during a vacancy at Canterbury. (One of those affected by the latter was Coenwulf's sister Cwenthryth, the new abbess of Minster-in-Thanet.) Wulfred then seized the disputed lands, but Coenwulf promptly expelled him and took control of Canterbury himself; apparently the Mercian kingdom was deprived of the archbishop's ministry for six years (816–22 [?]). Pope Paschal avoided demanding Wulfred's immediate restoration, and Coenwulf or his successor seems to have allowed Wulfred to return home provided that he did not exercise authority.

Around 820 Coenwulf resumed attacks on the Welsh, raiding Gwynedd and Powys and penetrating into Dyfed. He died while preparing for a second campaign in 821, predeceased by his son (Saint) Coenhelm, whose mysterious murder in the Clent Hills seems to be related to some sort of family feud. The usual version in his hagiographies blames his aunt and guardian, Cwenfryth, sister of Coenwulf, for ordering a thegn in her employ to murder the boy and hide his body – presumably to aid the chances of her own candidate for the throne. Coenwulf's brother Ceolwulf succeeded him. In retrospect, Coenwulf can be seen as the last great king of Mercia; the effective overlordship of southern England established by his predecessors in the later seventh century collapsed within two years.

CEOLWULF (821–3) The brother and successor of Coenwulf of Mercia, from a junior line of the Icelingas dynasty. He was probably already middle-aged when he succeeded in 821, and was chosen by the nobles to represent dynastic continuity. He was crowned on 17 September 822, the long delay from his accession possibly indicating political problems. Coenwulf had recently been achieving major successes against the Welsh of Gwynedd, Powys and Dyfed, but if Ceolwulf continued his campaigns this is not recorded. It may have been him rather than his predecessor who allowed Archbishop Wulfred to return to Canterbury. Ill health may have hampered his effectiveness or he lacked his brother's forcefulness over his nobles, for some time in 823 he was deposed in favour of the even more obscure Beornwulf.

BEORNWULF (823 – 6 (?)) The beneficiary of the overthrow of Ceolwulf of Mercia in 823. Ceolwulf, probably already middle-aged, had a distant link to the old dynasty; Beornwulf may have represented the line of Beornred, the usurper of 757 driven out by Offa. Within months he had launched a devastating attack on Powys which was claimed to have reduced that kingdom to ruin and subjection to Mercia. He then marched on into Gwynedd, overran Clywd, and sacked the main royal residence at Degannwy. Even if this was building on years of attrition by Coenwulf, it represented a major success; within two years Gwynedd was ruled by a new dynasty (that of Merfyn 'Frych') which put a premium on Welsh military recovery.

Beornwulf had less success against Mercia's Saxon rivals, and in 825 tackled the rising power of Egbert of Wessex – possibly a pre-emptive move after Egbert's acquisition of resources and reputation in the conquest of Cornwall. He was defeated at Ellandun, probably Wroughton near Swindon, which marked the end of Mercia as the major power in southern England and led to the loss of Kent to Wessex and East Anglia to Wessex-backed rebels. Beornwulf attempted to restore the situation with an invasion of East Anglia but was killed in battle, probably in 826. Ludecan, not Beornwulf's own relative (son or brother?) Beorhtwulf, succeeded him and was soon killed in turn.

LUDECAN (826 – 7 (?)) An ealdorman who assumed the kingship in 826 on the death in battle of Beornwulf in East Anglia. The Icelingas dynasty were now extinct and Mercia in crisis; the element of unstable successions had been supplemented by military defeat against Wessex in 825 and now revolt in Kent and East Anglia. Whether or not Ludecan was the nobleman who assumed command of the defeated army on Beornwulf's death and was the best military leader available, his priority was restoring Mercia's military power. Coenwulf's Welsh wars and the defeats of 825–6 would have made the task difficult due to falling manpower and morale, and within months Ludecan was killed in a second failed invasion of East Anglia. Wiglaf now took the throne.

WIGLAF (826/7 – 9 and 830 – 39/40) Chosen king in 826/7 following the death in battle of Ludecan against the East Anglians. Mercia had suffered major military reverses and had lost control of its satellite kingdoms Kent, Essex and East Anglia, and Wiglaf was taking over at a time of the kingdom's worst crisis for 170 years. His wife, Cynefrith, was possibly connected to the royal house from her name, and if local Evesham tradition is correct that his son Wigmund predeceased him as an adult, Wiglaf was married well before his accession. His name was that of the eponymous hero's nephew and successor in *Beowulf*, suggesting that that epic was popular with his parents and possibly that they had royal hopes. (The Evesham traditions remembered Wigmund as a descendant of King Coenred, who abdicated in 709, but not whether this was through Wiglaf or Cynefrith.) Wiglaf had a distinctly ignominious early reign, as he could not stand up to Egbert's military power and in 829 the West Saxon king deposed him and annexed

Mercia. No major battle on the scale of the recent disaster at Ellandun (825) is recorded and his outnumbered army, still weak after its losses in 825–7, may have disintegrated. Egbert secured the submission of all England and marched into central Wales, but in 830 Wiglaf was able to return. It is unclear if he waited until Egbert went home and marched back with a warband to expel Egbert's governors, or if Egbert realised that he could not rule both Wessex and Mercia and came to terms with him. He may have ruled as a West Saxon vassal, but had enough freedom of manoeuvre in Egbert's declining years to regain a degree of control over Essex whose governors witnessed charters on behalf of Mercia. He also presided over an impressive synod of the bishops of southern England at Croft with Archbishop Ceolnoth of Canterbury in 836.

He died in 839/40, apparently without heirs; the later Evesham traditions say his son Wigmund predeceased him and the latter's son (Saint) Wigstan refused the throne. Beorhtwulf succeeded him.

BEORHTWULF (839/40 – 52) A near relative of King Beornwulf who was killed attacking East Anglia in 826, probably his brother or son. Passed over for the throne on that occasion, probably due to youth or military inexperience, he was chosen as the new king on the death of Wiglaf in 839/40. The latter had male heirs, but it seems that his son Wigmund died before or soon after him; his grandson (Saint) Wigstan was under-age and Beortwulf would have been chosen as more experienced a leader. Wigstan's hagiography states that the saint had popular support but turned down the throne. Apparently Beorhtwulf sought to marry Wigmund's widow Elfleda to add to his security, but she refused; Elfeda was the daughter of Beornwulf's victim of 823, Ceolwulf, and possibly a family enemy. Beorhtwulf's reign seems to have seen extensive conflict with Powys, though with less success than Beornwulf had achieved; he may also have lost control of northern Berkshire to Aethelwulf of Wessex. But he had enough authority in the middle Thames valley to witness a land-grant at Pangbourne near Reading in 844 without reference to Wessex; his local ealdorman was the Mercian Aethelwulf, later a Wessex official killed by the Vikings in 870, who came from Derby.

In 851, a massive Scandinavian fleet of about 300 ships sailed up the Thames and started to ravage south-eastern Mercia; Beorhtwulf took them on in battle but was heavily defeated. The invaders moved on south into Wessex where Aethelwulf routed them at Aclea. Beorhtwulf died soon after, probably in 852 as his successor reigned for twenty-two years until 874, and was succeeded by Burghred. He had reigned for thirteen years according to a Mercian regnal list.

NORTHUMBRIA

EARDWULF (796–806 and 808–11) A contender for the throne in the chaos after the murder of Aethelred 'Moll' in March 796. The grandson of Eadwulf (or Eardwulf) and possibly related to the usurper Eadwulf of 704–5, he had been seen as a threat by Aethelred as early as 790 and was injured in a murderous attack ordered by that king, being left for dead outside Ripon monastery, but was found alive by the monks ordered to bury him and recovered to escape into exile. He either returned to challenge his would-be killer or, more likely, returned on the news of his death; within four weeks of Aethelred's death he was able to muster a force strong enough to overthrow the new king, Osbald. Aethelred's persecution of Eardwulf may have added to the support of his kin in his successful revolt. He assumed the throne on 24 April as Osbald fled to Lindisfarne and proved a strong ruler. Revolt was now endemic, and in May 798 he won the battle of Billington Moor against rebels apparently backing Osbald. He pursued as determined a pursuit of potential enemies as Aethelred had, driving them to take sanctuary on Church property. This led to tension with the new Archbishop of York, Eanbald, with the latter also accusing the king of deserting his wife for a mistress.

In 800 Eardwulf ordered the execution of a dangerous enemy, Alchmund, son of ex-king Al(ch)red, backed by Mercia. Revolt was headed off, and in 801 Eardwulf raided Mercia; the two kings were equally matched, and a long war ended when bishops mediated. They eventually came to terms. In 806 he was overthrown by an unknown Elfwald, possibly connected to the first king of that name and to the kin of the mid-eighth-century warrior-king Eadbert. He fled to the court of his principal ally Charlemagne in Francia, the most powerful ruler in Europe and more than a match for Coenwulf should the latter intervene; his patronage of the Church had helped in building up connections with clerics at Charlemagne's eclectic court, some of Northumbrian extraction. (The most well-known and influential, Alcuin, had died.) Charlemagne lent Eardwulf an impressive escort, probably soldiers as well as officials, and so did his ally Pope Leo III; the spectacle of papal backing that threatened excommunication on his foes showed that Eardwulf had built up his contacts to good effect. Resistance to Eardwulf's return in 808 was probably reduced by the open backing of the international Church. Elfwald's fate is unknown; Eardwulf held his throne until his death in 811, by which time he was probably in his forties or fifties, and he passed on his realm to his son Eanred. The latter was not challenged successfully in a thirty-two-year reign, and some of the credit must go to his father's vigorous and, when necessary, ruthless rule.

AELFWALD (II) (806–8) One of the most obscure rulers of an obscure era. His name may suggest a link with Aelfwald II, son of Oswulf, in which case he was the candidate of one of the three rival royal dynasties of the eighth century and had more of a hereditary claim to the throne than the man he replaced. He was chosen as the candidate of those who removed the strong Eardwulf in 806, and he reigned for two years before Eardwulf returned to York in 808 from the court of Charlemagne with a Frankish and papal escort. Aelfwald was deposed or killed; his fate is unknown.

EANRED (811 – 43 (?)) The son and successor of Eardwulf, who died in 811. The latter had restored a degree of stability after more than fifty years of rebellions, though he was briefly expelled in 806 and had to be restored with Frankish and papal help. Eanred continued his father's work, and kept his throne for either thirty-two (Simeon of Durham's version) or thirty-three (according to Roger of Wendover's *Flowers of History*) years – the longest reign in Northumbrian history. He submitted to Egbert of Wessex when that ruler overthrew Wiglaf of Mercia and marched as far as the Peak District in 829, preferring to treat than to rely on the size of his realm to exhaust an invading army (or to risk Egbert setting up a rival king?). The distance from Wessex to York made any exercise of authority by Egbert difficult and the return of Wiglaf to Mercia in 830 would have limited the latter's ability to threaten Northumbria. The conjunction of the Viking-threatened kingdoms of Dal Riada and the Picts under Kenneth MacAlpin, *c.* 843, would have posed an implicit threat to Northumbria at the end of Eanred's reign. He died in 843 (?), probably at least in his early fifties if not his sixties, and was succeeded by his son Aethelred. (One anomalous coin of a King 'Eanred', similar in style to the coinage of Aethelwulf of Wessex, *c.* 849/50, has been discovered, and may force a re-dating of the end of his reign to the late 840s.)

AETHELRED II (843 – 4 (?), 844 – 52 (?)) The son of Eanred of Northumbria, who he succeeded in 843 (?). This was the first time that the throne had passed directly from a Northumbrian king to his son and then his grandson. It seemed to indicate a return to earlier stability, but within a year Aethelred was deposed and expelled by a certain Raedwulf. In or soon after 844, Raedwulf was killed fighting a Viking incursion. Aethelred was recalled, but was killed some years later by the partisans of a certain Osbert who succeeded him. Given the length of the latter's reign (either thirteen or eighteen years to 866/7), this was some time between 848/9 and 852/3. Aethelred was the last of his dynasty.

RAEDWULF (*c.* 844) The usurper who temporarily displaced Aethelred, son of Eanred, early in his reign (which commenced in 843). It is possible that the nobles saw him as a better war-leader against Scandinavian raids. He was soon killed resisting a Scandinavian attack in 844, according to Roger of Wendover, and Aethelred reclaimed the throne.

OSBERT (849 (?) – 866/7) An obscure but relatively long-reigning ruler of turbulent Northumbria, he appears to have succeeded Aethelred II in 849. The difference in names probably indicates that they were not related, and he may have been connected to the previous kings with Os- names in the eighth century (Oswulf, d. 759, or Osred II, d. 790 [?]). He reigned for either thirteen (Simeon of Durham's chronicle) or eighteen (according to Roger of Wendover's *Flowers of History*) years, probably counted to his death in 867. He was forced to accept Aelle as his co-ruler some time prior to his expulsion if the latter reigned for five years to 867; alternatively the latter may have reigned for only a year from 866 (?). Possibly he was restricted to Bernicia by a revolt in York. His confiscation of lands from the monastery of Lindisfarne may reflect a weakening of royal power through a lack of land to endow his warriors, and/or a resort to seizing Church property which the latter resisted. He was expelled by Aelle in 866, but had enough aristocratic support to mount a counter-attack. The two kings were at war when the Scandinavian 'Great Army' arrived in Deira in autumn 866 and captured York, evicting Aelle, and they agreed to a truce and combined their armies to attack the city in March 867. The attack was unsuccessful and both were killed.

8

860 to 899

WESSEX

AETHELBERT (860 – 65/6 (east kingdom 855 – 65/6)) The second surviving son of Aethelwulf and (probably) his first wife Osburga; next brother of Aethelbald. He was old enough to be granted the eastern part of Wessex (Sussex, Surrey, Kent and Essex) when his father set out for Rome on pilgrimage in 855; this had been Aethelwulf's sub-kingdom under his own father Egbert in the 830s. He was probably at least in his mid-teens, possibly as much as a decade older. When Aethelwulf endeavoured to return with his new Frankish wife Judith in 856, Aethelbald refused him admission to his western part of the kingdom, but Aethelbert admitted his father to the east. Aethelbert's contrasting generosity and dutifulness to his father may have been tinged with political calculation that Aethelwulf would make him his heir to the whole kingdom if he managed to depose Aethelbald. But the latter was too strong to be dislodged, and Aethelbert had to grant his father co-rulership of the east.

When Aethelwulf died in January 858 Aethelbert became sole ruler of the east, and he succeeded the childless Aethelbald in the rule of the west on his death in December 860. The kingdom now remained united, ending an experiment in co-rule within the royal family which may well have been continuous since 825. Aethelbert's action, the only recorded initiative of an obscure but largely peaceful reign, indicated either masterful determination to avoid future inter-dynastic conflict among quarrelling athelings or practicality arising from the youth of his next brother, Aethelred (I), aged probably under twenty. According to Alfred's account in the 880s, he and Aethelred agreed to entrust their property inherited from Aethelwulf to the new king in return for later grants, thus enhancing the wealth available to the sovereign. Aethelbert possibly treated Aethelred as his sub-king in c. 862 from charter evidence, but there was no new allocation of a province to him.

A Viking force landed in Wessex at the start of Aethelbert's reign and advanced as far as Winchester, principal royal residence, before the shire militia cornered and defeated them. But the main threat to Wessex and all England developed in autumn 864, when an unprecedentedly large force, the 'Great Army' as it was subsequently called, arrived on what was to turn out to be systematic conquest. They wintered on Thanet; the locals confronted a raiding-force on the mainland and brokered a pact to leave Kent alone. The invaders broke their word and resumed plundering before sailing off northwards in spring 865. The lack of a major military response from the king may imply Aethelbert's ill-health. Before the 'Great Army' returned Aethelbert was dead, the second (or even third) of Aethelwulf's sons to die young, in his late twenties or early thirties. The exact date is not recorded, except that it was around New Year 866; he was buried at Sherborne so he probably died at the royal manor there. Aethelred succeeded him.

AETHELRED (ETHELRED) I (865/6 – 71) The third surviving son of Aethelwulf of Wessex, probably born in the mid-840s. Given his age and his closeness to his next brother Alfred, he was more certainly than his older brothers the son of Alfred's mother Osburh. His mother died before 856 and his father in January 858. The kingdom had been divided into western and eastern halves since 855, but on the death of his brother Aethelbald (ruler of the west) in December 860 the next brother, Aethelbert, did not pass on his own eastern kingdom to Aethelred. At the most he was given the honorary role of sub-king around 862, presumably on reaching adulthood. He succeeded Aethelbert around New Year 866, facing the danger that the massive Viking force which had wintered on Thanet in 864–5 would return to attack Wessex. Late in 867 the Vikings, led by the three sons of Ragnar Lothbrok, sailed up the Trent and established a bridgehead in Mercia at Nottingham. Burghred of Mercia sought help from his West Saxon wife Aethelswith's brother, Aethelred. Aethelred led a force from Wessex to assist the Mercians. The two armies had cooperated against the Welsh already (853), but unprecedently both the West Saxon king and his heir, Alfred, now aided Mercia. Both he and Alfred took Mercian wives; Aethelred married Wulfrida and had at least one son (possibly two by 871). The Vikings sat it out in Nottingham, able to bring in supplies by river so they were not vulnerable to blockade and a stalemate ensued; eventually Burghred sued for terms. Peace was made and the West Saxon army returned home; the Vikings moved to East Anglia late in 869.

The 'Great Army' invaded Wessex in late 870. Some settlers probably remained behind in East Anglia, as others had in York, and possibly one or more of Ragnar's sons had also left the invading force by this time; numbers were made up by new arrivals, with several major warlords of the rank of king or jarl among the commanders. The Vikings, probably led by Halfdan, sailed up the Thames and seized the strategically important, easily-defensible riverside town of Reading as their base for raids, as in Northumbria and Mercia, where they erected a rampart between the Thames and the Kennet to withstand attack. A few days later, Ealdorman Aethelwulf of Berkshire defeated a large raiding-party under two jarls at Englefield (west or east of Reading). Aethelred and Alfred then brought the main army forward to besiege Reading, pressing a quick assault with more vigour than Burghred had shown at Nottingham. They met defeat, Aethelwulf was among the casualties, and they had to retreat westwards onto the Downs. The Vikings moved out of Reading to give chase.

The crucial battle of Ashdown which followed on 4 January 871 (?) was the invaders' first serious check since their arrival, and a rare English victory in open conflict. The site is disputed except that it took place on the Berkshire Downs, a few days' march from Reading; it was later linked to White Horse Hill above Uffington, but was probably somewhere on the ridge of the Downs. An alternative site is at Cholsey or Streatley, on a lower chalk ridge nearer the Thames. Both armies fought in two sections, with Aethelred facing Halfdan and his fellow-king Bacseg and Alfred facing the jarls. Alfred's biographer Asser claimed that the Vikings started to advance while Aethelred was still at prayer and Alfred urged him to attack by surprise while they were still marching into place; the king preferred to finish prayers so Alfred attacked alone. The West Saxons scored a decisive victory with fighting raging until nightfall; Bacseg and five jarls were killed and the Vikings put to flight. The West Saxon success at Ashdown did not have any significance in the short term; the Vikings, reinforced by fresh arrivals, moved south to northern Hampshire. Aethelred and Alfred met them at Basing fourteen days after Ashdown, and this time they were defeated.

The West Saxon army remained in the field throughout what was subsequently called the 'battle-winter', putting up a stronger fight than the other kingdoms. It suffered a second defeat at Merton (perhaps Martin near Ringwood, or Merton Park near Winchester) in mid to late March. It is probable that Aethelred was seriously wounded, at least from Asser's account. Another Viking fleet arrived, tipping the balance further, but Aethelred died on 23 April, probably at Witchampton near Wimborne where he was buried. He was probably aged around twenty-eight. His infant son Aethelwold was superseded by the adult and military experienced Alfred, as was necessary in the crisis. Overshadowed by his younger brother's subsequent success and largely forgotten except as an adjunct to Alfred, Aethelred played a major role in the ultimately successful resistance which Wessex mounted to the first major Viking invasion. Aethelred's resolute resistance set the tone for what followed.

ALFRED (AELFRED) THE GREAT (871–99) The youngest of the sons of King Aethelwulf and Osburh, of royal (Wight?) Jutish descent, he was the crucial figure in the survival of Wessex – and indeed any Anglo-Saxon kingdoms as a political entity during the Scandinavain invasions of the 860s and 870s. The preserver of his kingdom and the enabler of its revival in the early tenth century to take over all England, he was, in a sense, the first king of all Anglo-Saxon England. With adminstrative gifts, a passion for learning, a clear mission as a royal Christian leader and a sense of history added to his generalship, Alfred rightly became a major figure to his successors and is still one of the best-known early English kings. But the number of myths makes it necessary to sift legend from fact, and the unique advantage of the survival of a near-contemporary biography attributed to his friend Bishop Asser has been challenged as a source. It is now claimed (Alfred Smyth, 1996) that the oddities in its language for an early tenth- rather than eleventh-century book, several stories which sound apocryphal or lifted from saintly biographies (e.g. that of an abbot of Cluny), and mistakes about Wales, indicate that it was put together in Asser's name by Byrtferth, a monk of Ramsey Abbey in *c*. 1000. But other historians continue to defend Asser as the author.

The king was born around 848, according to Asser, at Wantage – which some historians allege was still under Mercian administration then, so it could not have been a West Saxon royal manor. His date of birth depends on whether Asser's script can be read as meaning that he was twenty-three or in his twenty-third year at his accession in April 871; he was born between May 847 and April 849. He had at least three and possibly four older brothers, not necessarily all by the same mother. According to Asser, he was a precocious reader who was able to memorise a passage from a book set by his mother before his older brothers, a tale presumably told to him by Alfred but slightly dubious given how much older (at least a decade?) all his brothers were except Aethelred. As early as 853 Aethelwulf sent him with an embassy to Rome with gifts for Pope Leo IV, who conferred insignia on him; a risky journey for a five-year-old. Sceptics have insisted that it was invented so as to have him honoured by a Pope Leo like his exemplar, Charlemagne; others have suggested that Alfred's memory mistook confirmation into the Church as a personal sacring by the Pope which presaged his kingship, or chose to 'spin' it as such when he was an embattled king as proof of divine favour. He returned to Rome in 855 with the king, staying there for a year as a guest of the next Pope (Benedict) before returning via Francia where the widowed Aethelwulf married King Charles' daughter Judith in October 856. Possibly due to this threat to his inheritance, Aethelwulf's eldest son Aethelbald, left in charge of western Wessex, refused to allow his father home and Aethelwulf (and Alfred?) had to settle with the second son, Aethelbert, in the eastern counties. Commentators have seen in Alfred's subsequent angry editorial comment, in his translation of the works of Boethius about treacherous, unfilial sons, his anger at Aethelbald's greed for the throne.

Aethelwulf died in January 858 and Alfred continued as a minor atheling, increasingly closer to the once-remote throne as his elder brothers died off. He witnesses charters from 861. Aethelbald died in 860 and Aethelbert at New Year 865/6; the Scandinavian 'Great Army' arrived in England that winter and in 868 Alfred joined his next and only surviving brother, King Aethelred, to march to Nottingham and assist the Mercians against the invaders. King Burghred was married to their sister Aethelswith; now the brothers took Mercian wives, Alfred marrying Ealhswith, daughter of the ealdorman of the 'Gaini'. At least three sons and three daughters were born. Asser also dates the onset of his much-debated 'illness' to the time of his marriage, presumably on the king's own account of events; Alfred is supposed to have prayed for an infirmity less embarrassing than his current haemorrhoids at the site of the later shrine of Saint Neot in Cornwall. In December 870 the Scandinavians, having sailed up the Thames to Reading, launched their assault on Wessex and Alfred fought as Aethelred's deputy in the resulting campaigns of the 'battle-winter'. According to Asser, his was the decisive move at Ashdown on 4 January 871 (?). Due to command one of the two Saxon divisions, he urged the praying king to attack unexpectedly while the Danes were still maneovuring into line and Aethelred piously refused but let him do so. Alfred shared in the victory and his division killed five jarls. A subsequent defeat at Basing followed, and was followed in March by a belated defeat in an initially successful battle at 'Merton'. Aethelred was badly wounded here according to one source, and in any case he died on 23 April. Alfred now succeeded as the only adult contender; Aethelred's infant sons were set aside.

A new 'summer army' of Vikings had recently arrived in Wessex to make up the invaders' losses, and the West Saxons could not call on any reinforcements. Resistance continued with another battle at Wilton (indicating a Scandinavian advance on Wiltshire), where the West Saxons held the advantage for most of the day but lost. The effects of war-weariness must have been mounting in a campaign reckoned as nine major battles and countless skirmishes, and Alfred negotiated in order to survive. The West Saxons had to pay tribute, later covered up by their embarrassed propagandists, and the invaders retired from Reading to London. The settlement of Vikings in part of Mercia in 874 and the settlement of much of the 'Great Army' in Yorkshire (875) preoccupied enemy commanders and removed much of their manpower, but successes emboldened other land-hungry adventurers to try their luck and in 875 Guthrum led an army into Wessex. Probably marching overland, they took over the useful port of Wareham (on a navigable river for sea-access, like earlier bases) as a centre to ravage Dorset. Alfred blockaded them there successfully. They were forced to accept terms (876), probably due to lack of food and reinforcements, and swore oaths to depart Wessex. But the land-army broke out by surprise and headed for Exeter, another strategic site on a river whence they could pillage Devon; seaborne reinforcements arrived from overseas but the fleet

Previous page: 1. Statue of Bertha of Francia, queen of Aethelbert of Kent, Canterbury Cathedral.

Above: 2. The ruins of St Augustine's Abbey, Canterbury.

Below: 3. Site of a royal settlement of the Bernician kings, in a field near Wooler, Northumberland.

Above: 4. Statue of King Eadbald of Kent (d. 640), Canterbury Cathedral.

Right: 5. Statue of King Alfred at Winchester, erected for the millennium of his death.

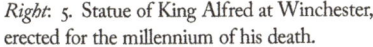

6. Winchester Cathedral, built on the foundations of the Saxon building in the 1080s. The original building had a shorter nave, with a tower standing separate at the far left. Alfred and most of his dynasty were buried here.

Above: 8. Stained-glass window depicting Edgar's coronation, Bath Abbey.

Opposite: 7. Bath Abbey, later building on the site of where King Edgar was crowned in 973.

Left: 9. Statue of King Edgar at Powis Castle, Wales.

Above: 10. Engraving of King Cnut by George Vertue.

Opposite bottom: 11. Tomb of Queen Emma and her son Harthacnut, Winchester Cathedral.

This page top: 12. Fourteenth-century painting of King Edward 'the Confessor' in his role as royal saint, as patronised by Richard II.

This page bottom: 13. Bosham Church, depicted (minus the later tower) in the Bayeux Tapestry. Harold II worshipped here before his 1064/5 visit to Normandy. His family's main residence was probably adjacent.

Above: 14. King Edward nominates Harold Godwinson as his successor (above) and dies (below), Twelfth Night 1066, from the Bayeux Tapestry.

Left: 15. Coronation of King Harold (II), from the Bayeux Tapestry.

from Wareham was destroyed in a storm off Swanage with 120 ships lost on the notorious rocky coastline. The losses of men and supplies probably weakened Guthrum's force at Exeter as Alfred starved him out here too in 877. Hostages were handed over in another (broken) peace-treaty and the invaders departed for Mercia.

The Scandinavians settled for the winter of 877-8 close to the Wessex frontier, and in the New Year Guthrum returned by surprise. Attacking the royal manor at nearby Chippenham while Alfred was there at Twelfth Night, he intended to kill his foe and then overrun the leaderless kingdom. Alfred ecaped and took refuge in the Somerset marshes at Athelney. He was reduced to a guerilla leader while the Scandinavians roamed at will across Wessex, probably unresisted by a leaderless army who at first thought their king dead; the *Chronicle* had to admit that most of Wessex was overrun and many people fled overseas. It is possible that Guthrum intended to set up a puppet king, as had been done in other kingdoms, but if so the 'quisling' and his supporters were expunged from the record. It is to this period that the apocryphal story of Alfred burning a poor cottager's bread (the 'cakes') and accepting her scolding belongs; it seems to have emerged from a hagiography of Saint Neot. Alfred rallied his men, and a seaborne descent on north Devon from Wales by the surviving Ragnarson, Ubbe/Hubba – probably intended to take Alfred in the rear at Guthrum's request – was crushed by Ealdorman Odda at Cynwit (Countisbury?). The dead invader's magical 'raven banner' was taken by the West Saxons, the victory inspiring them to rally to their king, and in the seventh week after Easter Alfred met up with his army at a rendezvous at 'Egbert's Stone', probably on the south-western edge of Salisbury Plain. The West Saxon army headed for Guthrum's headquarters at Chippenham, and he intercepted them en route at 'Ethandun', probably Bratton Down above Edington. The vital battle went the West Saxons' way, saving Wessex and England and fondly remembered for centuries (and possibly commemorated by the original 'White Horse', a Saxon war-symbol, on the Down). The defeated Guthrum fled back to Chippenham, where Alfred blockaded him for a fortnight and he had to seek terms. This time he was required to become a Christian – as Alfred's godson – as well as give hostages and depart Wessex for good, in the Treaty of Wedmore. Baptised at Aller, he led his men back to Cirencester and in 879 moved on to London en route to settle East Anglia. This time the peace lasted and Alfred's unexpected victory discouraged ambitious Vikings from trying their luck in Wessex for fourteen vital years.

Military victory was followed by Alfred's famous administrative reforms, which reorganised Wessex for defence – with the caveat that he may have begun some of them before 878. Wessex had been divided into a network of counties run by royal officials (led by the ealdormen) not by semi-autonomous sub-kings since Ine's time, with the local levies for the army led by the ealdormen. Now Alfred arranged for a Wessex-wide network of fortified towns, the 'burhs', which served to gather troops and supplies and deny these vital positions to invaders; the Scandinavians could no longer attack suddenly, seize a major town and build a fortification there to sit out a siege and plunder the countryside. The advantage of a safe defensive position in any confrontation from now on belonged to the West Saxons; and the presence of the defenders in a strong position, dominating the invaded countryside, would force attackers to spare many men from plundering to watch them. If they gave up and moved on, it diminished the amount of territory they could plunder; if they stayed to besiege the 'burh' it gave Alfred time to arrive with the main army. The extensive network served to add to royal-led centralisation with one plan being adopted for sites across the kingdom, and the secure sites also stimulated revived trade (and hence revenue). Around thirty were built, at least some (e.g. Twynham/Christchurch in Hampshire and Lydford in Devon) on new sites which were not existing towns. The fortifications by Charles the Bald in northern Francia in the 860s may have inspired the idea. The 'burhs' thus ended several Scandinavian advantages used in 870–8 and acted as rallying-points for the future defence of Wessex – and were to be extended into reoccupied territory by Alfred's son and daughter after 899. Next time a raiding fleet tested Wessex, at Rochester in 884, the locals held out in the fortified town; the invaders had to build their own camp outside, could not storm the town, and were duly starved out and forced to leave by Alfred (885).

In 886 he took over the vital position of London, which guarded the lower Thames from invasion, and handed it over to his new ally Aethelred, the ealdorman of Mercia, who had taken over from Ceolwulf II. Mercia had legal claim to the place and Alfred avoided antagonism by not using his military supremacy to secure it; Aethelred, now or recently married to Alfred's daughter Aethelfleda, proved a staunch ally for Wessex – to whose king he had made some sort of formal oath of dependency *c.* 884. His (diplomatic) aid was successfully sought against Anarawd of Gwynedd, the most powerful and predatory prince of the Welsh, by the latter's intended victims in south Wales, Hyffaid ap Bledri of Dyfed and Eliseg of Brycheiniog, some time in the early 880s. Alfred seems to have warned Anarawd off, and the latter's retaliatory alliance with the Scandinavians of York was abandoned in favour of some form of dependence on Wessex, *c.* 890–2; Asser, from Dyfed so an interested party, wrote that all the Britons as well as Saxons submitted to Alfred's leadership.

Alfred also rebuilt a powerful navy, able to challenge raiders at sea, and in 884 raided the Stour estuary in East Anglia to defeat a local fleet and sink sixteen ships. Victory at sea was not always secured, and Alfred was not the 'founder of the English navy'; Aethelwulf had also had a fleet and the Scandinavian settlers in the Danelaw and 'hit-and-run' raiders remained able to attack Wessex. But it put raiders on the defensive and discouraged the less bold, adding to his kingdom's defensibility. The main Scandinavian 'raiding-army' was occupied in the divided realm of Francia (mainly in Belgium) through the late 880s, but in 892 it returned to Kent after being fought to a standstill by the Franks in Flanders. Denied their usual fortified towns as bases by the West Saxon 'burhs', the invaders had to build their own camps but varied tactics with one invasion and camp in northern Kent (Milton) under Haesten and a second in the south (Appledore). Alfred positioned himself between them, and outsmarted the invaders when they sat it out waiting for the West Saxons levies' term of military service to expire so their army would have to disperse or else leave their agricultural work at home neglected. Alfred instituted a rota whereby only half the army was in service at any time and when one half had to be discharged the second took over – one of many inspired and logical improvisations.

The second major Viking war turned into a mixture of prolonged sieges and occasional breakouts for plundering expeditions across-country. Alfred's son Edward won his first victory at Farnham in 893, as the blockaded southern army at Appledore broke out to plunder across Sussex into Hampshire; the defeated raiders had to flee to the Thames valley in a failed attempt to get to the northern army, which Haesten had evacuated to a new camp at Benfleet in Essex. A diversionary attack on north Devon and Exeter by an allied fleet drew Alfred off, but on his return Benfleet was blockaded and (in Haesten's absence) stormed. The Scandinavians in Essex, reinforced from the north, moved off to western Mercia, but West Saxons and Welsh came to the Mercians' aid and the invaders were besieged at Buttington, starved out, and defeated in battle. The remnants escaped back to Essex. The year 894 saw a Scandinavian defeat in north Wales and a second campaign in Essex, this time based on a camp on Mersea Island, while more raiders attacked Exeter and the Chichester region, and in 895 the West Saxons besieged the invaders' camp on the River Lea upstream from London. Alfred protected the harvest so the raiders could not damage it and built fortified bridges across the river so they could not bring supplies in by river, and they broke out to try their luck in western Mercia only to be cornered and besieged again (this time at Bridgnorth). The Scandinavian army managed to break out in spring 896, but this time they did not return. Alfred also had some success at sea against continuing 'hit-and-run' raids on the South Coast in 896 with a new type of longship superior to enemy vessels. Beyond this military success, he also seems to have been recognised as overlord by the rulers of Wales; he was sought out as their senior ally against raiding Vikings and his alliance with Wales prevented attacks by Aethelred's Mercians. The autonomous Anglian enclave of Bernicia established a relationship with him, which the West Saxon propagandists interpreted as vassalage. All the English not under Danish rule recognised his authority, although any such terms were only honorary.

In military matters Alfred had managed to drive back two prolonged and serious attacks, and this was the last serious invasion for three generations. The successful defence of Wessex (and Mercia, where his daughter and son-in-law adopted the 'burh' system and received military aid during invasions) was centred on his planning, and this was duly adapted for reconquest of all England in the 910s. But he also did his best to revive learning for the future of Christian English culture, allegedly lamenting the fact that there was not one man able to read Latin books left in his war-ravaged kingdom, bringing in foreign scholars, and establishing his own palace school to educate the sons of the nobility. As stated in his preface to his translation of Pope Gregory the Great's *Pastoral Care*, he saw his role as restoring the greatness, contentment and wisdom of the 'English race'. Moreover, he required wisdom and moral authority from the entire leadership class as well from as the king, possibly influenced by the eighth-century scholar Alcuin as well as by Gregory. His circle of scholars, copying out vital or useful literary works, included Asser from Dyfed, John the 'Old Saxon' from Germany, and Grimbald of St Bertin, a Frank. The stories in Asser may be influenced by Einhard's *Life of Charlemagne*, but this need not mean they were invented; Alfred had visited Francia and Rome at an impressionable age and modelled himself on Charlemagne. Keen on maximising literacy, he learnt to read and write Latin himself and undertook translations – historians differ if he was illiterate or just unable to use Latin until Asser taught him. His significant choices for translations showed his concept of Christian rule, justice, and ethics as well as personal spirituality and interest in Rome – Pope Gregory the Great's *Pastoral Care*, Boethius' *Consolation of Philosophy* and Saint Augustine's *Soliloquies*. He did his best to revive monasticism as well as learning, founding one monastery (which needed a foreign abbot) at Athelney and (probably) a nunnery at Shaftesbury. His interest in the past of his own people is seen in his commissioning of the *Anglo-Saxon Chronicle*, which glorified (and sanitised?) the record of the West Saxon monarchy, playing up its right to lead the English, and set down the record of the heroic wars against heathen conquest for future generations. The claim that Alfred may have composed part of the text himself is now thought unlikely. According to less certain records, he even invented a new type of candle-lantern for dividing up his time more profitably. The *Chronicle* recorded his meeting interesting visitors like Irish monks as well as prestigious diplomatic contacts and gift-exchanges with the Popes and Jerusalem, and Alfred's fame and known curiosity (and generosity) seems to have brought travellers from far afield, such as the Arctic adventurer Ohtere, to his court.

Probably the most significant and outstanding ruler of Ango-Saxon England, Alfred died on 26 October 899, probably aged between fifty and fifty-two. Even his health is a subject of legend and controversy, with Asser's stories about his chronic sickness and repeated physical collapses dismissed by some as written into his biography to make him seem like a saintly sufferer chastised by God. He was supposed to have prayed for relief from one illness (or lust?) and promised to accept any infliction which God imposed on him without complaint. The confusing account of his illness defies accurate analysis, and certainly any recurrent (psychosomatic?) problems he had did not seriously hamper a remarkably active adulthood. The large number of early deaths among the males of his house suggests some hereditary ailments. His death led to a military confrontation between his elder son Edward and the disinherited atheling Aethelwold, son of King Aethelred, which Edward won. Edward and his heirs went on to create a kingdom of all England on Alfred's foundations, vindicating his judgement, and Alfred himself became the centre of a laudatory cult as the founding Christian hero-king which was revived in Victorian times. His combination of successful warfare, moral exhortation, Christian piety, promotion of learning, and the 'foundation of the Royal Navy' made him an appropriate role-model, and heroic paintings were duly installed in the new Palace of Westminster and statues erected at Wantage and Winchester – the latter unveiled in 1901 by former Prime Minister Lord Rosebery as part of the millennial Alfredian celebrations. Nowadays, the role and image of Alfred as a would-be imitator of Charlemagne is thought more relevant than his supposed 'founding role' in the greatness of the former British Empire.

EALHSWITH (Queen/'Lady' of Wessex, 871–902) Mercian wife of Alfred the Great, who he married in 868 as part of the Wessex-Mercian alliance to evict the Scandinavian 'Great Army' from Nottingham. Her father was the ealdorman of the 'Gaini', around Gainsborough in eastern Mercia; her mother was the formidable scholar Eadburh, prominent at Alfred's court, and her brother Aethelwulf was ealdorman of Worcester in the 880s. She had at least five children – Aethelfleda, 'Lady of the Mercians', born in c. 869 and married in 886 to Ealdorman Aethelred of Mercia; King Edward 'the Elder', born around 870; Aethelweard; Aethelgifu, abbess of Shaftesbury; and Aethelthryth/Elfrida, married to Count Baldwin of Flanders. She outlived her husband, who left her the probably emotionally significant estates of Wantage (his birthplace?) and Edington (site of his great victory in 878). She died in December 902; she appears to have been the main patron of the new nunnery in Winchester, the 'Nunnaminster'. Some commentators have noted that despite his regard for her, Alfred, unlike Aethelred I, never allowed his wife to attest charters; Asser implies that her formidably learned mother Eadburh was a stronger character.

EAST ANGLIA

(SAINT) EDMUND (854–70) The royal saint and martyr of the Anglo-Saxon era who made most impact on later centuries. Little is known about his reign, and his subsequent legend may have distorted events in seeking to present him in appropriate terms for his cult. He succeeded an unknown king in 854, being crowned on Christmas Day, and was sixteen or so at the time. His father and/or predecessor was probably Beorhtric, unless an unknown ruler intervened between them. By this stage the earlier alliance with, and overlordship of, Wessex of Egbert's era (825–39) had probably lapsed, and East Anglian military strength lessened since its two defeats of Mercia in the mid-820s. Edmund's obscure reign was probably peaceful apart from Viking raiding, but in winter 865–6 the Scandinavian 'Great Army' arrived in the Fens (probably by sea) from Kent and set up winter quarters there. The defensive forces were clearly outnumbered even if subsequent legend built up the attackers' numbers, and they had three experienced and ruthless commanders in the sons of Ragnar Lothbrok. Events were to show that they were intent on conquest and settlement, not merely raiding, but this may not have been obvious at first.

This was implicitly the greatest challenge in the East Anglian monarchy's history, and Edmund did not challenge the attackers but let them camp unmolested and granted them supplies and horses. The invaders' main target appears to have been York, possibly as a result of a blood-feud, and Edmund had every reason to speed them on their way out of his kingdom. No aid had been forthcoming from the main military powers of southern England, Wessex (whose king had just died) and Mercia. If he was calculating that the invaders would be defeated by the larger forces of Northumbria or be content to settle there, this proved inaccurate. After overthrowing Northumbria and fighting the Mercians to a standstill at Nottingham, in autumn 869 the Scandinavians returned to winter quarters at Thetford in the heart of his kingdom. Unusually, they did not bother to choose a site easily reachable by their ships – possibly a sign of confident contempt of their opponents.

At this point the legend of Saint Edmund takes over from contemporary chronicles, with the king portrayed as a Christian hero prepared to sacrifice himself for his people – according to one account he dismissed his main army to minimise casualties. He may have rejected a summons to hand over at least part of his kingdom for settlement; it is unlikely that he was ordered to abjure Christianity. He took on the Viking army in battle at Hellesdon/Hoxne in November 869 and was defeated and killed; the stories that he was captured alive and tortured to death, probably by being tied to a tree and used as target-practice, are persistent enough to be based on genuine memories. He may have had the 'blood-eagle' carved on him like Aelle of Northumbria; he was apparently beheaded and his remains later recovered by local followers and buried near the site. East Anglia was settled by the victors, but a few scattered coins of a subsequent Anglian ruler in the 870s (Oswald) suggest that Halfdan Ragnarsson and his brothers temporarily installed a puppet-king. A cult of Saint Edmund grew up in later decades, encouraged by the newly Christianised Scandinavian warlord Guthrum and serving as a unifying factor for Anglians and Danes. By 915, Edmund was an important enough figure to have his relics translated to Bedricsworth (later renamed 'Bury St Edmunds') as the centre of a cult based at a major shrine; the cult grew in importance after the West Saxon annexation of East Anglia and King Edward appears to have called his fourth son after the saint. By the fourteenth century, Edmund was one of the patron saints of England.

OSWALD (870 (?)) A very obscure ruler, only known by his coins and omitted from all chronicles. He seems to have been the king over parts of East Anglia not occupied by the Scandinavians after his predecessor, (Saint) Edmund, was killed in November 869. Any ruler in his position would have been at the mercy of the triumphant 'Great Army', and it is likeliest that they set him up as a client to administer those areas not under direct control as they did with Egbert in Northumbria and with Ceolwulf II in Mercia. The invaders moved on to tackle Wessex in winter 870–1, and formal settlement by the army based on Cambridge did not commence until Guthrum took up office as king on his return in 879. Oswald probably administered the kingdom in the interim.

MERCIA

BURGHRED (852 (?) – 74) The successor of Beorhtwulf of Mercia, probably in 852. He is not known to have been connected to any earlier kings, and was probably a senior ealdorman. He abandoned hostility between Mercia and Wessex in favour of a close alliance to add to Mercian resources, marrying Aethelwulf's daughter Ethelswith at Easter 853 and possibly surrendering any remaining control within Berkshire. The two kings campaigned together as allies against Powys in 853, and had such success that King Cyngen ap Cadell abandoned his people and fled to Rome; Powys was now reckoned to have been subjected to Mercia. Powys was never fully conquered and fell under the control of Cyngen's nephew Rhodri 'Mawr' of Gwynedd. Burghred now turned against Gwynedd, and in 865 was able to advance along the coast as far as Anglesey; further successes were prevented by the landing of the Viking 'Great Army' in England that autumn.

The Scandinavian force, led by the sons of Ragnar Lothbrok, marched across eastern Mercia from East Anglia to invade Northumbria in 866. Burghred made no move to come to the aid of the embattled Northumbria, thus missing a crucial chance. In autumn 867, the invaders moved south up the Trent to Nottingham – like their first target, York, a defensible town with river-access for their longships. Burghred summoned the forces of Wessex to his aid, and King Aethelred and his brother Alfred arrived to join the siege. Either then or before the campaign, they took Mercian wives. The invaders stayed within the walls of Nottingham, endeavouring to sit out the siege with supplies available by river while the English had to live off the land; according to Alfred's biographer Asser, they refused to fight. After a long stand-off the Mercians reached terms wth the Scandinavians. Presumably the latter received money and supplies, and promised to leave, which they did in 869 (either for York or for East Anglia); the West Saxons returned home and the tone of the *Chronicle* suggests some discontent at Burghred's caution.

Mercia survived unmolested as the Scandinavians proceeded to settle Deira and, from 870, East Anglia. Burghred sent no aid to Wessex in the crisis of 870–1 though the conflict centred on ex-Mercian Berkshire, and next winter reached terms with the invaders' army as it moved back from Wessex to (Mercian) London. In 872 they moved on to Torksey in the eastern Midlands, and in 873–4 they wintered further inland at Repton. In 874, the invaders moved to formally take over Mercia and drove Burghred into exile; a 'foolish king's thegn' called Ceolwulf was installed as their puppet ruler of the western part and the east was seized. Burghred and Ethelswith journeyed overseas to Rome, where he later died at an unknown date; he had clearly given up the will to resist.

CEOLWULF II (874 – early 880s) One of the English rulers regarded with most contempt in the records, he was chosen by the Scandinavian 'Great Army' as their candidate for the vacant Mercian throne on Burghred's flight in 874. The *Chronicle* calls him an 'unwise king's thegn', an ambitious royal official who was prepared to collaborate with the enemy currently occupying the centre of Mercia in return for the throne. A dynastic link with Coenwulf and Ceolwulf (I) is possible; he ceded eastern Mercia beyond Watling Street (the later Danelaw) to the invaders and remained king of the west as their vassal, allegedly promising to hand that over too when they required it. In his favour, he did at least preserve part of Mercia from occupation although he had to put up with Guthrum operating from Cirencester, deep in his territory, after the failure of the latter's invasion of Wessex in 876–7.

The Mercian Cotswolds were Guthrum's base for his attack on Alfred at Chippenham at New Year 878 and occupation of part of the kingdom, and the departure of his force in 879 added to Ceolwulf's ability to operate effectively. He seems to have allied with Alfred as the two subsequently issued joint coinage. Without the presence of his Viking overlords, Ceolwulf may have been a more acceptable king than hostile tradition maintains and he had some success raiding Gwynedd, but the end of his reign is masked in obscurity and it is uncertain if the five years ascribed to him dates from Guthrum's departure. He presumably died around 884, and was the last king of Mercia.

AETHELRED, EALDORMAN (*c.* 884–911) He emerged as the national leader of the part of Mercia excluded from Scandinavian settlement after the death or deposition of its last king, Ceolwulf II, in the early 880s. Probably a local West Midlands nobleman, he does not appear to have had any connection to Mercian royal families and he did not take the title of king like his Viking-appointed predecessor had done. Aethelred emerged as the most vigorous local figure in the weakened half-kingdom left to the Mercians under Ceolwulf. His accession was apparently not agreed by his Scandinavian neighbours, and logically the departure of the army of Guthrum from Cirencester to East Anglia in 879 deprived them of the military force to coerce the Mercians. Aethelred's avoidance of the royal title – he called himself 'ealdorman' or 'lord' – may have been to avoid seeming to claim the entire kingdom, or a practical reflection of the limits of his power and legitimacy.

By 886, Aethelred was the unchallenged ruler of western Mercia and in that year King Alfred entrusted the control of recently-reconquered London, controlling access to the Thames valley for Viking fleets, to him. He was the junior partner in the alliance of the two surviving Anglo-Saxon states, and probably recently married to Alfred's daughter Aethelfleda. The latter, the 'Lady of the Mercians', was to prove an equal partner in leadership to her husband as they rebuilt the reduced kingdom. The 880s saw Aethelred confident enough as a military leader to return to warfare with his Welsh neighbours. The eclipse of Mercia at Viking hands had been a boon to the united kingdom of Powys and Gwynedd, under major military threat in the early ninth century; his fortification of Gloucester, apparently his main residence and moving the centre of administrative power well away from the Viking frontier, and Worcester may also have been linked to setting up bases for the Welsh wars. His main foe was Anarawd of Gwynedd, who succeeded his father Rhodri 'Mawr' (killed by the Vikings) in 878 and sought alliance with the Vikings in York. Mercia's Welsh targets resorted to sending emissaries to Alfred, already the overlord of the south Welsh princes, to treat for alliance so he would use his influence on Aethelred to prevent further attacks.

In 893, Aethelred faced the arrival of the next large Scandinavian raiding army in England, constantly harassed by Alfred's force of rotating county levies and unable to plunder at will. Pursued from Essex up the Thames into the Severn valley, the raiders were unable to stop to plunder; Alfred's successful tactics were used in Mercia. The Vikings were surrounded and besieged at Buttington, probably in Gloucestershire, starved out, and forced to withdraw into Northumbria. In 895 a similar joint reaction met the next raiders, who were blockaded at Bridgnorth and forced to withdraw northwards. Serious attacks on the Mercian heartland now ceased, though a Scandinavian force briefly established itself on the Wirral. After the deaths in battle of the Wessex rebel Aethelwold and his Viking allies in 903, Aethelred is called lord of the Northumbrians, so he possibly exploited a leadership vacuum to enforce some sort of vassalage on York.

Aethelred was probably constrained by ill-health in his later years. In 910 a major Danelaw raid took place west into the Severn valley, but Edward brought West Saxon aid and the raiders were defeated at Tettenhall on 6 August. Aethelred was not present at the battle, and died in 911. Aethelfleda succeeded him as the first female ruler of Mercia.

NORTHUMBRIA

AELLE (Northumbria, 862 (?) – 7) The last king of independent Northumbria. He reigned for five years according to the Durham tradition recorded by the chronicler Simeon, probably from 862; four years according to the twelfth-century annals of Lindisfarne; one year according to an eleventh-century source. Due to the need to accommodate his predecessor's reign of either thirteen or eighteen years before 867, it is possible that he reigned jointly with the latter, Osbert (against whom he had perhaps revolted), from around 862 to 866. Aelle's power was based in Deira, probably excluding his rival. Aelle is said to have lacked royal blood, but he was called after the first king of Deira, which may indicate high pretensions by his family. According to legend he captured the pirate Ragnar Lothbrok and threw him into a pit full of snakes, occasioning the retaliatory invasion of England by the victim's sons; the motif is, however, common in sagas and may be a later story justifying invasion.

Whether the landing of the 'Great Army' under Ragnar's sons in 865 was as a result of blood-feud or opportunism, Northumbria was its first major target. In 866, soon after Aelle had expelled Osbert, the invaders occupied York. Aelle returned with an army in March 867, joined by Osbert; the two kings attacked on 21 March but were defeated and killed. According to the saga the sons of Ragnar captured Aelle alive and carved the 'blood-eagle' on him, a form of sacrifice to Odin. York became Scandinavian for the following two centuries.

EGBERT I (867–72) The king appointed as their vassal in Northumbria by the 'Great Army' in March 867, following the deaths of Aelle and Osbert in battle at York. It is unlikely that the Scandinavian settlement of Deira began now, the formal start being dated at 875; Egbert may thus have exercised authority in York as well as in unconquered Bernicia. His two rival predecessors having been killed and their armies destroyed, he had no known challengers. After the conquest of East Anglia in 869–70, part of the Viking army returned to settle Deira. Egbert now seems to have exercised authority over the English in Northumbria (probably living in Bernicia) while one of the sons of Ragnar in command of the 'Great Army', Ivarr the Boneless, ruled from York, now the military and trading base of 'Yorvik'. In or around 871, Ivarr moved on to attack fellow Danes in Dublin which may have emboldened the restive English. In

872 Egbert was driven out by his fellow countrymen in favour of Ricsige, and fled to Mercia where he died the following year.

RICSIGE (Bernicia, 872–6) A Northumbrian nobleman who led the successful revolt against the Scandinavian nominee Egbert in 872, aided by the absence of much of the 'Great Army' from York in the Midlands. He succeeded in taking over Bernicia, but does not appear to have regained York; in 875, the invaders returned and started to parcel out the land in Deira for settlement. The Bernicians would have been no match for the Scandinavians under the experienced Halfdan Ragnarson, and probably relied on distance to protect them from much interference from the invaders, whose primary concerns were Deiran settlement and inter-Viking politics involving claims to Dublin. Ricsige disappears from history after 876, being succeeded by Egbert II, but it is not known if the invaders killed him or he died naturally.

EGBERT II (Bernicia, 876 – c. 888) The successor of Ricsige in Bernicia from 876; it is not known if he had any connection to his eponymous predecessor-but-one. The Scandinavians in York, led by Halfdan Ragnarrson, had formally parceled out land in 875 so any authority which Egbert exercised within Deira was limited. Halfdan departed to Dublin on his second invasion attempt in 877 and subsequently died there, which must have reduced the military threat to Bernicia. Anglo-Scandinavian conflict now centered on southern England, and the sporadic clashes between Scandinavians (mainly based in Dublin) and the new Scots kingdom would have kept Bernicia's potential challenger for control of Lothian preoccupied. Egbert died or was expelled around 886–8, and was replaced by Eadwulf, who was to found a long-lived dynasty of warlords in Bernicia.

EADWULF (EARDWULF) (Bernicia, c. 888–913) The nobleman who replaced Egbert II as ruler of Bernicia in around 886–8 and thus ruled the surviving Anglian portion of Northumbria while the Scandinavian settlers held York. Possibly the hereditary lord of the rock-fortress at Bamburgh, which became his dynasty's centre of power, Eadwulf was clearly a strong ruler as he retained authority for around twenty-five years. He was usually known by the term of 'ealdorman' rather than king, unlike predecessors Ricsige and Egbert II, except in Irish records which may not have known the distinctions of Anglian terminology. Possibly his use of a lesser title reflected a lack of royal blood, or the West Saxon records wished to play down his status as subordinate to their own rulers. But he formed some sort of alliance with Alfred of Wessex, the successful defender of southern England and probably informal overlord of English Mercia, and seems to have accepted his ally as the senior ruler (and possibly as his overlord). Eadwulf died in 913, and was succeeded by his sons Uhtred and Ealdred, who faced a York attack on their domains in 914; following their eviction of the occupiers, the dynasty held Bernicia well into the eleventh century.

VIKING YORK (YORVIK)

HALFDAN RAGNARSSON (871/3 – 7) The most prominent of the three sons of Ragnar Lothbrok ('Leather Breeches'), a famous figure of Viking saga who was a leading raider in the 840s and 850s. Most of the stories told of him are stock ones, including his being thrown into a pit of snakes when captured by King Aelle of Northumbria in *c.* 862. This supposedly brought about the revenge mustering of the Scandinavian 'Great Army' by his sons Halfdan, Ivarr the Boneless and Ubbe/Hubba to invade England in 865. The size of the invasion was unprecedented, though it grew with legend; the Ragnarssons set up their initial base in small East Anglia, extorting horses and supplies from King Edmund, and then methodically reduced Northumbria in 866–7 (see article on Aelle), invaded Mercia in 867–8 (see Burghred and Aethelred I) and overran East Anglia late in 869 (see Saint Edmund). After this, they sailed up the Thames to seize Reading and attempted to conquer Wessex in the 'battle-winter' of 870–1, but met with several serious defeats such as Ashdown (see Aethelred I and Alfred). The peace with Wessex in summer 871 left the latter intact through tributary, and Halfdan and Ivarr led their army back to Northumbria whence Ivarr departed to conquer Dublin (where the brothers had been active fighting for King Olaf the White in the 850s).

Halfdan ruled the Danes based in Yorkshire, having to deal with his rebellious local puppet king, Egbert, in 872 on returning from aiding his brother in Ireland and in 874 marching his army to Mercia to seize Repton, depose Burghred, and impose a client king called Ceolwulf II (q.v.) who ceded the eastern half of Mercia for settlement. His main interests were in the north, where he arranged the formal Danish settlement of Deira in 875. Ivarr, titular co-ruler of York though now in Dublin as king, died in 873; later in 875 Halfdan proceeded to Dublin to expel Olaf's son Eystein and secure the kingdom. His precarious double kingship of York and Dublin, a precedent for later Viking warlords, was secured by control of the land-route across central Scotland from Clyde to Forth and intimidation of the Scots kings as he traversed their lands. But he was soon deposed from Dublin while absent in York, and in 877 he launched an unsuccessful invasion to be killed in battle on Strangford Lough. Ubbe, the last of the brothers, was now ruling a pirate lordship in south Wales; in spring 878, he died in battle invading Devon to aid Guthrum against King Alfred and the brothers' mythical 'raven banner' was captured.

9

899 to 959

WESSEX AND ENGLAND

EDWARD (EADWARD) 'THE ELDER' (Wessex, 899–924; England, 918/20 – 24) The elder son and second child of Alfred and Ealhswith. Born around 871, he was experienced enough to be put in charge of part of the army during the Scandinavian invasions from 892. The invaders repeated their usual tactic of seizing a fortified strongpoint with access to the sea as a base for ravaging the countryside and sitting out a blockade, but with new refinements. They chose to attack Kent on two sides, with one army based at Milton near Sheppey (north), linked via their shipping to their kinsmen in East Anglia, and the other based at Appledore (south). In 893, the Viking army at Appledore broke out suddenly and raided westwards across the Weald in search of supplies and loot. Their intention was to take their booty back to the Thames and cross into Essex to settle at their evacuated northern army's new base at Benfleet, but Edward intercepted them at Farnham in eastern Hampshire and inflicted a heavy defeat (traditionally on the hill north of the town). The survivors escaped with their badly wounded king, but were caught up with on the River Colne and blockaded on an islet there. They held out until the West Saxons' term of military service had expired and Alfred, bringing reinforcements to the siege, had to leave to deal with a diversionary raid on Exeter. The war continued with 'hit-and-run' ravaging and occasional sieges until 896, when the raiders gave up hostilities; Edward was presumably acting as his father's deputy.

At Alfred's death on 26 October 899, Edward, in his late twenties, was an experienced commander used to the army, and seems to have been his father's choice to succeed him. This passed over his cousin Aethelwold, elder son of his father's brother Aethelred, who was a little older and probably lacked his experience; the aggrieved atheling seized Wimborne Minster (probably his own manor) and Twynham (Christchurch) in revolt. Edward moved swiftly and advanced to Badbury Rings to cut him off from the hinterland. Besieged in Wimborne, Aethelwold boasted that he would die rather than surrender, but fled by night to the Scandinavians in Northumbria, apparently with a nun who the king had forbidden him to marry (which dispute may have sparked off the confrontation). Aethelwold was accepted by the Scandinavians in York as their king, though his position was soon disputed, and in 902 he moved south to win the adherence of the settlers in East Anglia. In 903 Aethelwold launched a major raid across the Thames at Cricklade, probably as a probe to gain loot and assess his support; he shied away from battle and retreated into East Anglia before Edward could catch him. Edward eventually called off the chase in the Fens, probably because of extended communications in enemy territory and because his men's term of service was expiring, but during the West Saxon return march the contingents became separated and the disobedient Kentish troops were caught alone and attacked. A battle followed with many senior casualties on both sides, and though the Scandinavians held the battlefield, Aethelwold and the East Anglian Danish king Eorhic/Eric were killed. This ended the challenge to Edward's throne.

Some years of peace followed, apart from opportunistic raids away from the West Saxon heartland. In 906, Edward confirmed peace with the Scandinavians of East Anglia and Northumbria. In 910 a large army of raiders from the Danelaw invaded Mercia, and Edward sent an army to assist the defence; the raiders retired from the Severn valley and were caught and heavily defeated at Tettenhall (Staffordshire). Ealdorman Aethelred died, probably early in 911, and Edward succeeded to the crucial border fortified towns of London and Oxford; close cooperation with his sister Aethelfleda, now sole ruler of Mercia, followed and it appears that they coordinated building new fortified 'burhs' to defend old (and soon new) territory. In spring 913, while Aethelfleda was creating new strongholds in the west and central Midlands, the West Saxon advance began with Edward building his first new 'burh' beyond the earlier English/Danish border of Watling Street, at Hertford. This protected the area north of London and threatened the Danish settlers in Essex. Next summer he invaded Essex to build a fortification at Witham, and the locals submitted. A major raid by the Danes in Northampton and Leicester on Bedfordshire was driven off, and in 914 Edward had to deal with the arrival of a large raiding-force from Brittany (led by Ohtar and Hroald) in the Bristol Channel. The small south-east Welsh kingdoms were plundered, but when the invaders moved into Archenfield (English south-western Herefordshire) they were defeated and Hroald was killed; the survivors had to promise to leave Edward's lands, and his fortified positions along the southern side of the Channel kept their resulting raids to a minimum. Attacks on Watchet and Porlock were driven off and Edward ransomed captured Welsh clergy, building up a good reputation with their kingdoms. Having secured the west, Edward then proceeded to Buckingham to build strongholds both sides of the river there, and with his army threatening the East Midlands Jarl Thurcytel and the men of Bedford and Northampton submitted. In 915, he built a new stronghold at Bedford to control this annexed area, and in 916 returned to Essex to fortify Witham. Thurcytel and some of his men left for Francia with the king's agreement. All this time Mercia was also building new 'burhs' as far north as Cheshire, evidently in coordination with Edward.

In 917, the process of annexation moved onto a new phase, preceded and possibly instigated by a retaliatory Scandinavian attack from Northampton and Leicester in breach of treaty. The raiding army attacked Edward's recently-built 'burh' at Towcester but were held back by the townsmen until help arrived. Another raid around Aylesbury followed, and the East Anglian and Huntingdon Danes moved west to build their own fortification at Tempsford (on the upper Ouse) and raided Bedfordshire. An East Anglian attack on the English stronghold at 'Wigingamere' also failed, and the English stormed the enemy stronghold at Tempsford and killed the local Danish king and several jarls. Next the Danes invaded Essex to besiege Maldon after the harvest but were driven back, and Edward launched an autumn campaign which protected the building of a new 'burh' at Towcester and led to the submission of Jarl Thurferth, Northampton and all the Danes south of the Welland. The takeover and refortification of Huntingdon and Colchester followed, and the settlers and the raiding army in East Anglia and Essex submitted. The settlers and their army in Cambridge then chose Edward as their lord, and he secured full control of East Anglia.

In late May/early June 918 Edward marched to Stamford and built a new stronghold, upon which the local Danes submitted. Leicester meanwhile submitted to Aethelfleda. The two armies were moving north in concert, but the campaign was halted as Aethelfleda died just before midsummer, leaving only a daughter, Egwynn. Edward marched immediately to Tamworth to secure control of Mercia. He was already undertaking military leadership within Mercia and had probably secured control of their armies with his sister's agreement (no Mercian commanders in the recent campaigns being recorded). His niece could not lead armies and there is no evidence of any threat to his domination of Mercia, but he preferred to annex it outright and deny Egwynn the right to succeed; there was no known resistance except a Chester mutiny in 924. It is possible that he had promised the Mercian leadership that his eldest son Athelstan, brought up at Aethelfleda's court, would succeed him as their king. In effect, his coup was the first stage in the creation of the kingdom of England, coinciding with the takeover of the Danelaw; he may have intended to divide the kingdom again among his sons rather than a permanent creation of one kingdom.

As full ruler of Mercia as well as Wessex, Edward now completed his military/political takeover of the Danelaw. The division of the land among the separate authorities of the Danes settled in different areas, principally the 'Five Boroughs' and recent Danish losses in the unsuccessful raids on English territory would have aided his advance. The Mercians' western neighbours, kings Idwal of Gwynedd/Powys and Hywel and Clydog of Dyfed, sought his alliance and according to the *Chronicle* recognised him as overlord. Later in 918 he marched to Nottingham, improved an earlier fortification, and received the submission of the locals, which gave him control to the Humber; in 919 he moved on to Cheshire to secure the line of the Mersey with a new 'burh' at Thelwall. Manchester was then rebuilt. He moved back to Nottingham in summer 920, and then fortified Bakewell to control the Peak District. He had now methodically secured control of all of England south of the Mersey-Humber line and his joint Wessex/Mercia/Danish army had military supremacy over the north; the rulers of the region duly recognised his power. Later that year, Ragnall of York (grandson of Ivarr the Boneless) and the kings of the Scots (Constantine) and Strathclyde (Donald) submitted to Edward; the mutual antagonism of Ragnall and Constantine and Ragnall's other concerns as overlord of Dublin probably aided the peaceful resolution of the northern confrontations. With the Anglian line of Bernicia also accepting Edward as their lord he was effectively, if nominally, the first king of all England.

The dominant position of the kingdom over its newly annexed territories in the Danelaw and East Anglia and its northern vassals was a result of Edward's military and administrative success, and was a personal triumph. The loyalty of Danes in paticular was not irreversible, and a Danish military challenge from York was to break up the new kingdom temporarily in 940–1. York had only nominally submitted to Edward and Ragnall died in 921 with his successor Sihtric not recognising Edward as his lord. But Edward remained unchallenged until his death on 17 July 924, at Farndon-on-Dee in north-western Mercia (a location which shows that he was still spending much of his time in his new lands to secure personal loyalty). He was probably around fifty-three. He left an unprecedently large family by three wives (or one mistress, Egwynn, and two wives, Elfleda and Edgiva) – one surviving son by his first 'wife', two by his second, and two by his third, plus at least ten daughters. One daughter had married Charles of Francia in *c.* 919. His intentions for the succession are unclear, except that his choice for Wessex was his elder son by his second (first legitimate) wife, Aelfweard, who died only a fortnight later; Athelstan derived his subsequent support from Mercia and may have been intended as its king in a division of kingdoms. The unity of England from 924 may thus not have been Edward's intention; but he created the kingdom of England as a unit and welded the disparate elements into one state. His military successes were less spectacular than his father's, and based on a solid military and adminstrative footing created by Alfred; his own steady advance north was cautious and based on piecemeal annexation of territory and its incorporation into his father's military ('burh') and administrative system. It would have been impossible without coordination with Mercia, in which his sister was his partner. But he was clearly a highly competent and inspiring leader who was able to use his father's creation in the new Wessex to take over control of all England when the military situation allowed it.

ELFLEDA (Queen/'Lady' of Wessex, 900s) Queen of Edward 'the Elder'; daughter of Ealdorman Aethelhelm. It is unclear if Edward had married before, as illegitimacy marred the career of Athelstan (born c. 894), his son by his previous 'wife' Egwina. Nor is it certain if Edward married Elfleda before he acceded in October 899, though it has been suggested that a new 'ordo' of coronation was written for Edward so its reference to crowning a queen means that he had married Elfleda. They had at least two sons – Aelfweard, who succeeded briefly to Wessex and died within a month of his father in 924, and Edwin, who was drowned in suspicious circumstances in 933. Their numerous daughters included Eadgifu (married in c. 919 to Charles the Simple, king of the Franks, and later to Count Herbert of Vermandois); Edhilda (married to Charles' rival, Count Hugh of Paris); Edith/Eadgifu (married to Otto of Saxony, later Holy Roman Emperor); Elgiva (married to Duke Boleslaw of Bohemia); and four nuns – Eadflaed, Elfleda, Aethelfleda and Aethelhilda. Elfleda must have been pregnant for much of her marital career; she died in 920. Her husband quickly married again, producing two more sons.

EDGIVA (EADGIFU) (Queen/'Lady' of Wessex and (informally) England, 920s) Third wife of Edward the Elder, and daughter of Ealdorman Sigehelm of Kent. She was probably married to Edward in 920, when his previous wife Elgiva died; their sons Edmund and Eadred were born in 920/1 and 921/2. There were also at least two daughters, Eadburh (a nun who died in 960) and Elgiva (who married Louis, king of Arles, a minor Carolingian dynast). Edward was already around fifty by the date of marriage; Edgiva was probably much younger than him as she lived until 968. He already had two sons by his previous marriage (the elder of whom, Aelfweard, was his heir) and a third, Athelstan, by a legally dubious first marriage, plus numerous daughters, so he was not in need of heirs. The marriage to Edgiva may have been an 'insurance policy' to provide more sons, given the opposition to Athelstan (the heir to Mercia?). When Edward and then Aelfweard died in quick succession in July 924, the succession to Wessex was not resolved for a year. Athelstan had to nominate Edgiva's sons as his successors, either then or when Aelfweard's full brother Edwin (much older than them) died in 933; it is less clear if he had to promise not to marry in order to assure their succession. Her sons ruled from 939 to 955. She was still regarded as an important political figure as late as 955/6, when she was one of the partisans of (Saint) Dunstan, exiled when her grandson Edwy fell out with him. Her lands were seized, but restored on her other grandson Edgar's accession in 959.

ATHELSTAN (924/5 – 39) The second effective 'King of England', eldest son and ultimately successor of Edward the Elder. He was probably born in 894 or 895, the elder of two sons of Edward and his first wife Egwina; later legend was to make her a shepherdess, though contemporaries called her of noble birth. There was some doubt over the legitimacy of the marriage; Edward's parents may have opposed it, and Edward married her in secret. On or before Edward's accession in October 899, he seems to have made a more prestigious marriage whose offspring were regarded as his heirs. Athelstan was sent to be brought up at the court of his aunt Aethelfleda, 'Lady of the Mercians', probably as his father's intended heir to that kingdom (Aethelfleda had only a daughter) as much as to avoid tension with his stepmother Elfleda and the supporters of their sons, Elfweard and Edwin. The idea may have been Alfred's. A story claimed that Alfred had given the infant Athelstan a purple robe and sword to wear some time in the late 890s, thus designating him for political rule. It is possible that his equivocal origins, surprise succession and massive achievements made him a subject of legend in subsequent centuries, and literary argument has raged over whether the twelfth-century stories come from a tenth-century heroic poem.

The complex events of 924–5 were obscured by the careful editing of the *Chronicle*, but it appears that Athelstan was not intended to rule Wessex and that even after the chosen heir, Elfweard, died a strong 'rearguard' action was mounted by partisans of his full brother Edwin and the infant sons of Edward's third marriage. Edward had extinguished Mercian independence by a swift military coup on his sister's death in 918, disinheriting her daughter and taking control of Mercia's armies which he needed for his northern campaigns, but Athelstan was probably regarded as heir in that kingdom. When Edward died on 17 July 924 in north-western Mercia, Elfweard is said to have been elected as king of Wessex by its council; the Mercian magnates elected Athelstan, presumably as per his father's wishes. His stepmother's more powerful kin may have swayed the West Saxon magnates against him. But Elfweard died a short time later at Oxford (1 August), probably en route with the late king's entourage to Winchester or to his crowning at Kingston-on-Thames, and Athelstan claimed the united throne. It is only supposition that Elfweard was murdered, logically by Athelstan's supporters to preserve the recently-imposed unity of Wessex and Mercia under their more able candidate. One later story even says that Elfweard was a hermit uninterested in the throne of Wessex who was thus put up to his claim by Athelstan's enemies.

The *Chronicle* plays down the resulting stand-off between rival groups of magnates, which meant that Athelstan was not crowned at Kingston until 4 September 925. There is no record of warfare and the need to preserve military strength and Edward's new kingdom against its Scandinavian and Scots vassals restrained both parties. But Athelstan appears to have promised that his half-brothers would succeed him, and his avoidance of marriage may have been a concession to their partisans. His elder half-brother Edwin, apparently not content to wait for the throne, died in odd circumstances while fleeing abroad in 933, according to a later version cast adrift to drown in the Channel by the king. Edwin may have been involved in an obscure plot in Winchester in 924/5, centred around a certain Alfred, to seize and blind Athelstan.

Despite his disputed succession, Athelstan preserved the unity of the new kingdom and proved as vigorous and successful a ruler as his father, both within Britain and in relations with his Continental peers. His generosity was noted, though it was politically wise to win over support in a Wessex where he had met substantial resistance in 924–5, and he seems to have followed a policy of dazzling his subjects as a worthy ruler with a collection of treasures including prestigious religious relics (many of which he gave away to the Church). His suzerainty was accepted by Sihtric 'Caoch' of York, with their alliance cemented at New Year 926 by Sihtric's marriage to Athelstan's full sister Eadgyth. But Sihtric refused to accept baptism, as required in West Saxon treaties with a pagan Scandinavian ally. The death of Sihtric months later ended that attempt to secure York, and the late ruler's brother Guthfrith arrived from Dublin to stake his claim. Athelstan marched north to defeat, capture and evict him, showing him politic hospitality, and annexed York to bring the kingdom's borders up to Bernicia and Cumbria for the first time.

The king of England could not be in the North to enforce obedience for more than limited periods, a weakness which claimants to York were to exploit for decades. Like Edward, Athelstan used his army to persuade the northern dynasts into alliance. (The English sources portray these as submission to English overlordship; the Scots are more equivocal.) Athelstan summoned King Constantine of the Scots and Owain of Strathclyde to a 'summit' at Eamont Bridge in Cumbria, where they had to pledge alliance and promise not to support Guthfrith and other Viking claimants to York; it also seems that they had to agree to suppress paganism.

Athelstan pursued a similarly aggressive policy against the Welsh princes, a particular threat due to the union of Gwynedd with Dyfed under Hywel 'Dda', which left only small Morgannwg independent. A military demonstration similar to those in the north took place between Athelstan's two marches to York, with his court and army arriving in Hereford in 926 to meet the summoned Welsh rulers (Hywel, and Owain of Gwent) who did not dare stay away. They were forced to accept his overlordship, pay heavy tribute, and agree to his demarcation of the southern Anglo-Welsh frontier at the Wye. Hywel in particular was to show signs of learning new methods of displaying and augmenting kingship from Athelstan's example. A Cornish revolt was then defeated. The peace established by decisive action in 925–7 held for another seven years, with the kingdom's prestige augmented by marital alliances and gift-giving with the nearer kings on the Continent. Early in his reign Athelstan married his half-sister Eadgyth to Otto, duke of Saxony and later

(962) Holy Roman Emperor. Two other sisters had been married by his father to the rivals Charles the Simple and Duke Hugh the Great in Francia and in 936 the exiled son of the former, Athelstan's nephew Louis 'd'Outremer', was to return to the French throne with English help. Athelstan also fostered a son of his gift-exchanging ally Harald 'Finehair', first king of Norway, and appears to have taught him the arts of kingship; Haakon was able to return to his homeland to evict his brother in the mid-930s. Another fostered exile who returned home to rule with Athelstan's aid was Count Alain of Poher in Brittany, in 936; in practical terms, a stable Brittany would evict raiding Scandinavians' settlements there.

Relations with Scotland had become fraught enough for Athelstan to undertake the first West Saxon invasion of Scotland in 934, both by land and sea. The catalyst seems to have been the Scots king's marrying his daughter to Olaf Guthfrithson, king of Dublin and claimant to York; the English invasion was probably intended to head off a move on York. The logistics involved and the distance which Athelstan had to travel testify to Athelstan's confidence, and agreement about borders and non-interference in York was reached. But Constantine was roused to seek allies for a retaliatory attack, and created a coalition of Celtic and Scandinavian warlords including Olaf and probably the rulers of Man, the Hebrides (Gebeachan), and Strathclyde. Little is known about the campaign except for Athelstan's crushing defeat of the invaders at 'Brunanburh', a victory lauded with a heroic poem in the *Chronicle*. Many of the invading leadership were killed, though Constantine escaped; the site has vanished from history but topographical clues have led to attempts to place it, most convincingly in the Wirral or at Brinkley Wood in South Yorkshire (indicating a seaborne landing in Lancashire in one case, in the Humber estuary in the other). The victory secured the security of the English kingdom, but only for Athelstan's lifetime.

Events showed that Danish notables within York (and the local Church) were ready to exploit any weakness in Wessex, and on 27 October 939 Athelstan died unexpectedly at Gloucester. He was probably around forty-five, still unmarried, and left an adult and capable heir in the elder son of Edward's last marriage, Edmund (his fellow-commander at Brunanburh). The news caused a revolt in York in favour of the exiled family of Sihtric and Guthfrith, which spread to the Danelaw before Edmund could halt it militarily; possibly the onset of winter delayed a West Saxon response. To this extent Athelstan's achievement was ephemeral, and his kingdom was only permanently reunited in 954. But the more successful kings were to follow the joint examples of Edward and Athelstan, not least towards the Scots, for centuries to come and it is clear that he was one of the most outstanding leaders of his gifted dynasty.

EDMUND (I) 'THE MAGNIFICENT' (939–46) The elder of the two sons of King Edward by his third wife Edgiva, daughter of Ealdorman Sigehelm of Kent, born in 920/2 and named after the martyred king of East Anglia. He and his bother Eadred were too young to be contenders on their father's death in 924, but the resistance to the new king, Athelstan, their eldest half-brother, led to some sort of dynastic compromise, making them his heirs. Athelstan possibly agreed not to marry so as not to jeopardise their claim; at the latest the mysterious death of their half-brother Edwin in 933 made Edmund heir. Athelstan entrusted him with a joint command in the crisis of the major Scots-Scandinavian invasion of 937, probably indicating that he had already shown signs of military ability as well as absolute loyalty. As such he fought with distinction at the English victory of Brunanburh, probably in Lancashire or south Yorkshire, and was honoured with his brother in the celebratory battle-ode in the *Chronicle*. Athelstan died in his forties in October 939, and Edmund succeeded aged eighteen. The Scandinavians of York, reluctantly incorporated into Athelstan's realm in 927 and with exiled claimants at large in Dublin, took advantage to invite back Olaf Guthfrithson, king of Dublin. Invading with a force of warriors later that autumn, Olaf took over York; Archbishop Wulfstan preferred to back this pagan invader to a Christian West Saxon and even became his chief adviser, indicating the strength of local particularism against the claims of the distant English kings.

The onset of winter aided Olaf's success and Edmund's caution in marching north, and in 940 he marched on south into the Danish-settled Five Boroughs. He had enough support, or his army's ravaging intimidated enough of the local leadership, for him to sack Tamworth; Edmund then arrived with his army and besieged the invaders in Leicester. Olaf and Wulfstan escaped a dangerous blockade by night, and Edmund was unable to bring them to battle. A stand-off ended with an agreement whereby Olaf accepted baptism as Edmund's godson (the usual terms for a West Saxon treaty with a Scandinavian warlord) but allowed him to retain York and the Five Boroughs. The imbalance of the terms in Olaf's favour suggest that Edmund feared widespread Danish desertion to the invaders; Olaf was a more experienced commander with hardened Dublin Vikings in his army, but Edmund may have underestimated the mutual antipathy of eastern England's Danes and the invading Dubliners. His ignominious caution surrendered all that his father and brother had won since 915, but luckily Olaf was killed raiding Bernicia within eighteen months.

The latter's cousin, Olaf Sihtricson, then returned from Dublin to seize York, but he was less effective a ruler and in spring 942 Edmund invaded and recovered the Five Boroughs. Edmund now had the confidence to march into Northumbria, and Olaf submitted and accepted baptism as an English ally (943); Wulfstan probably negotiated the compromise. Edmund had the caution to rule York via a Scandinavian vassal rather than attempt to do do directly as Athelstan had done, but it remained chronically unstable; Olaf's cousin Ragnall Guthfrithson deposed him within months, backed by

Wulfstan as Olaf had returned to paganism. Ragnall also reached terms with Edmund and accepted baptism from him, sponsored by Wulfstan and at risk of invasion by Olaf who was at large in Strathclyde. The balance of power had shifted in Edmund's favour, and in 944 he was able to take York and kill Ragnall; York was annexed and the full kingdom of Athelstan in 927–39 was restored. In 945 Edmund invaded Cumbria, currently under the control of Strathclyde (ruled by junior princes of the Scots kingdom) and its king, Donald (Domnhall). Donald was defeated, probably at the pass of 'Dunmail's Rise' between Grasmere and Thirlmere, and had to come to terms and hand over Cumbria; Olaf, his ally, fled to Dublin to take over its kingship.

Edmund had now restored the unity of his brother's full realm after five or six years and extended it to the Solway Firth, or possibly the later Cumberland–Westmorland county boundary if Strathclyde retained part of Cumbria. His ability as a king outside the field of warfare is less easy to assess, and he seems to have been hot-headed and not as close to the Church as Athelstan. The hagiography of Saint Dunstan, who Edmund made abbot of Glastonbury in *c.* 943, has the king only recognising the saint's abilities belatedly and granting him the abbey out of gratitude for divine preservation when his horse bolted in the Cheddar Gorge and nearly threw him off a cliff. Edmund's nickname of 'the Magnificent' would suggest a fondness for display and the physical demonstration of kingship, and it is possible that he would have been as renowned a ruler as Athelstan had he lived longer. But on 28 May 946, he was stabbed in a brawl at his hall at Pucklechurch near Bath, apparently by accident when he recognised a thief he had earlier exiled illegally attending the feast; the man resisted arrest, and Edmund came to the aid of his servants. He was probably twenty-four or -five. His two sons, Edwy and Edgar, were under-age so his surviving brother Eadred succeeded him.

EADRED (EDRED) (946–55) The younger son of Edward the Elder and Edgiva; probably born in late 921 or 922, possibly 923. Eadred succeeded his full brother Edmund on his murder on 26 May 946, the latter's sons being infants. It is recorded that he suffered from a chronic stomach condition and was only able to swallow food with difficulty, though it is unclear if this was a lifelong problem or only developed during his reign. This did not affect his ability as a vigorous warrior who preserved his half-brother Athelstan's new kingdom of England. At his accession York had recently surrendered after rebelling at Edmund's accession in 939, and Eadred quickly marched north to secure the submission of Archbishop Wulfstan and the other magnates. Despite their promises, in 947 they revolted for the Norwegian ex-king, Erik 'Bloodaxe'. Eadred invaded Deira; eventually the leading men surrendered and Erik fled, but their allegiance remained insecure whenever there was no army there to enforce it. In 948 Wulfstan and his faction invited back the former ruler of York, Olaf Sihtricson; Eadred marched north but agreed to recognise Olaf as ruler provided that he kept out Erik. Erik returned to York as Wulfstan's nominee in 952. Eadred's invasion in 954 was successful, Wulfstan was captured, York submitted and Erik was ambushed and killed on Stainmore during his journey back to his Hebridean lordship. This time the kingdom of England was permanently reunited, but Eadred was unable to enjoy his status long.

He died at Frome, Somerset, on 23 November 955, aged probably thirty-three or thirty-four, and was succeeded by his brother's elder son Edwy.

EDWY (EADWIG) (955–9 (not Mercia or Northumbria from 957)) Born in 940/1, he was the elder of two sons of King Edmund and his first wife, Elfleda. He was too young to be chosen king on his father's death in a brawl in May 946, when his adult uncle Eadred succeeded, but took the throne when the latter died on 23 November 955. According to the *Chronicle*, he was supposed to succeeed only to Wessex and his younger brother Edgar was designated for Mercia and Northumbria, but the latter was judged too young to rule so Edwy was given the entire kingdom until Edgar's majority. He was only fourteen and little is known of his reign; despite his youth his accession saw no renewed challenge to the kingdom's unity (York had only been recovered the year before). He was lucky in that the worst threat that could aid the York Danes, their ex-king, Erik Bloodaxe, had been killed and the usual claimants in Dublin were preoccupied.

Unfortunately our main source for the reign is the biography of Saint Dunstan, who fell out with Edwy and was exiled. Their quarrel supposedly commenced at the coronation banquet, when Edwy left the feast early and Dunstan found him in compromising circumstances in a side-chamber with his fiancée Aelfgifu and her mother. Sulky at being forced to return to his duties, the spiteful teenage king let his wife talk him into exiling Dunstan and his partisans. In reality there may well have been political struggles at court and Aelfgifu, who had powerful kin but was vulnerable to Church attempts to nullify her marriage as she was related to her husband, had every reason to fear the sternly moralist abbot. She won out and those deprived of their lands included Edwy's grandmother Eadgifu, a rival influence at court; the struggle may have been linked to the resignation in 956 of the most powerful man in Mercia and East Anglia, Ealdorman Athelstan 'Half-King', a patron of Dunstan's Glastonbury. A year later, in 957, the leading men of Mercia and Northumbria revolted against Edwy's authority and raised Edgar to be their king. He was still only fourteen and this early and forced implementation of the suspended succession plan of 955 seems to have been carried out against Edwy's wishes, probably arising from resentment at the dominance at court of a hostile faction. Dunstan now joined Edgar. Edwy, reduced to rule of Wessex, had his marriage annulled in 958 and took a second wife, probably in a search for extra aristocratic support and/or an attempt to make amends with the

Church. His early death on 1 October 959, aged probably eighteen, prevented any clash with Edgar, who now succeeded to all England. The triumph of his enemy Dunstan and brother Edgar, neither of whom had reason to honour his memory, resulted in a record hostile to him and his reign. His nickname according to his distant cousin Aethelweard, the 'All-Fair', seems to refer to an easy-going character, and this may have made him more vulnerable than a stronger ruler to ambitious court flatterers and unable to control faction. But if he had survived to maturity, these problems could have decreased and Edwy been as adequate a king as his father, uncle and brother.

MERCIA

AETHELFLEDA (886–918) Eldest daughter of Alfred the Great and Ealhswith; born in 869/70. She was married to her father's ally, Ealdorman Aethelred, the new ruler of western Mercia, in 886 as the personal symbol of cooperation between the two kingdoms, with Alfred handing the recently-recovered town of London over to Aethelred on or soon after the marriage. (By maternal descent she was half-Mercian.) A worthy daughter of Alfred and sister of Edward the Elder, she proved the equal of her husband as a ruler and assisted him in rebuilding Mercia after its loss of half its territory. The 'Lady of the Mercians' ('*Myrcna hloefdige*') became a venerated figure in the region's history, and founded a new minster of Saint Peter at her principal residence, Gloucester, to which the relics of the Christian hero-king Saint Oswald were brought in 909, after being acquired in the East Midlands. After Aethelred's death in 911, she took over as sole ruler at a time of renewed conflict with the Danelaw. There had been a major raid on the Severn valley from the Danelaw in 910 which the West Saxon army had helped to defeat at Tettenhall (Staffs); now Aethelfleda and Edward coordinated a systematic advance from the Watling Street frontier to annex the East Midlands piecemeal.

The divided nature of Danish settlement, with the settlers in each area (mostly the nuclei of later English counties) grouped around the local fortified town in separate 'armies', aided the Anglo-Saxon advance. The English probably had the edge in numbers over their enemies, who lacked recorded good commanders (many competent warriors seem to have fallen in the battles of 903 and 910), and opportunity was taken to incorporate the Danish settlers in the English kingdoms. The use of defensive fortified 'burhs' as the basis of Anglo-Saxon warfare – to concentrate men and supplies, deny food and strongpoints to Danish ravagers, and serve as the basis for administration, military recruitment/garrisons, and trade – was now turned into a means of offense. It is uncertain whether Edward or Aethelfleda designed the overall strategy, but both would have seen their father implement the defensive version of it in Wessex. Now the two leaders worked together to strengthen the defences of western Mercia from future raids, and then to overrun the East Midlands.

Aethelfleda concentrated in the north while Edward worked on the south; in 912 she built new 'burhs' at 'Scergeat' and Bridgnorth and in 913 she advanced to Tamworth and Stafford. In 914, a major Scandinavian attack on Herefordshire from south Wales was driven back by the militia backed by Edward, who now took on coordinating defence on both sides of the Bristol Channel. Aethelfleda built 'burhs' at Eddisbury and Warwick, and in 915 at Chirbury, 'Weardbyrig' (thought to be in Cheshire), and Runcorn in an evident move north to ward off attack from York and the threat of Norse settlers in Lancashire. In 916, she led her army in person into the Welsh kingdom of Brycheiniog (Brecon) to break down a fortification on Llangorse Lake and took prisoners, including the king's wife.

Edward took the lead in fortifying Tamworth and 'Wigingamere' in the central Midlands and driving back a counter-attack in 917, being gradually introduced to command within his sister's kingdom in a creeping merger of their armies – a sensible move with no male heir to succeed Aethelfleda. But in 918 she was in command in person again in the advance to Derby, a crucial stronghold controlling the route into the north-eastern Midlands and the lower Trent valley. The town was stormed with Anglian losses including several senior thegns, and became a key part of the northern frontier. Edward was now completing his control of the south-east Midlands, and from an Irish Annals account it is possible that Aethelfleda led her army as far as Corbridge to secure victory over Ragnall, ruler of York, in spring 918. If so, the English military domination of York from 919/20 was commenced by her, not her brother, and was played down by the Wesssx-based *Chronicle*. Edward's final campaign to secure the land up to the Trent was underway when Aethelfleda died at Tamworth on 14 June 918. She was probably forty-eight or forty-nine. The commanders of Mercia were already used to Edward's leadership, and his eldest son Athelstan had been brought up at Aethelfleda's court which suggests that he was intended as a future ruler of Mercia. But it is uncertain if Aethelfleda was aware of her brother's intention to merge the kingdoms immediately, disinheriting her daughter Egwynn; as soon as he heard that Aethelfleda was dead Edward marched to Tamworth to seize full control and assumed the government. Egwynn was placed under West Saxon control, and in December 918 was deprived of her lands and deported. There may have been an anti-Wessex revolt at Chester (principal military base of the north-west) in 924. Aethelfleda was thus the last ruler of Mercia. Overshadowed by her brother and portrayed as less important than Edward by the *Chronicle*, she was nevertheless the only recorded Anglo-Saxon female sovereign to lead troops and was a highly competent and well-loved ruler with many of her father's qualities. The 'Lady of the Mercians' was the only long-lasting and successful female English ruler before 1558. Reflecting a long tradition of veneration, Henry of Huntingdon wrote in *c*. 1120 that she was regarded as equal to a king.

ELFWYNN The daughter of Ealdorman Aethelred and Alfred's daughter Aethelfleda, rulers of Mercia; probably born in the late 880s or early 890s. Her being female was crucial to the future of English unity, as it gave her uncle, Edward, excuse for annexing Mercia when her mother died in June 918. Denied the governance of Mercia in 918, despite being (probably) fully adult and placed under West Saxon supervision, Elfwynn was deprived of her lands and deported to Wessex in December. If Edward intended to restore Mercian independence, the chosen candidate was his son, her cousin Athelstan; a marriage between them would have been logical if the Church allowed it. Her date of death is not recorded.

VIKINGS – EAST ANGLIA

GUTHRUM (879–90) Guthrum was one of the leaders of the Scandinavian army occupying Repton in 874, who (with Anund and Oscytel) then marched part of it to Cambridge. In 874–5 they settled East Anglia. Later in 875 Guthrum invaded Wessex, probably by land, and established a base at Wareham with easy sea-access; intending to ravage untouched Dorset, he was blockaded by Alfred and forced to promise to leave Wessex. He broke out by surprise and headed west to occupy Exeter and terrorise Devon instead, but his fleet was destroyed by storms off Swanage and he was starved out at Exeter in 877. He and his captains had to swear peace on their sacred arm-rings and were allowed to leave, but after moving to western Mercia he treacherously attacked Alfred at Twelfth Night 878 at Chippenham. The king narrowly escaped, but was a fugitive in the Somerset marshes for several months while most of Wessex submitted to Guthrum, who may have set up a puppet king. A Danish seaborne attack on north Devon by Ubbe/Hubba Ragnarsson was defeated, and after Easter Alfred rallied his people and raised an army which won the vital battle of Ethandun (thought to be Bratton Down, Edington). Starved out in Chippenham, Guthrum had to accept baptism as Alfred's godson (Aller, May 878) and agree to leave Wessex permanently in the treaty of Wedmore. This time he kept his word, moving back to Cirencester, and on to London in summer 879, and then to East Anglia where he set himself up as king. Under his baptismal name, 'Athelstan', he kept peace with Alfred, except possibly in 884–5 when there was a naval clash, and issued coins as a Christian king. He died in 890; his successor Eric was killed fighting for Alfred's nephew Aethelwold, pretender to Wessex, in 903.

YORK

AETHELWOLD (899/900 – 903) The elder of probably two sons of Aethelred of Wessex and his Mercian wife Wulfrida. Born around 869/70, he was an infant when his father died during the first Scandinavian invasion of Wessex (23 April 871) and he was passed over for the throne in favour of his adult uncle Alfred. His role during his uncle's reign is unrecorded; if he did have military experience during Alfred's wars, this was not regarded as significant. On Alfred's death in October 899, he was passed over again by the royal councillors in favour of the king's son, his cousin Edward, who was younger but was already an experienced battle leader. He seized the royal manors of Wimborne (Minster) and Twynham (Christchurch) in revolt, centring his attempt on eastern Dorset. The army rallied to Edward, and the rebel was quickly besieged in Wimborne. Bragging that he would stand and die there if necessary, he was forced to flee by night; Wimborne may well have been his inheritance. He appears to have taken his choice of wife, who had been made a nun, with him into exile or recovered her later.

Aethelwold made his way to Northumbria, and was accepted by the Danes of York and later by the Angles of Bernicia as their new ruler. The Danes were apparently leaderless; their acceptance of a West Saxon prince with no local connections was unusual but may have been due to his promises of a share in or loot from his cousin's lands. He may already have been known to some ex-warriors from the armies that had fought Alfred in the 890s as a capable commander. He ruled over Northumbria for three years, defeating a first incursion by an exiled Danish prince called Cnut but later having to accept the latter as co-ruler; his rival was murdered a year later.

In 902/3 he was confident enough to march south into East Anglia to secure the adherence of Eowils, Danish king. The local Danes joined his army for a major raid south across the Thames into Wessex in 903, and in retaliation Edward led his army after the raiders into East Anglia. Aethelwold outpaced the West Saxon pursuit and reached the Fenland safely, but succumbed to the temptation to attack Edward as the enemy retired. The resulting battle of Holme was bloody, with major losses on both sides, but although the Danes held the field, both Aethelwold and Eowils were killed. Aethelwold's younger brother and his descendants seem to have survived as loyal subjects of their cousins within Wessex.

RAGNALL (910–21) Grandson of Ivarr the Boneless and brother of Sihtric (q.v.), he was among the Viking leaders expelled from Dublin in 902, later building up a precarious lordship in the Hebrides and Man. The leadership losses of the York Danes in battle against King Edward at Tettenhall in 910 left a hiatus which he exploited to seize the city, and his ambitions extended to Bernicia (where he temporarily evicted the Anglian Bamburgh earls in 914) and Strathcylde. He was absent assisting Sihtric in regaining Dublin in 917 and so he missed the Wessex takeover of the Danelaw; he returned to secure York from pro-English Danes advocating surrender in 919, but the following years was forced to accept Edward as overlord. He died in 921, and was succeeded by Sihtric.

SIHTRIC 'CAOCH' 'THE SQUINT-EYED' (Dublin, 917–21; York, 921–7) A grandson of Ivarr the Boneless, he was king of the 'Fair-Haired' and 'Dark-Haired Foreigners' (Norwegians and Danes) in eastern Ireland when he was driven out of Dublin with the Norse in 902. Possibly aiding his brother Ragnall in the Hebrides or else the 'Jarl Sihtric' who ruled the Danish settlers in Cambridge before King Edward's 916 conquest, he returned to Carlow, Ireland, with a fleet in 917 and retook Dublin. In 919 he killed the attacking High King Niall Glundub, but he left Ireland in 921 to succeed Ragnall as king of York. In this capacity he ended Ragnall's vassalage to Edward, but he submitted to Athelstan sooner than face invasion and met him at Tamworth on 30 January 926 to accept him as overlord, be baptised, and marry his overlord's sister Eadgyth. He soon abandoned Christianity and expelled his wife, but died in spring 927 before the expected clash with Athelstan. York fell to the latter, but Sihtric's brother Guthfrith secured Dublin.

ATHELSTAN, King of England, q.v., 927–39

OLAF GUTHFRITHSON (Dublin, 934–41; York, 939–41; Five Boroughs, 940–1) Born around 917, he was son of Guthfrith of Dublin, brother of Sihtric and Ragnall of York. The most successful Viking commander of his generation, he was commanding armies for his father in his teens, and in 933 sacked Armagh and raided Monaghan. After succeeding Guthfrith he united the Scandinavian settlements along the east coast of Ireland, destroying his rivals' fleet on Lough Ree in 937, and later that year joined his new father-in-law Constantine, king of Scots, and other Celtic rulers in a massive Danish-Celtic attack on Athelstan. This was defeated at Brunanburh in northern England (thought to be in Lancashire or south Yorkshire), but after Athelstan's death in October 939 he was able to exploit his brother Edmund's youth and anti-Wessex feeling in Danish York to invade again and take that city. He was backed by Archbishop Wulfstan despite his Viking and pagan background. His successful march into the Danelaw in spring 940 led to Edmund (outnumbered or wary of his military skill?) ceding rule of the Danish territories in eastern England to him, but his achievement was short-lived. He was killed raiding Bernicia in 941, and succeeded by his cousin Olaf Sihtricson; his under-age sons remained in Ireland.

OLAF 'CUARAN' SIHTRICSON (York, 941–3, 948–52; Dublin 945–8, 952–80) 'The Shoe/Sandal' (so-called from his Dublin footwear). Cousin of his predecessor and son of Sihtric of York (d. 927); born in 926/7 if he was Sihtric's son by Athelstan's sister, a little older if not. A refugee in Ireland after his father's death, he took over York and its Anglo-Danish dependencies when his namesake died in 941 but had to surrender the Five Boroughs to Edmund in 942 and agree to become Christian in 943. He reneged on this but was shortly expelled from York in favour of his cousin Ragnall Guthfrithson; he fled to Strathclyde and made an unsuccessful attempt to regain his kingdom. Returning to Dublin in 945, he evicted Blacair

Guthfrithson and ruled there to 948. In the winter of 947–8 he returned to York to overthrow his Norwegian rival Erik Bloodaxe (lord of the Hebrides and ex-king of Norway) and received King Eadred's backing as less dangerous to Wessex than the latter. He allied with Eadred against Erik but could not win over Archbishop Wulfstan, who preferred the Norseman; in 952 the two combined to expel him. Returning to reclaim Dublin, he survived for another twenty-eight years as king there in sporadic conflict with his Viking rivals and local Irish rulers, abdicating in 980 after a bloody battle with his principal foe High King Mael Sechnaill at Tara. Finally turning Christian, he died in 981 on Iona.

RAGNALL GUTHFRITHSON (943–5) The brother of Olaf Guthfrithson, he was chosen by Archbishop Wulfstan and the leading men of York to replace his evicted cousin Olaf 'Cuaran' in 943. Forced to agree terms with King Edmund and be baptised later in that year, he ruled as an English vassal and fought off his cousin; he was killed in battle in 945 as the more confident Edmund invaded to take over York.

ERIC 'BLOODAXE' (Norway, 933–5 (?); York, 947–8 and 952–4) The eldest son of the unifying King Harald 'Finehair' of Norway, Erik was probably born around 895. He succeeded his father in 933, but his violent nature and oppressive rule are said to have caused his swift deposition; he fled to the Norse settlements in the Hebrides and built up an extensive lordship, ruling Orkney and Man. Possibly acquiring his brother and successor's (King Haakon) patron Athelstan's agreement to rule York in *c.* 939, but was unable to act on it due to Olaf Guthfrithson's coup, he finally gained York in 947 after an anti-Wessex revolt on King Edmund's death. Backed by Archbishop Wulfstan, an unlikely alliance given Erik's paganism and bloody reputation, he held York against King Eadred for a year but was then driven out by Olaf Sihtricson with Scots aid; he returned with Wulfstan's backing in 952. After Wulfstan's capture by the invading Eadred in 954, Erik, deprived of his principal ally, was driven out and fell in battle gainst Earl Maccus during his retreat north on Stainmore. His sons Ragnfred and Gordred led his forces back to Orkney along with their warlike mother Gunnhilde, daughter of King Gorm 'the Old' of Denmark, and all three continued a career in Hebridean affairs for another two decades. His murderous daughter Ragnhild married three successive brother jarls of Orkney (killing two of them).

959 to 1016

ENGLAND

EDGAR (EADGAR) 'THE PEACEABLE' (Mercia, 957–9; England 959–75) The second son of Edmund (I) and Elgiva, probably born in 943. His father died in a brawl in May 946, and on his uncle Eadred's death in November 955 his elder brother Edwy became king of England. On his mother's death, Edgar was placed in the household of Ealdorman Athelstan of East Anglia and the eastern Danelaw, the king's principal lieutenant in eastern England and known from his wide-ranging authority as 'Half-King'. The connection proved vital in giving him local support in the crisis of 957. He may have been intended as king of Mercia by his father – in which case the reunion of England was not the long-term West Saxon royal policy in the 940s. Edwy proved unpopular with his nobles as weak, easily-guided and impetuous, at least according to subsequent memories. Local particularism against rule by Wessex may have played a part in both Mercia and Northumbria renouncing allegiance by November 957 and choosing Edgar as their king instead. Separate rulers for Wessex and Mercia may have been Edward the Elder's intention, and Edmund's too had Edgar been adult at his death. The two realms remained separate until Edwy died on 1 November 959 and Edgar succeeded to Wessex, reuniting England.

Edgar recalled the forceful (Saint) Dunstan, exiled by his brother after a contretemps at his coronation feast, to act as his bishop of Worcester and close adviser while he ruled Mercia. On succeeding to Wessex, he removed the Archbishop-elect of Canterbury and made Dunstan archbishop, giving him full power over the Church for reforms. Under Dunstan's influence Edgar made monastic reform on Continental lines a centrepiece of his policies, bringing in current Lotharingian practices. Secular canons were ejected from monasteries in favour of fully-professed monks, who also took over the staffing of the cathedral chapters of each bishopric. The pioneering cathedral was in Edgar's capital, Winchester, the bishopric of which went to Dunstan's ally (Saint) Aethelwold. New monasteries were founded and all were granted extensive lands to fund them, arousing resentment among the nobility at the diversion of lands from secular personnel. Both lands and grants of local jurisdiction built up abbots as leading conduits of royal authority, particularly in the lands most recently taken under the control of Wessex such as the Danelaw. The northern sees, with York being held with the wealthier bishopric of Worcester under Saint Oswald from 972, also served as props of royal rule and were endowed with extra lands. In political terms Churchmen were more reliable than secular magnates, with hierarchical loyalty to their superiors and their royal patron. Edgar's building up of the Church as a bond of national order was, however, to lead to a violent reaction among aggrieved lords after his death.

In secular matters Edgar's sixteen-year sole reign was notable for the absence of revolts or external challenges, reflecting on his military power and ability to secure loyalty, though also to international luck. Unlike Athelstan, his kingdom did not face a major threat from Viking attackers from Dublin, the Hebrides, or Norway or a Celtic coalition. An impressive fleet helped to ward off challenges. To bind the men of the Danelaw closer to the new order, they were permitted to retain their laws and customs rather than conforming to those of Wessex. In 973 Edgar staged a special coronation at Bath, probably chosen for its impressive Roman ruins as a sign of past glories which he wished to revive – a local equivalent to Charlemagne's coronation at Rome in 800. He had already been crowned like his ancestors at Kingston-on-Thames at his accession; he was now specifically crowned as 'King of the English' rather than just Wessex. The second coronation may have been chosen as he was now thirty and eligible to conduct priestly rites, giving an extra sacral element to his kingship. The ceremony was masterminded by Dunstan, who probably drew up a new and more sacramental coronation rubric (the 'Second Recenscion') using ninth-century Frankish practice. Edgar then proceeded to march his army to Chester, the headquarters for the Irish Sea fleet which undertook a similarly impressive demonstration of force at sea. Six (the *Chronicle*) or eight (Aelfric and John of Worcester) kings of the Celtic and Scandinavian realms of northern and western Britain attended on him at Chester, summoned en masse to recognise his authority and encouraged to obey by the demonstration of his military strength. They included the rulers of Gwynedd, Strathclyde, and Cumbria. The fact that the kings of Scots (Kenneth II) and probably Man (Maccus/Magnus) attended reflects on the reach of Edgar's power; Edgar now formally recognised the earlier occupation of Lothian, a former part of Northumbria, by the Scots rather than fight. Kenneth may have done a form of homage for it. According to later legend, the kings were required to row Edgar in a barge on the Dee as a sign of their submission to the new kingdom of England. This may be a garbled interpretation of a ceremonial voyage which the sovereigns at the 'summit' took on the river which showed off Edgar's superiority. In practical terms, the location of the visitors' lands suggests agreement to enforce peace in the Irish Sea area. Edgar maintained a large fleet, the only naval power around his coasts (in implicit contrast to what followed) according to Aelfric in c. 1000; by the twelfth century, the reputed size of this had grown to 3,600 or 4,000 ships. He probably instituted a system whereby each 300 'hides' of land in his kingdom paid for a warship.

Edgar married twice, and showed signs of the sexual recklessness which had marked his elder brother. The stories may have been exaggerated in retrospect to enhance the role of Dunstan in successfully chiding him to mend his ways. In retrospect, he was also accused by Abbot Wulfstan of favouring foreigners and importing Flemings and Scandinavians (probably mercenaries as well as traders), which caused increased drunkenness and ferocity. His first wife, Aethelfleda, died in the early to mid-960s having given him a son, Edward; either before or after this, he became entangled with Wulfthryth, who gave him a daughter, Edith (later abbess of Wilton) and then became a nun, which may be the origin of the story that Edgar abducted a nun. It is uncertain if they (briefly?) married and whether she left Edgar due to religious impulses or was banished for political reasons to make way for his next wife, the notorious Aethelthryth/Elfrida. Scandal, exaggerated in retrospect given her later actions and Church hostility, later claimed she (or the king, with her connivance) disposed of her previous husband, Ealdorman Aethelwold of East Anglia, chief stalwart of royal authority in eastern England and Edgar's former foster-brother as son of the 'Half-King'. They had two sons in the mid-late 960s, Edmund (who died young) and Aethelred.

Edgar died suddenly at an early age, probably only thirty-two, at Winchester on 8 July 975. There are no hints of earlier ill-health, but he may have shared the weak constitutions of his male ancestors which produced so many early deaths. At the most his elder surviving son Edward was around fourteen, and the resulting succession dispute, regicide, and Viking attacks that troubled England made Edgar's reign seem a golden age. The alliance of king and Church and his patronage of Dunstan aided his favourable reputation, although he was never required to prove himself in battle. The eulogies seems deserved, apart from a note of caution about his alienation of many landowners over the extent of his grants of land to the Church.

ELFRIDA (AETHELTHRYTH) (Queen of Edgar) One of the most notorious figures of Anglo-Saxon history in legend, she was the daughter of Ealdorman Ordgar of Devon (probably appointed on her marriage) and was probably born in the early to mid-940s. She was first married to Ealdorman Aethelwold, son and successor (956) of Athelstan 'Half King', governor of East Anglia and parts of the East Midlands, the senior prop of royal power in the ex-Danish lands. Her first husband died in 962, with legend accusing her of murdering him – possibly in collusion with her next husband, King Edgar, who had been brought up in her father-in-law's household and may still have been there when she married Aethelwold. Edgar's marital affairs are unclear, but he had at most one son by 964; his marriage or affair with his 'second wife' Wulfthryth only produced a daughter. Elfrida gave him two sons in the mid-late 960s, Edmund (died 971) and Aethelred; when her husband died early in July 975 she backed the rights of Aethelred, despite him being under ten. She or, more likely, Ealdorman Aelfhere of Mercia took the lead in the plan and intended to be the regent. The family of Elfrida's late husband, led by the new ealdorman of East Anglia, Aethelwine, probably also backed Aethelred. The crisis was complicated by local opposition (thought to have been mainly in the Midlands) to Edgar's wide grants of land to the Church, which was being masterminded by the late king's clerical advisers under Archbishop Dunstan, who now backed Edgar's son Edward as king. The latter won out, but widespread disturbances and plundering of Church lands followed. Edward, possibly disliked for his impetuous nature and logically resented by ambitious nobles like Aelfhere as being unamenable to their influence, was unable to halt it.

On 18 March 978 Edward was murdered while visiting Corfe (Castle [?]) in Dorset, apparently being stabbed in his saddle while seeking refreshment. Contrary to legend Corfe Castle was not Elfrida's manor, being owned by the abbess of Shaftesbury, but as early as the *Life of Saint Oswald* (*c.* 995) the murderers were being named as Elfrida's attendants. The exoneration of the queen may have been to avoid embarrassment to the reigning sovereign, her son, and if Edward had called there on impulse after hunting there was hardly a long-standing murder plot. There is no contemporary indication that Elfrida was present. But whether or not the murderers had been acting on her orders, subsequent legend blamed her as a murderess and a legend arose of her as an evil stepmother and a bad influence on her weak, incompetent, and treacherous son Aethelred. In real life, there is no evidence of her participation in the government, though her impressive landed estates in the Fenland (and possibly also Suffolk), probably her dower from her first marriage, indicate that she was acquisitive. Church partisans of her stepson's overthrown regime disliked her as a political enemy. She was a generous patron of the Church in her later years (traditionally put down to repentance), particularly of the monasteries at Ely and Peterborough, and founded and endowed the new nunnery at Wherwell in northern Hampshire. Even in her ecclesiastical dealings she caused controversy and had a clear desire to promote her allies, sacking the abbess of Barking in favour of her own candidate when she took over as lay patron. She seems to have spent an increasing amount of time at Wherwell. She died on 17 November, between 999 and 1001, at Wherwell where she was buried, probably aged a little under sixty. Her reputation was hopelessly lost due to the circumstances of her son's accession and his later failings, but Church hostility was a crucial factor and it may be that she was no more than a shrewd and political noblewoman, politically active and intent on defending her interests.

(SAINT) EDWARD (EADWARD) 'THE MARTYR' (975–8)

Son of Edgar by his first wife, Aethelfleda. He was probably born in *c.* 961, and was not a unanimous choice as his father's successor when Edgar died on 8 July 975. Edgar had left one survivor of two sons by his second wife, the reputedly ambitious Elfrida (Aethelthryth), Aethelred. He was only aged around seven, but was a serious candidate. It is possible that there was some question-mark over Edgar's first marriage, with Aethelred being preferred by some as 'born in the purple' (after his father's accession), in which case Edward may have been born before his father succeeded to Wessex late in 959. Edward's principal lay backers were the ealdorman of East Anglia, his father's foster-brother Aethelwold, and the ealdorman of Essex, Byrtnoth (later to be killed by the Vikings at Maldon in 991). The current political dispute over the 'excessive' grants of land made by Edgar to the Church led to frustrated would-be grantees, keen to see this policy halted, opposing the Church (led by Archbishop Dunstan) and its candidate Edward. Led by Earl Aelfhere of Mercia, they may have been concentrated in the East Midlands, where the landed power of the Church (lapsed since the Viking invasions and settlement in the 870s) had been boosted by Edgar to assert royal control. They rallied to Aethelred's cause. Aethelred was young enough to be controlled by a regency; Edward was at least in his mid-teens and so less easily influenced, which possibly alienated ambitious men keen on a weak ruler under a regency. He was also to be accused of having a reputation for bad temper and hasty, violent action, even at this young age, though West Saxon royal males reached maturity early; as this charge survived his sanctification, he was clearly not able to be portrayed realistically as a passive, godly youth in the usual manner of hagiographers.

Edward was crowned on 18 July, probably in 975, but there appears to have been strong antagonism to his Church allies and outbreaks of violence against lands granted to the Church on his accession. Famine followed, implying divine displeasure and probably bringing hungry and superstitious recruits to the ranks of those determined to overset Edgar's grants. Assorted monasteries were pillaged and monks expelled in violence that escalated in 976 and was thus widely-supported by aggrieved lay personnel; the *Chronicle* accuses Aelfhere of coordinating it. The new king and his ministers were unable to control it; possibly it centred in Aelfhere's Mercia, and Edward dared not leave Wessex. The pillaging and the famine cast a blight over his reign, and early in 978 a disastrous accident at a royal council meeting at Calne (Wiltshire) saw the floor of an upper-storey chamber fall in, leading to the death and injury of assorted people; Dunstan narrowly escaped, as the beam he was standing on was not affected.

On 18 March 978 Edward was murdered in Dorset, at 'Corfe gate' (probably the gate of the royal manor at what is now Corfe Castle, or Corfe as the 'gate' in the Purbeck Hills, but possibly Corfe Mullen). His legend said that he was visiting his stepmother Elfrida at her manor when her attendants – or even Elfrida in person – stabbed him, probably as he reached down from his horse to take a goblet. The *Life of Saint Oswald*, the earliest account, *c.* 995, blames the attendants without mentioning the queen and implies that he turned up on impulse for refreshment or a night's stay after hunting nearby. His horse galloped away carrying him, and he fell to his death; he either bled to death or broke his neck. Corfe was not a royal manor, belonging to the abbess of Shaftesbury. He was at most eighteen or nineteen. He was hastily buried at nearby Wareham without royal honours and Aethelred succeeded to the throne, but embarrassingly the locals were soon claiming that Edward's body was performing miracles and regarding him as a saint. The Church encouraged, if not instigated, the campaign, and a year later he was reburied at Shaftesbury amidst more appropriate splendour with the royal family and nobles in attendance. The shrine remained a centre of pilgrimage for centuries. As 'king and martyr', the first of two royal Edwards of England to be sanctified, he was the only post-Alfredian king to have a church – which still survives – dedicated to him, at Corfe Castle.

AETHELRED (ETHELRED) II 'UNRAED' (978–1013 and 1014–16)

One of the few Saxon kings whose memory survived into the succeeding era, albeit for negative reasons. His unsavoury reputation and notorious lack of success seems enshrined by his garbled sobriquet, 'the Unready' – a corruption of 'Unraed', 'ill-counselled', a pun on his name ('noble counsel') and criticism of his reliance on bad advisers. His reputation was already poor among his contemporaries, as seen from the tone of the 'official' record in the *Chronicle*. It was claimed that Aethelred had begun a long career of misdeeds by sullying the baptismal font (a charge also used against the anti-clerical Byzantine emperor Constantine V, and possibly borrowed from that story). Aethelred's reign began inauspiciously, through no fault of his own. Indeed, he owed his candidature to the early death of his elder (full) brother Edmund, first son of King Edgar and his second wife Elfrida. Born probably in 967 or 968, Aethelred was backed by his mother and her partisans (led by Earl Aelfhere of Mercia) for the throne when Edgar died in July 975; the rival, older candidate was his half-brother Edward. Edward's temper and strong character may have made ambitious men prefer his half-brother as a younger puppet ruler, and matters were complicated by opposition to Edgar's extensive monastic grants. Edward was successful but was murdered on 18 March 978 by his stepmother's partisans while visiting Corfe (Castle [?]) in Dorset. Aethelred assumed the throne, as the beneficiary of fratricide and regicide; the 'pro-monastic' party led by Archbishop Dunstan now lost influence to Aelfhere's grouping and promoted a cult of the murdered king. Popular belief in the 'martyr' led to Edward's translation to a grand shrine at Shaftesbury as a centre of veneration with official backing. This preceded the coronation in May 979, and may have been the Church's price for accepting the new regime.

Aelfhere remained the leading figure until he died in 983, with the lack of an adult king contributing to the new wave of Viking raids (including Southampton in 980 and London in 982). Dunstan returned to a limited degree of influence until his death in 988, and Bishop Aethelwold of Winchester (d. 984) was also regarded as influential in secular affairs. Some tension with the Church marred the 980s, with the king ravaging the diocese of Rochester in 986 (an early example of his sporadically violent actions?), but abated. Modern historians have seen the emergence of a group of more responsible ministers in the 990s, led by Ealdorman Aethelwaerd and his son Aethelmaer, the king's uncle Ealdorman Ordwulf and a group of younger clerics trained under Edgar like Bishop Aelfheah of Winchester and Abbots Wulfgar (Abingdon) and Aelfgar (New Minster, Winchester). As an adult ruler Aethelred seems to have endeavoured to be more generous to the Church, and the retirement/ deaths of the three ealdormen in *c.* 1005 led to marked deterioration in his conduct. He also showed a desire to appear as a just Christian king in his law-codes, where the Wantage Code of 997 endorsed the survival of local legal particularism within his lands (especially in the Danish-settled areas of eastern England) rather than imposing one system on all subjects. His imagery and the tone of his court remained that of an inspiring warrior-king, the father of his people.

This became increasingly at odds with reality, as from 991 he failed to meet the new threat of ever-larger Viking probes as his ancestors had done. But offering a militarily superior enemy 'geld' to leave his kingdom was not an innovation – even Alfred had done so (871). How much of Aethelred's military failure was due to a loss of nerve, as opposed to excessive caution, is open to question – the raiders grew in boldness year by year. Aethelred clearly had no willingness or ability to fight, or to trust and inspire competent subordinates; the lack of coordination between his armies became ever more apparent and the *Chronicle* makes it clear that morale steadily worsened until the defences became largely paralysed.

The Scandinavian attacks commenced with a descent on south-east England, probably by the Norse prince Olaf Tryggvason, in 991. Ealdorman Byrtnoth of Essex mounted a strong military resistance, but he allowed himself to be outflanked at Maldon and was killed. The defeat of this veteran commander was avoidable if the near-contemporary *Song of Maldon* can be trusted, given that he is supposed to have allowed the Vikings to cross a causeway onto the mainland to fight him without intercepting them 'unsportingly' as they were crossing. Even if he was overconfident of defeating the invaders in an equal fight, his rashness cannot be blamed on his king – but the disaster set the pattern for the future. Aethelred chose to pay Olaf a large ransom (£10,000) rather than to meet him in battle, allegedly on the advice of Archbishop Sigeric of Canterbury. Olaf moved on from Essex to ravage elsewhere; the coasts remained terrorised, and in 992 Aethelred brought together a large fleet at London only to find that one of his ealdormen warned the Vikings ahead of the confrontation, enabling them to evade a trap, and then himself abandoned his position. This mixture of timidity and treachery among Aethelred's senior advisers was to become endemic. The Vikings moved on to ravage Northumbria in 993, and the English commanders fled battle.

In 994 Olaf and his ally Swein Forkbeard failed in an attack on London, but ravaged the coasts from East Anglia round to Hampshire and then took horses to plunder inland. Faced with the enemy encamped at Southampton for the winter, Aethelred paid them £16,000 to leave and endeavoured to bind their commander as an ally like Alfred had done with Guthrum, requiring Olaf to come to Andover to be baptised and swear to leave his kingdom alone. Olaf left, but more loot-hungry Viking captains started to follow his precedent, ravaging England until they were paid off. Devon suffered in 997 and then the raiders moved into the heartland of southern England in 998; in 999 the raided locals in Kent resisted but were defeated for lack of outside support; in 1001 the Hampshire levies were defeated in West Sussex, and the Vikings attacked Devon again before returning for another assault. Aethelred did endeavour to put together large fleets to meet the Vikings' ships, but either they were not ready on time or they failed to sail, usually amid recriminations among their commanders. Aethelred's only major personal contribution was a large-scale land and naval campaign in Cumbria in 1000, evidently to secure or regain control of it from Scotland or Strathclyde. Even then his fleet did not operate adequately. Logically he should have used all his power to tackle the raiders across England in person. By this point some of his commanders, such as his Danish recruit and brother-in-law Pallig, were treating him with disdain and defecting; Aethelred received the latter back unpunished, still could not trust him, and had him murdered.

In 1002, Aethelred made the decision to buy off the endemic raiding with a huge sum of £24,000, leading to their main fleet temporarily leaving. He took a major diplomatic initiative to deny the raiders a safe haven across the Channel for their descents, allying with Duke Richard II of Normandy; widowed with at least five sons, he married Richard's sister Emma. Aethelred now endeavoured to rid himself of one supposed threat, that of the Danes resident in England linking up with the unchecked Scandinavian army. He ordered the notorious St Brice's Day Massacre (13 November), presented in retrospect as a concerted effort to wipe the Danes out by simultaneous massacre, which predictably failed to kill all its intended victims and only led to a heightening of hostility between English and Danes. It may not have been as wide-ranging as later believed, as the only recorded massacre was in

Oxford. The survivors escaped, demanding vengeance, and Swein Forkbeard arrived from Denmark with a large army to destroy opposition province by province. Given the location of most of Swein's support in the coming years, it is probable that Aethelred's killings loosened the ties of some settlers of Danish origin in eastern England to the West Saxon dynasty, but the Danelaw and East Anglia resisted ravaging as determinedly as Wessex, as seen at the battle of Ringmere.

In 1003, Swein sacked Exeter and then marched east into Wiltshire and Hampshire. In 1004 it was the turn of East Anglia, and after a brief respite while England suffered from famine in 1005, the raiding army returned to the south in 1006–7. The tax which eventually bought them off amounted to £30,000 this time and during the resulting respite Aethelred put a massive effort into raising a new fleet, which he based at Sandwich for the 1009 raiding season. Disaster followed as usual, this time due to accusations of treason against one of the fleet commanders (Wulfnoth, probably father of the later Earl Godwin) who fled and turned pirate; after his defeat the fleet was left inactive and dispersed early. The feuding among Aethelred's councilors, leading to sporadic executions by the king, now centred on Eadric (later nicknamed 'Streona') the new earl of Mercia, widely regarded as a disastrous choice and with a murderous career of repeated treachery to all sides.

The Vikings ravaged East Anglia and the East Midlands through 1010, with the *Chronicle* lamenting that the English army was rarely in the right place to catch them, and when it had a chance to do so it failed to act. Aethelred's latest attempt to buy the invaders off with another huge tax was accepted but they contemptuously failed to keep their word once they had the money. The attack on Canterbury in 1012 left Archbishop Aelfheah a prisoner in the Viking camp, and when his ransom failed to arrive he was murdered by drunken Vikings at a feast. That atrocity led to a competent commander, Thorkell the Tall, deserting to Aethelred with forty ships, but by then the enemy were too numerous and spread out over England. In 1013 Swein returned to eastern England with a new army, based himself on the Humber, and secured the submission of the Danelaw and Northumbria before marching south to enter Wessex again. Outright conquest was now his aim, and Aethelred shut himself in London; Swein was driven off by a determined English military effort. Deserted by more and more of his abandoned subjects, Aethelred temporarily held out with his fleet in the Thames as even London despatched emissaries to Swein in the north, sending his wife Emma to Normandy. As his position deteriorated, he retired to the Isle of Wight and in midwinter 1013 fled to Normandy.

All England now submitted to Swein, but his sudden death at Gainsborough on 2 February gave Aethelred an unexpected second chance. The councillors who had gone over preferred to have their 'natural lord' to Swein's son Cnut, 'if only he would govern them more justly than before' as the *Chronicle* tellingly put it. They sent envoys to Normandy recalling him, and he returned to England to buy off the Viking fleet and lead his army against Cnut. The resulting campaign in Lindsey ended with Cnut in retreat to the Continent, but Aethelred's recovery of his kingdom was short-lived. The crucial Anglo-Danes of the East Midlands were alienated by the shocking murder of two of their leading figures, Siferth and Morcar, at court by Earl Eadric; the king supported him and sent Siferth's widow Eadgyth/Edith captive to Malmesbury, only to have her carried off and married by his estranged eldest son, Edmund. The East Midlands then transferred their allegiance to Edmund, a vigorous and inspiring commander in the renewed war for England when Cnut returned to attack Wessex in 1015. Aethelred lay ill at Cosham (near Portsmouth) with his army inactive and his chosen deputy, Eadric, quarreled with Edmund instead of joining him and then deserted to Cnut. Wessex submitted to the latter, and early in 1016 the reinforced Cnut joined Eadric to march north into Mercia; at his men's request Aethelred himself led his troops north but soon abandoned the campaign amid the usual rumours of treachery.

The king died in London on 23 April 1016 as Edmund was moving back south to link up with his army for the expected confrontation with Cnut (also heading for London). He was probably a year or two under fifty, and had ruled for one of the longest reigns in Anglo-Saxon history (thirty-eight years) amid unprecedented misfortunes, which his own failings and misjudgements had made worse. The unanimity of his recall in 1014 shows the immense latent goodwill which he still possessed, by virtue of his office and lineage if not personally, even after decades of defeats and poor leadership. His incompetence may have been overestimated, and his lack of skill or commitment as a military commander at a time of crisis (rare for his dynasty) was his most crucial failing. He was too ready to resort to violent intimidation which failed in its main effect. He could not choose or inspire competent subordinates, he trusted people who aroused antagonism and were liable to betray him, and was a damaging failure in the personal leadership which acted as the binding force of a state in a time of crisis. But his bad reputation owed much to hindsight and to subsequent events, with twelfth-century writers lamenting him as the originator of foreign conquest and high taxation.

SWEIN FORKBEARD (Denmark, c. 985–1014; England, 1013–14) Born around 960, he seized control of Denmark from his father, Harald Bluetooth, around 985 and thus took over the pre-eminent organised military machine of the aggressive and militaristic Scandinavian world. His father was probably responsible for the combination of centralisation and organisation evident in the network of round military camps built in mid-tenth-century Denmark, of which Trelleborg is the most notable, and for the new system of roads which added to the dynasty's grip on the country. As a new and untried ruler, he needed to prove himself and cement his soldiers' loyalty by external aggression, collecting loot to add to his prestige as a reliable employer and giver of gifts. This was clearly in tune with his own restless and ruthless personality, and although he had ambitions in disordered Norway, where central kingship had lapsed in c. 980, they were challenged by local jarls of royal descent, particularly Swein's rival Olaf Tryggvason. His first target appears to have been the pagan Wends on the southern coast of the Baltic Sea in 983, in association with which he allied with the latter's Polish enemies (the kingdom of Poland was emerging to the Wends' south at this time) and married a Polish princess. His sons Harald and Cnut were the result, probably born in the mid- to late 980s.

Agriculturally rich England, with towns and monasteries, offered a more lucrative as well as an easier target, and Swein may have been attacking it as early as 991 (though his participation in the Maldon campaign is unclear). Conversely, allowing ambitious and potentially threatening minor warlords to build up armies and amass loot there could lead to a challenge to his rule in Denmark; possibly Olaf's growing reputation and success in England drove Swein to intervene to safeguard his own control over the raiding forces there.

From 993/4, Swein was active in raiding England. Following up the success of his ally/rival Olaf Tryggvason, and a major threat as a reigning king, a competent and ferocious commander with a large army, he and Olaf attacked London with ninety-four ships in 994 and ravaged across the South-East before wintering at Southampton. They were bought off with £16,000 tribute by Aethelred, and although Olaf kept his oath never to return Swein continued raiding. The death of his sister Gunnhilde and assorted countrymen in Aethelred's Danish massacre in 1002 added an element of blood-feud as he led his army back to England for a sustained assault, and his relentless and merciless ravaging in the following years included Devon, Dorset and Wiltshire in 1003, East Anglia in 1004, and across the south (based on Wight) in 1006. (See article on Aethelred II.)

Finally, in summer 1013, having exhausted England by widespread ravaging across most of Wessex and Mercia and extorted huge payments of Danegeld, he turned to conquest and brought his fleet into the Humber to establish a base at Gainsborough. The Danelaw and Earl Uhtred's Northumbria submitted, and he raided south via Oxford into Wessex, forcing submission en route, before heading for Aethelred's base in London. Aided by Thorkell the Tall and his Viking fleet, the king held out; Swein returned west to Bath to receive the submission of Ealdorman Aethelmaer and western Wessex and then headed back to Lincolnshire. Englishmen and Danes alike now submitted, including the independent Viking fleet at Greenwich, and after London sent envoys to Swein, Aethelred sent his family to Normandy and fled from the Thames to Wight. The king's councillors came to Swein to recognise him as king in December, and he was titularly king of all England for around two months with Aethelred in exile. His sudden death at Gainsborough on 2 February 1014 forestalled any crowning, and enabled his disgraced predecessor to return as the senior English nobles deserted his second son Cnut. His elder (?) son Harald almost certainly inherited Denmark as king rather than merely Cnut's viceroy. Evidently an able and energetic commander, Swein's death prevented any signs emerging of whether he shared Cnut's statesmanlike qualities or was nothing but a glorified pirate.

EDMUND (II) 'IRONSIDE' (1016) The second son of Aethelred Unraed by his first wife Aelgiva; from his activities he was adult by 1013, probably born in c. 988. Succeeding his elder brother Athelstan as his father's heir and being bequeathed his best swords (1014 [?]), Edmund showed the vigour, military ability and talent at attracting loyalty which his father lacked. He probably had some military experience in the wars of 1010–13 which saw his father's position steadily eroded and his provincial elites deserting to the Danish forces of Swein Forkbeard. There is no record of him leaving the kingdom for exile in winter 1013–14, unlike his father, stepmother, and half-brothers, and he (or the sickening Athelstan?) possibly remained in loyal parts of Wessex, Northumbria, or English Mercia away from Swein's army. He first appears in history in 1015, challenging his father's latest blunder of following the advice of Earl Eadric of Mercia in executing Si(g)ferth and Morcar, two leading nobles of the Danelaw. The men were probably suspected of links to the new Danish challenger Cnut, but killing them alienated their supporters; Edmund carried off Siferth's widow Edith (Eadgyth), imprisoned at Malmesbury, and married her in defiance of his father's wishes. She may have been a substantial heiress in her own right, and his action led much of Mercia (English and Danish, the latter led by Siferth and Morcar's supporters) to transfer its allegiance to Edmund in September 1015. He raised an army, still technically loyal to his father, and when Cnut landed the latter's progress across Wessex unchallenged was aided by Aethelred falling ill. Eadric raised his own army in Mercia and met Edmund, but they failed to reach an agreement and Eadric, believed to be intending treachery, deserted to Cnut; Edmund remained in the Midlands while Eadric led his men into Cnut's seized territory in western Wessex.

In 1016, Cnut and Eadric marched north into Warwickshire to attack Mercia. Aethelred moved out of London to take his army north and join Edmund. But there may have been problems in raising and motivating enough men for the king, the two armies failed to achieve anything, and Aethelred returned to London. Edmund, outnumbered, marched north into Northumbria and achieved the support of Earl Uhtred, and they moved south into Staffordshire and Shropshire but avoided an open battle. Cnut, doing likewise, moved across the north Midlands up towards York, and Uhtred had to return home. He then submitted to Cnut, leaving Edmund to return to London.

Aethelred died in London on 23 April, and Edmund was elected king. Cnut had now secured Northumbria and was sailing south, and Edmund chose to avoid being penned up and retired into Wessex to raise an army. The Danes arrived at Greenwich, and the Londoners held their fleet back at the bridge, but were outmanoevured as Cnut dug a ditch around the Southwark end of the bridge and hauled his ships across. London withstood a siege, and a Danish army pursued Edmund into Wessex but was defeated by him at Penselwood. The men of Wessex had rallied to Edmund as they had not to his father, and a second success followed in a two-day battle in midsummer at Sherston (thought to be in Wiltshire or Hwicce). Cnut's men returned to London, abandoning the Wessex campaign, and Edmund followed with the third army he had managed to raise in a year (a sign of his charisma to his exhausted subjects). The besiegers retreated to Greenwich, and a few days later Edmund won a third victory at Brentford which was marred by large numbers of the English being drowned in the Thames through carelessness. When Edmund returned to Wessex to raise more men the Danes made a second assault on London, but this was beaten off and they retired to eastern Mercia.

Edmund now returned to the Thames valley, and drove a Danish raiding army that had attacked Kent back from the Medway onto Sheppey and thence onto their ships. Sensing which side was winning, Earl Eadric surrendered to Edmund at Aylesford and was received back – a decision which the *Chronicle* calls the worst ever made for the English nation. It seemed so in retrospect, but at the time Edmund probably needed Eadric's men and dared not execute him like the wiser Cnut did later. The Danes retired into Mercia, and Edmund followed; they eventually met in a crucial battle at Ashingdon, Essex, on 18 October 1016. Edmund had raised five armies in a year and revitalised his war-weary people, using his nation's administrative structure for warfare and uniting his nobles in a way that Aethelred had failed to do; he had also made up for any initial military inexperience compared to Cnut. But in the battle that followed Eadric and his Mercians fled, losing the battle with serious English losses including much of the leadership such as Ulfcytel of East Anglia. It was interpreted as deliberate desertion to aid Cnut by prior arrangement, but it may have been a genuine panic by the soldiers which Eadric took advantage of to aid the man who now seemed likely to win. The decisive reverse forced Edmund, possibly wounded and certainly outnumbered, to retreat into western Mercia; Cnut, joined by Eadric, followed him to Gloucestershire and on Eadric's advice the two leaders met at a safe site in the middle of the Severn ('Ola's Island') to negotiate terms. Cnut was either too cautious or had lost too many men to force another battle yet, and the treaty gave Edmund rule of Wessex and Cnut rule of Mercia and Northumbria. Cnut returned to London.

The truce gave the majority of the Anglo-Saxon lands to the English contender and the Danish lands to his Scandinavian rival. A lasting settlement was unlikely. But within a month or so, on 30 November 1016, Edmund died at Oxford. Later stories had it that Cnut had treacherously had him assassinated, possibly by a poisoned statue with a spring or by sending someone to stab him on the privy, but he may have died of a wound from Ashingdon. He was no more than twenty-eight or twenty-nine years old. The lack of an adult English leader gave his surviving full brother Eadwig/Edwy no chance against Cnut, and Edmund's councillors recognised Cnut as king of all England; Edmund's widow Edith and infant sons Edward and Edmund fled to Scandinavia, whence the boys later ended up in Russia. A capable and possibly outstanding war-leader and an inspiring leader, Edmund had all the qualities that Aethelred lacked and might have proved a king of the quality of Alfred, Edward, and Athelstan had he succeeded in driving out Cnut. It is uncertain if his generosity to Eadric alone caused his failure, given the advantages of manpower and leadership which Cnut also possessed.

II

1016 to 1066

CNUT (CANUTE) (England, 1016–35; Denmark, 1018–35) Thought to be the second son of King Swein 'Forkbeard' of Denmark by his first wife, Gunnhilda of Poland. His birth-date is unknown and has been put as late as 995, given that he only appears as an active commander in 1012. He may have been only forty when he died in 1035. Alternatively, one source indicates that he was present at the Danish sack of Norwich in 1004 and would have been likely to be in his early to mid-teens if trusted with a command; a late reference to him dying aged fifty-seven has been interpreted as a mistake for 'forty-seven', implying a birth-date around 988. He served his military apprenticeship with his father's army in England while his elder brother Harald acted as Swein's deputy in Denmark, and was present as Swein's heir as the provincial notables of England went over to Swein in autumn 1013. Based in the Danish-settled Danelaw close to his fleet in winter 1013–14, Swein died unexpectedly on 2 February 1014. Cnut succeeded in command of his armies with the support of the local nobility, but the defecting councillors of Aethelred who had come to Swein's camp deserted in favour of the legitimate king and returned to Wessex to recall him. Aethelred returned from Normandy and led a large army into Lindsey to confront Cnut, and the Dane had the worst of it and retreated to his ships. Sailing for Denmark in an unsuccessful challenge to Harald's accession, he savagely mutilated the hostages his and Swein's faithless English supporters had had to give and dumped them ashore at Sandwich, a useful reminder to future opponents that he was as ruthless and bloody if thwarted as his father.

Having failed to secure Denmark, he returned to England in 1015 with the advantage that Aethelred had started alienating his leading subjects again, particularly in the Danelaw. Edmund Ironside, a far more formidable foe, cut that potential source of support off from Cnut by rescuing the arrested widow of the executed noble Sigferth and marrying her, but Cnut seems to have copied his marital tactics with a relationship (not certainly Church-sanctioned) to Aelfgifu of Northampton, another heiress and daughter of the murdered Ealdorman Aelfhelm of Northumbria. She gave him two sons. The 1015 invasion saw Cnut land at Sandwich, move west, and plunder Dorset and Wiltshire, aided by Aethelred falling ill at Cosham. With the royal army paralysed and Edmund busy raising men in Mercia, Cnut then received the adherence of Earl Eadric of Mercia, Aethelred's leading but most controversial supporter, who had quarelled with Edmund. This arch-opportunist secured him enough support to be recognised as king in Wessex, and at midwinter 1015–16 they moved across the Thames into Warwickshire. Cnut appears to have gained control over eastern Mercia while Edmund, avoiding battle as too weak, operated in the west and temporarily won over Earl Uhtred of Northumbria; after Edmund had moved south-west, Cnut in turn marched north to force Northumbria's submission. Uhtred swore loyalty to him but was executed anyway; Cnut took no chances and put his own man, Eric, in as Earl.

Before he could take his fleet south to attack the sick Aethelred in London he died and Edmund was recognised as king. London held out against Cnut, who had to send his army after Edmund into Wessex. It is not clear if Cnut was at the siege of London or in Wessex as his army was defeated at Penselwood and Sherston, but when the action moved back to London Cnut was driven back to his ships. Having raised three armies in quick succession and rallied his people, Edmund then defeated Cnut again at Brentford; while he was absent in Wessex Cnut returned to attack London again, but was driven off. His attack on Kent was defeated and his army fled to their ships on Sheppey, and Eadric went over to Edmund and was pardoned. After this defection Cnut was probably outnumbered as well as on the defensive against a repeatedly victorious enemy, with inevitable effects on morale, but his leadership skills are apparent as he held his army together. Another raid across Mercia was met by Edmund, and on 18 October 1016 Cnut won a decisive victory in the crucial encounter at Ashingdon in Essex. Eadric is supposed to have deserted to him and/or ordered his men to run away in mid-battle, breaking Edmund's battle-line, though this may be a guess to explain an outbreak of panic or Eadric's attempt to assure Cnut (whose support he now needed again) that the incident was deliberate. Many of the senior English nobles were killed, decimating the military command, morale was crushed, and Cnut pursued the retreating Edmund as far as the Severn valley. He was not sure enough of his victory to force Edmund into a final battle or the latter evaded him, as their advisers were able to persuade both into talks at 'Ola's Island' in the Severn and they signed a treaty leaving Edmund the rule of Wessex.

Edmund died on 28 November 1016 at Oxford – possibly of wounds, though later accounts accused Cnut of having him poisoned or stabbed. He left one inexperienced brother (Eadwig) and infant sons, and his councillors recognised Cnut as king. Not prepared to take chances, Cnut exiled the infants (allegedly with a failed request to their hosts to kill them), and now or later killed Eadwig too. A revolt by Eadwig the 'ceorls' king', some sort of peasants' revolt against the submissive nobility, was suppressed; the arch-traitor Eadric, initially given Mercia, met his just desserts with peremptory execution.

Cnut anticipated the position of the next foreign conqueror, William in 1066. There was substantial unrest at first, with the *Chronicle* noting successive executions and exiles among the nobility. Another purge followed Cnut's return from Denmark in 1020. Cnut relied on a large standing army and fleet, for which an exorbitant tax of £72,000 was raised in 1018; his bodyguard was the nucleus of the later 'housecarls' who fought for Harold II. But there were fewer confiscations of land than under William, and much of the senior landholding class survived; there were a number of native ealdormen such as Leofwine, father of the later Earl Leofric, in south-west Mercia. Cnut relied on a narrow basis of support from senior provincial governors, giving a few well-endowed earldoms to trusted deputies rather than spreading out power. Arguably, this policy weakened the monarchy by making the earls more powerful locally than an absent king – as seen in 1052 – and extending this from the northern provinces, often trusted to a few men under Aethelred, to Wessex. He initially kept Wessex for himself, divided up Mercia, and gave Northumbria to Eric and East Anglia to Thorkell the Tall, a formerly independent Viking war-leader. Thorkell, a potential rival with military experience and his own following, was exiled in 1021 but was pardoned in Denmark in 1023 and made regent there. Part of Wessex was given, in *c.* 1020, to a Saxon (probably from Sussex), Godwin. Cnut thus set up the Godwin dynasty which dominated national life under his successors, and the earl married Cnut's sister-in-law Goda. Cnut set aside Aelfgifu, for the audacious step of marrying Aethelred's widow Emma in 1017; she had fled to Normandy with her sons by Aethelred (who remained exiled) and securing her ended any threat from her homeland. This marriage was a major factor for political continuity, and Emma's experience and political ability were invaluable as Cnut presented his regime as a continuation of traditional English kingship, reissuing the old law-codes in consultation with Archbishop Wulfstan of York (and later using them in Denmark). He worked closely with the Church as a Christian sovereign, a generous patron mindful of his duty. Laws were enforced and the king ruled in accordance with tradition, though dependant ultimately on military force.

Harald of Denmark died childless in 1018, leading to Cnut's departure for his homeland. He used his English troops and finance to extend his power in Scandinavia, with his son by Emma (Harthacnut) being made titular governor of Denmark as heir. Cnut's attempt to invade Sweden, which had aided a rebellion, in 1026 was repulsed with defeat at the battle of the Holy River. Norway, however, fell to him in 1028; in 1030 its expelled monarch St Olaf returned to be killed by Cnut's troops at the battle of Stiklestad. Cnut's elder son by Aelfgifu, Swein, now ruled Norway with his mother as regent. Cnut thus created a family 'federation' of monarchies in Scandinavia, becoming the most powerful king of England (or Denmark) to date. In 1027 he went on pilgrimage to Rome, and was treated as an equal by Emperor Conrad (whose son duly married his daughter Gunnhilde). He used his power to mount a major invasion of Scotland in 1031, making up for long neglect of his northern border; this was the most serious English military demonstration since Athelstan's in 934. Malcolm II probably avoided engagement due to military inferiority, and the two kings came to terms. The English sources claim that Malcolm accepted Cnut as his overlord, and two other rulers – Macbeth, sub-king of Moray, and Margad Ragnallson of Man – probably also agreed treaties. There is no record of Cnut's taking a similar interest in Welsh affairs.

Cnut's later years were mainly peaceful, although his domination of Norway was never accepted by the inhabitants and late in 1034 or early in 1035 Swein and Aelfgifu were driven out by a revolt led by Olaf's son Magnus. Cnut did not respond to this, possibly due to ill-health. A notably generous Church patron in his later years and clearly accepted by his Anglo-Danish nobility with no evidence of real or feared plots after 1020, he died on 12 November 1035 at Shaftesbury aged somewhere from forty to about forty-seven, usually assumed to be the former. The event was sudden enough for Cnut or Emma not to have brought Harthacnut, only around seventeen and with a half-brother (Harold, son of Aelfgifu) in England ready to challenge his accession, from Denmark to England first. The nobility were divided over which son should succeed Cnut, with no incontrovertible evidence of the late king's wishes though he probably favoured Harthacnut. As a result, a stand-off with a country divided between their factions followed; Harold eventually won. This illustrates the essentially personal nature of Cnut's grand multi-national kingdom; as with Athelstan in 939, a great war-leader's early death brought challenges to his monarchy. Within seven years his dynasty was extinct and Aethelred and Emma's son back on the throne, and England and Denmark were never ruled by one king again. Despite the insubstantiality of his creation Cnut was an outstanding leader, as brutal as Offa or any of his own ancestors (at least in his youth) but capable of transmuting from the fierce young warlord of 1014 into a mature and generous statesman emulating the most virtuous Christian kings of England. Tenacious in military crisis in 1016, when he seemed destined to miss out on two thrones, he became the effective 'emperor' of the North. A comparison may be made with the Viking-descended Duke William of Normandy, who was also to take England by conquest after a great victory fifty years later but created a longer-lasting dynasty. Could Cnut's empire have lasted had his sons been of stronger mettle, and was the lack of English revolt after c. 1019 testimony to his abilities at reconciliation or just to the size of his army and taxation-revenues? The most well-known of the stories about him, in which he showed up his flattering courtiers by vainly ordering the tide to go back, is probably apocryphal. It was popular enough for various places to vie for the honour, most plausibly Bosham in Sussex (where he had a manor and a daughter of his was buried) or Southampton. The moral of it, namely his refusal to be taken in by toadies and a pointed joke at their expense, is certainly in keeping with what can be surmised about the mature Cnut.

EMMA (a.k.a. AELFGIFU) (Queen of England, 1002–16, 1017–37, 1040–52) Probably born around 985/7, she was the daughter of Duke Richard I of Normandy (d. 996) and was married off by her brother Richard II to King Aethelred in 1002 on the occasion of an Anglo-Norman treaty banning the Normans' Scandinavian kin from using the land as a base for raids on England. She was possibly too young to have children immediately, but gave Aethelred two sons (Edward, born by 1005, and Alfred) and a daughter, Goda. Aethelred's many semi-adult sons by his first marriage had prior claims as heirs. When Aethelred was abandoned by his nobles to the overwhelming forces of Danish King Swein Forkbeard in autumn 1013, Aethelred sent Emma and her children from London to Normandy, and he followed shortly before Swein's death on 2 February 1014 allowed his restoration. His eldest son by Aelfgifu, Athelstan, died *c.* 1014 but his second son, Edmund Ironside, led the resistance to Swein's son Cnut in 1014–16 and on Aethelred's death in London on 23 April 1016 was acclaimed as king. He had at least one son by this date and Emma and her sons were marginalised in the conflict with Cnut which followed; when Edmund died on 30 November and Cnut succeeded they fled to Normandy again.

Cnut requested Emma's return to England in early summer 1017 as his bride, probably in a treaty with Duke Richard extending the Anglo-Norman alliance. The ex-queen chose to resume her status rather than stay in exile, and whether on Cnut's orders or not she left her sons in Normandy. Their alienation, and particularly Edward's grievances, has been the subject of much speculation. She gave Cnut a further son, Harthacnut (*c.* 1018), who seems to have been her favourite, and a daughter, Gunnhilde; the boy was sent to Denmark as titular regent in 1023 and the girl was married off to the German Emperor Conrad's son Henry after 1027. Emma proved invaluable to Cnut in teaching him the expected way to operate as a respectable English king instead of a Viking warlord, acting as intermediary with Churchmen and senior nobles who she knew from her earlier period as queen, and assisted his transformation into a wise statesman, lawgiver, and religious patron; on her own account she built up a substantial landed endowment and a network of lay and ecclesiastical patronage. A skilled operator who knew the value of ideology and image as well as acquisitive and protective of her rights, Emma centred her activities on her 'dower-town' of Winchester, where she was a major religious patron and a surviving illustration in a manuscript shows her and Cnut presenting a cross to Hyde Abbey. (She is the first English queen whose portrait has survived.)

It is speculated that the practical and politically skilled Emma, descendant of a family of ruthless Norman dukes, found Cnut much more to her taste than the battle-wary and devious Aethelred. She was also the older of the two, though Cnut may not have been the full decade younger that has been assumed. On his death on 17 November 1035 she backed Harthacnut for the succession, holding Winchester with her husband's housecarls and treasure and backed by Earl Godwin of Wessex. It is not certain that Cnut wanted Harthacnut as king of England as well as Denmark, though she claimed this, and if so his wishes were defied; the nobles of Mercia and Northumbria chose Harold Harefoot, the surviving son of Cnut by Aelfgifu of Northampton. Cnut had probably married her by Danish common law while in eastern England in 1014–15, as a link to the nobility, but set her aside to marry Emma; her detractors, probably led by Emma, claimed that Aelfgifu had only been a mistress and that Harold was not even Cnut's son. Harthacnut failed to sail to England, due to the need to protect Denmark from Magnus of Norway, who he was fighting until 1039, and Emma's two sons by Aethelred tried to visit her in Winchester but were neutralised. Edward landed at Southampton but had to fight a battle and was driven back by the local levies, not definitively on Emma's orders as she may not have known he was coming (there is a later story about Harold sending him a forged invitation in her name). Alfred landed in Kent, was intercepeted and 'welcomed' by Godwin, but was arrested treacherously at Guildford and handed over to Harold for fatal blinding, which must have soured Emma's subsequent relations with Godwin. Godwin thus deserted to Harold, and in 1037 Emma had to flee to the Continent and abandon England to Harold. She settled at Bruges and raised a fleet; Edward visited her there and in 1039 Harthacnut finally joined her after agreeing peace with Norway. Their invasion of England was not needed as Harold died on 17 March 1040, and they arrived peacefully for Harthacnut to assume the throne.

Restored to power for the third time, Emma commissioned the laudatory *Encomium Emmae* to present her image as the wise, virtuous and divinely-protected queen, with inconvenient facts left out of a carefully spun story. Aethelred and his sons by his first marriage were marginalised, the king not even being mentioned, and her connection with Cnut was played up. But her favourite son died unexpectedly without heirs on 8 June 1042, and her relationship with Edward as the next king was difficult. Too much may have been made of his anger at being abandoned as a child, but it was Godwin who is stated as the main supporter of his election and in November 1043, Edward rode with his earls to Winchester to arrest her and deprive her of all her treasure and lands. According to Goscelin of Canterbury she was accused of plotting to put Magnus – with whom Harthacnut had had a mutual succession pact, neither having sons – on the English throne, though she was later exonerated and her property returned. It would seem unlikely that she would turn against her own son in favour of a Scandinavian prince she had probably never met, an enemy of Cnut, but at least it was considered plausible by contemporaries and her enemies could work on a distrustful king. A more unlikely twelfth-century story, recounted by Richard of Devizes, had her accused of adultery with the bishop of Winchester, Cnut's protégé Aelfwine, and forced to undergo trial by ordeal which miraculously proved her innocence thanks to her prayers to the local Saint Swithin. (The identity of the bishop involved – Aelfwine was not in office in 1043 – was probably muddled with her son's protégé Stigand, who was temporarily dismissed about this time.) Another story, one of the miracles of Saint Mildred, has Emma praying to the saint for Edward to pardon her after being reduced to poverty, and Edward duly changing his mind and restoring her wealth. In fact, she continued to witness charters at court until at least 1045.

She died on 6 March 1052, aged around sixty-five to sixty-seven, after an unprecedented half century at the centre of English politics in which she had operated (usually) successfully as an active and model queen well aware of both her image and her rights.

HAROLD HAREFOOT (1036/7 – 40)

One of the two sons of Cnut by Aelfgifu of Northampton, apparently the younger. Given the support which he had in the Danish parts of England in 1036–7, he seems to have been personally known to its nobility; he was probably born in 1016/17. His brother Swein was sent to rule Cnut's conquest of Norway in 1030 and went with their mother who was regent; they were driven out in winter 1034–5 and fled to Denmark where Swein died.

On Cnut's death on 12 November 1035 the nobility of Mercia and Northumbria, dominated by men of Danish stock and probably marshalled by Aelfgifu and/or her Northamptonshire kin, chose Harold as their next king. Earls Siward (governor of Northumbria south of the Tees), Ealdred (governor north of the Tees), and Leofric (governor of western Mercia) were among them. A stand-off followed with Queen Emma in Winchester supporting her son Harthacnut with Cnut's bodyguard and treasure, and her supporter Godwin of Wessex. The *Chronicle* claims that many men did not believe that Harold was Cnut's son, but it is unknown if this was propaganda by the victors (Harthacnut and Emma). Harthacnut's continued absence damaged his cause though it helped to prevent war. When Emma's younger son by Aethelred, Alfred, arrived in Kent en route to visit his mother, he was intercepted by Godwin, treacherously seized by surprise at Guildford and handed over to Harold, who fatally blinded him and sent him to die at Ely. Godwin was protecting his future as earl; the blinding and its deliberate brutality were Harold's responsibility.

Harthacnut and his Danish fleet failed to invade, and Wessex accepted Harold as king in 1037 and Emma fled to the Continent. The new king's regime was under threat of invasion but nothing transpired in his lifetime, and nothing is recorded of his reign except for a dispute with the Church over lands at Sandwich. He died on 17 March 1040 at London, probably in his early twenties and forestalling a civil war with Harthacnut (and Emma) whose fleet was ready to invade. He was buried at Westminster, temporarily as Harthacnut had Harold's body dug up and thrown in a marsh when he arrived. It was retrieved and buried properly in London in secret. A little-known character who seems to have had Cnut's streak of cruelty in self-preservation, he was later nicknamed 'Harefoot' which presumably refers to his ability in running. If it was so well remembered, his interest in sport rather than administration may have noticed by contemporaries.

HARTHACNUT (King of Denmark, 1035–42; of England, 1040–2) The only son of Cnut and Emma who married in summer 1017, he was probably born in 1018. He was sent to Denmark as nominal ruler for Cnut in 1023, under the regency of Thorkell the Tall, but was probably intended by his father as heir to England as well. But his long absence jeopardised his position, and when his father died in November 1035 he failed to act quickly – due to fear of invasion from Norway, where his father's regime under his half-brother Swein had recently been evicted by Magnus Olafsson. He was recognised as king in Wessex, where his mother held Winchester, but Mercia and Northumbria backed his half-brother Harold. The stalemate ended when Godwin of Wessex went over to Harold and in 1037 Emma was forced to flee to Flanders, setting up her base at Bruges (a centre for shipping, useful for recruiting invaders). Harthacnut joined her with his own fleet in 1039, and the invasion of England was probably imminent when Harold died unexpectedly in March 1040. The reason for delay was the danger from Magnus in Norway rather than lack of interest in his English inheritance, though his Danish councillors would have been encouraging caution; his voyage to England was preceded by an agreement with Magnus in 1039, which was later said to have centred on each (childless) king agreeing to the other being his heir. Magnus later claimed this included England as well as Denmark.

As king of England from March 1040 to June 1042 he relied heavily on Emma and the earls. The queen had brought her son Edward to meet Harthacnut in Bruges earlier, and in 1041 Edward was recalled to England – probably as heir until Harthacnut had a son. Crowned on 18 June 1040 at Canterbury, Harthacnut pursued the building of a large fleet to protect his far-flung double realm and like Cnut used England as a 'milch-cow' for his ambitions. His taxation led to riots in Worcester and the murder of his tax-collectors, to which he replied by ordering his men to lay waste the county – such collective punishment for killing the king's men was perfectly legal and was ordered by his successor Edward for Dover in 1051. The killing of Earl Eadwulf of northern Northumbria in 1041 also had its reasoning, as this head of the Bamburgh dynasty had more local support than the distant king and was a potential threat; swift execution might head off a rebellion. He died suddenly on 8 June 1042 while drinking at the wedding-banquet of the prominent thegn Osgod Clapa at Lambeth, aged around twenty-four. An alcoholic, epileptic, or diabetic fit or poison have all been suggested as causes. He was succeeded by his half-brother Edward, and has generally been written off as a rash and vindictive wastrel like his half-brother Harold. A more positive reference attests to his generosity and free spending – which possibly included too much alcohol if his collapse testifies to a medical condition, not poison.

(SAINT) EDWARD (EADWARD) (Later known as 'the Confessor', 1042–66) The best-known of the Anglo-Saxon kings in later centuries, his reign benefited from nostalgia after 1066 as he was the last king of the old royal line and disasters, allegedly foretold by him, followed his death. William the Conqueror and his successors used his reign as a template for government, with their promises to adhere to the laws of King Edward, and the landholding situation at the end of his reign was one of the basic parameters of the Domesday Book. The first king since Alfred to have his biography written, dedicated to and probably commissioned by his widow Edith, the twelfth-century campaign to make him a saint led to an amplification – and distortion – of his memory to turn him into a suitable candidate and play up his holiness. The *Vitae Aedwardi Regis* of *c.* 1068 was extended with sanctification in view by Osbert of Clare in the 1130s, and subsequently the latter wrote his own biography of Edward as a saint; as a senior monk of Westminster Abbey, where Edward was buried, he had commercial motives in attracting pilgrims to the holy king's tomb as well as boosting the abbey's legal claims as a saintly shrine. Analysis is thus problematic. He has to be viewed through the prism of the events of 1066. Did he intend to make Duke William his heir as the latter insisted, what was his attitude to Earl Godwin and his sons, and why was he childless?

Edward's date of birth is uncertain. His parents Aethelred 'Unraed' (a widower with six sons) and Emma of Normandy married in 1002, as part of a treaty with her brother Duke Richard II to halt Normandy's use as a base for Scandinavian raiders. Edward was born at Islip in Oxfordshire, and first witnesses charters in 1005; as Emma was only in her mid-teens at the time of marriage, his conception was probably some time after the marriage so his likely date of birth is 1003 or 1004. Even in his infancy legends distort his career, as it is unlikely that he was ever really named as heir to England; there were many older half-brothers, militarily experienced as needed at a time of war, and it was the Witan not Aethelred who made the choice. It is possible that Edward did spend some time at Ely Abbey as later claimed (perhaps by monks eager to annex his reputation), but it would have been to keep him safe from Scandinavian kidnap while his parents were traveling. In autumn 1013, he and his full siblings were taken into exile in Normandy by Emma as the Danes ravaged and the magnates started to recognise Swein of Denmark as king; Aethelred followed but Swein's sudden death in February 1014 led to his recall. He sent Edward back from Normandy ahead of him to meet the Witan, and presumably to deliver his pledges of good government. The subsequent wars between Edward's eldest surviving older half-brother Edmund Ironside and Swein's son Cnut ended with the latter's victory at Ashingdon and Edmund's death a few weeks later in November 1016, and Edward and his mother and siblings went into exile again. A Scandinavian source, *Olaf's Saga Helga*, says that Edward was Edmund's co-ruler, which is possible as a move by the latter to placate Emma and her allies, and that he nearly killed Cnut in a battle for London – which is highly unlikely as he was only thirteen at the most.

In summer 1017, Emma returned to England to marry her stepson's successor Cnut. Much has been made of her 'Viking' allegiance as a Norman and her preference of the successful warlord and talented administrator Cnut to the incompetent failure Aethelred, with due note of her failure to promote her sons by Aethelred and the probable psychological effect on the abandoned Edward. In practical terms, the shrewd and ambitious Emma had made a brilliant match which restored her as queen and gave much-needed legitimacy to Cnut; the latter would not have been likely to tolerate Emma's sons, potential centres of plots, at his court. Edward and Alfred remained in exile for all Cnut's reign, and despite the subsequent legends is unlikely to have seriously considered a monastic career; he was able and ready to fight in 1035. He probably spent his youth at the court of Emma's brother Richard II (to 1027) and nephews Duke Richard III and Robert (to 1035), training as a knight – he brought in Norman knights and military tactics to fight the Welsh in the 1040s and clearly knew their advantages. He also seems to have spent time at Jumieges Abbey and acquired clerical friends and an appreciation of Continental religious developments.

When Cnut died late in 1035 leaving two young sons, one by Emma, he assembled enough supporters to sail to England; Duke Robert had recently died on pilgrimage to Jerusalem and the insecure regency for his son William had enough problems that the initiative was clearly Edward's; he had the influence to gather armed followers. He was en route to his mother's dower-city of Winchester when he landed at Southampton, but he was refused admission and driven back to his ships after a clash; it is unclear if his landing was intended at the throne. His mother was backing her son by Cnut, Harthacnut, who was absent in Denmark, against Cnut's (illegitimate?) son Harold who had the backing of Mercia and Northumbria; either Emma or her ally Earl Godwin of Wessex, gave orders to drive Edward away. His brother Alfred had landed in Kent with his followers, possibly in coordination with Edward, to head for Winchester via the Pilgrim's Way; he was intercepted by Godwin, promised the Earl's support, and then treacherously seized in his overnight lodgings at

Guildford and handed over to Harold to be (fatally) blinded. This was supposed to have poisoned Edward's relationship with Godwin, his chief minister in 1042–51, though this may be subsequent guesswork based on their quarrel in 1051. Emma, unable to hold Wessex for Harthacnut, fled to Bruges (principal sea-port of Flanders and a potential source of naval support) and Harold took over all England. Edward seems to have visited Emma at Bruges in 1039 and used her to form a relationship with Harthacnut. Normandy had fallen into anarchy and no support could be expected there; however, Harold's death in March 1040 led to the peaceful recall of Harthacnut before his planned invasion. The new king recalled Edward in 1041, logically as his (temporary) heir as he was still unmarried, and his surprise death at a banquet on 8 June 1042 led to the principal nobles electing Edward as the new king. The principal backer of his cause was Earl Godwin, Emma's close ally. In return for confirming Godwin in office and ignoring the unanswered questions about the killing of his brother Alfred in 1036, the new king received a valuable war-galley from the earl – possibly seen as a form of 'weregild' for the murder. The *Vitae Aedwardi Regis* commissioned by Edward's wife Edith claimed that her father Godwin served Edward as loyally as David served Saul, and was treated just as ungratefully – somewhat of an exaggeration, not least as Godwin was the elder by about a decade.

The last of his dynasty apart from Edmund's exiled sons, Edward was inexperienced in government and had not been in England long; after a twenty-year exile he lacked knowledge or established support, though temperamentally he was probably not as averse to the military duties of kingship as hagiographers later implied. He commanded fleets in the 1040s. Given his inexperience and his own lack of English associates, he inevitably relied on the veteran Godwin and the other two principal administrators and commanders on whom local government had devolved, Earls Leofric of Mercia (an Englishman) and Siward of Northumbria (either Danish or an Anglo-Dane). The creation of a small tier of senior earls, viceroys of large regions, to replace the earlier multitude of county ealdormen under Cnut (often abroad) had reflected his needs, but now placed local patronage and authority under powerful figures. Edward's reliance on a few earls, all Cnut's men, was inevitable and he was to promote Godwin's elder two sons, Swein (western and southern Mercia) and Harold (East Anglia), and nephew Beorn (the north-eastern and south-eastern Danelaw). The monopoly of new earldoms in one family heightened his reliance on the Godwins, as did his marriage to Godwin's daughter Edith in January 1045, and there have been questions as to its wisdom and over whether Edward was unwillingly bullied into it. He rid himself of the family, Edith included, in 1051, so had he been forced to make the concessions – and did his childlessness imply that he deliberately avoided sexual relations with Edith to prevent Godwin dominating his own grandchildren, the next rulers? Later eleventh- and twelfth-century stories claimed Edward remained celibate as an act of holiness, but this may have been subsequent guesswork as well as appropriate behaviour for a potential saint. Modern writers have claimed that Edward was homosexual, or that he had a difficult relationship with all women due to his neglect by Emma (who was briefly arrested and stripped of her property in November 1043, apparently for alleged plotting with King Magnus of Norway about an invasion). But there were complex manoevures in English politics in the 1040s, and it is not impossible that Emma resented her exclusion from influence by her son and, as the widow of Cnut with treasure and bodyguards to hand, contacted the greatest current Scandinavian warlord, Magnus. Alleged to have been promised Harthacnut's Denmark (and England?) by the late king, and currently overrunning Denmark to evict Cnut's and Godwin's nephew Swein Estrithson (Earl Beorn's brother), Magnus posed a constant threat in the mid-1040s. Edward led his fleet in person at Sandwich to await him several years running and the chronicler Adam of Bremen claimed that he named Swein as his heir in *c*. 1043, though he refused Godwin (Swein's uncle)'s request for direct aid. Luckily Magnus died in 1047 (allegedly foreseen by Edward); his military threat may lie behind Edward's reliance on the Godwin family and several contemporary banishments, e.g Osgod Clapa's. In 1049, Edward also used his fleet at Sandwich to assist the Emperor Henry III in a naval blockade aimed at the latter's rebel vassal Count Baldwin of Flanders, an ally of Godwin's and soon to marry his daughter to Godwin's younger son Tostig. Edward also brought in his sister Goda's eldest son by her first marriage, Ralph of the Vexin, as an earl in south-western Mercia and may well have thought of him as a possible heir.

The king remained childless and the question of the succession may be connected to the visit to his court in 1051 by his sister Goda's second husband, Count Eustace of Boulogne. The count's entourage had an affray with townsmen in Dover on his return journey over lodgings, and Edward ordered their lord, Godwin, to punish them; he refused and raised his and his elder sons' earldoms' armies in revolt. Tension had been rising between Edward and Godwin, particularly over the king's choice of a Norman, Robert of Jumieges, bishop of London, as his new Archbishop of Canterbury (instead of a Godwin client, the Canterbury monk Aelfric). Edward had brought in a few other Continental clerics – not all Normans – as bishops (e.g. Giso of Wells, 1047) and minor clerics in recent years, but this did not amount to embryonic Normanisation of the English Church; he mostly promoted royal household clerics (such as Cynesige, the new Archbishop of York in 1050), as had his ancestors and Cnut. There was little sign of sympathy with the 'reformist' zeal of Pope Leo. An evidently worldly English client of Godwin's, who was also the king's goldsmith, Abbot Spearhafoc of Abingdon – hardly a 'reformist' candidate – was promoted to London in 1051 when Robert was given Canterbury. Some historians believe that the Church was somewhat intellectually and administratively stagnant (as did the Normans after 1066) and Edward, aware of overseas developments from long experience, sought to reverse this.

There were military reasons for bringing in a few Norman knights to test out their military skills (and castles) against the resurgent Welsh in Herefordshire, as Edward did with Osbern Pentecost and Richard (of Richard's Castle); the first castles in England thus preceded 1066. Earl Swein had been (temporarily) exiled for abducting the abbess of Leominster on his way back from a campaign in Dyfed in 1046 and replaced by Harold, and Beorn had been murdered by Swein in a notorious incident in 1049 while trying to persuade him to call off a pirate campaign against the king in the Channel. Edward had forgiven Swein at Godwin's and Ealdred's behest despite the rape and the murder, and the crisis of September 1051 blew up unexpectedly, although he took full advantage of it. Godwin and his sons, based at Beverstone on the Cotswold ridge, confronted Edward's court at Gloucester, but Leofric and Siward joined the king and the outnumbered Godwin had to agree to a peace conference. His military support seems to have ebbed, as when the court and the armies arrived in London the king, in the city, was able to face down the Godwins at Southwark. Allegedly Edward promised to pardon Godwin when he brought him his brother Alfred and his companions, betrayed and murdered by the Earl's actions in 1036; if this is not pro-Norman propaganda it showed that he still bore resentment despite the Earl's exoneration of the charge in 1042/3. The entire Godwin family was exiled, evidently with the other earls' backing. The first literary account of the crisis, the *Vita* of c. 1067 (written for Edith), claims that Edward usually relied on the faithful Godwin dynasty but was persuaded to exile them by evil counsellors led by Archbishop Robert; as Robert apparently wanted the king to remarry, Edith was hostile to his reputation.

The confrontation of autumn 1051 could be said to have given control of England to Edward for the first time, and he proceeded to split up the Godwin earldoms among his own supporters (Leofric's son Aelfgar received East Anglia, and Ralph received Hereford). A few more Norman clerics were promoted, such as Bishop William of London, and the queen was sent to a nunnery – either to Wilton, a royal residence and school, or to the stricter Wherwell. Sending her away was possibly the first step in a divorce, as allegedly urged by Archbishop Robert (who thus wanted the king to have a son, not for his fellow-Norman William to succeed). Alternatively, Edward may have feared she would pass on secrets to her family. The events of 1066 cloud our knowledge of the supposed visit to court by William, Edward's kinsman and already apparent as a vigorous and talented ruler; did Edward promise him the heirship as William's writers later claimed? Did the visit, unrecorded in all but one (the 'Worcester') version of the *Anglo-Saxon Chronicle*, take place at all? (Some historians even think this one mention is a post-1066 addition.) Edward apparently gave William captive relations of Godwin as hostages (unless Archbishop Robert kidnapped them later in 1052), but in practical terms he (like Aethelred) needed Norman support to offset naval attack. The Godwins were at large in Flanders and raising ships, and William was married to a daughter of Count Baldwin (as was Godwin's son Tostig) and could influence him. But when Godwin crossed to the South Coast to raid in June/July 1052 and Harold brought another fleet from Dublin, raiding

Somerset en route to joining his father off Wight, Edward's fleet under Earls Ralph and Odda at Sandwich was outmatched. He had no experienced military commanders except his senior earls to match the Godwins (who had some Wessex backing?), and seems to have suffered (like his father) from poor morale, poor commanders and defections. The Godwin fleet sailed into the Thames unhindered, the Godwins landed at Southwark with apparent reinforcements from within Wessex, and when Earls Leofric and Siward joined Edward in London they persuaded – or forced – him to pardon the Godwin family and return their earldoms. (Swein was on pilgrimage and soon died there, so Ralph kept Hereford.) The Norman clerics fled, apparently with some Normans given lands in Herefordshire and other Frenchmen at court; Archbishop Robert was illegally replaced by a Godwin candidate, Bishop Stigand of Winchester.

The flight of Archbishop Robert back to Normandy probably resulted in him making mischief for his Godwin enemies with Duke William, with long-term results; he may have taken Earl Godwin's hostage son Wulfnoth and grandson Haakon to the Norman court and he may have (falsely?) told William that Edward wished him to be the next king of England but was constrained by the Godwins from acting on it. William of Poitiers, one of the main Norman chroniclers and a vehement supporter of the legitimacy of his duke's claim to be heir in 1066, has it that (presumably after Godwin's return) Edward required Godwin, Leofric, Siward, and Stigand to swear an oath to accept the duke as the next king, and then Archbishop Robert took the news to the duke. In fact, the archbishop fled England before Godwin's return.

The desertion of the senior earls, the only men with the troops and skill to match the Godwins, left Edward helpless in late summer 1052 and showed up the weakness of the monarchy. His personal clientage and popular support was insufficient to meet the threat, though the purge of senior English nobles by Cnut and the creation of the new 'super-earldoms' was ultimately to blame rather than Edward's weakness. He had attempted to restore the monarch's power and centrality in patronage in 1051–2, and might have succeeded had Leofric and Siward been prepared to back him fully; it is possible that his promotions of Frenchmen had been exploited by the Godwins to rouse popular feeling and increase defections within the army and fleet. But Edward was far from a puppet after 1052, although he had to adhere to Godwin's demands and accept Edith back, and luckily Godwin died in April 1053. The extent of Edward's grudge against Godwin over Alfred's death (they were supposedly quarrelling over it when Godwin had a stroke) and desire to seek revenge has been muddied by later legend. But Edward's relationship with Harold, who succeeded to Wessex and became chief minister and commander-in-chief, was clearly better and the government from 1053–66 was more harmonious. The king took no more part in warfare, but there he had never commanded a land campaign earlier either.

Harold now took the lead in warfare against Gruffydd ap Llewelyn of Gwynedd, who had seized Dyfed in 1055 to reunite the Welsh kingdoms and posed a major military threat. Ralph proved a poor commander, losing his only recorded battle, as did the fighting Bishop Leofgar of Hereford, and with Hereford sacked and the Welsh annexing part of Herefordshire, Harold took over the earldom on Ralph's death (1057) and drove the enemy back. His final, brilliant Gwynedd campaign of 1063, launched in mid-winter, saw the enemy heartland ravaged until Llewelyn's men killed him and sent his head to Harold seeking peace; the late ruler's half-brothers became English clients. Welsh unity was ended and English power restored to its optimum tenth-century position of overlordship of a divided people. In the north, Edward had given sanctuary to the refugee princes Malcolm and Donald Ban of Scotland, sons of King Duncan (killed 1040), and it would have been Edward's orders that led to intervention to restore them. In 1054 Siward marched into Scotland to defeat King Macbeth and probably restore Lothian and/or Strathclyde to Malcolm, who the English were to regard as Edward's client and vassal, and in 1057–8 the latter finally killed Macbeth and his stepson Lulach. Edward's generals thus defeated strong warlords in both Wales and Scotland and installed English allies, presenting an advantageous military predominance which Duke William could build on after 1066. Crucially, Edward had introduced Norman cavalry and castles (which gave the English extra military strength in the next centuries) to the Welsh battle-front, even though they were only a minor element – and ineffective – in his reign.

The evidence of administrative documents shows that Edward did not retire into holy works, principally building his new Abbey of St Peter adjacent to his palace at Westminster, and let Harold run the adminstration. (The abbey's illustration in the Bayeux Tapestry shows it to have been modelled on Jumieges.) He remained an active administrator though there were fewer foreign appointments, and seems to have been personally active as a huntsman well into the 1060s. Nor is it clear that he regarded either Harold or William as his heir, as their supporters alleged. Edith seems to have been treated as a daughter not a wife, and may have been barren. In 1054 Edward sent his leading diplomat, Bishop Ealdred of Worcester (also Archbishop of York from 1060, in defiance of canon law rules against pluralism), to Germany on a mission including a search for the missing sons of Edmund, Edward's nearest family apart from Goda's half-foreign sons. Edward 'the Exile' was located in Hungary, where he and his late brother Edmund had accompanied the successful invasion of exiled Prince Andrew from their mutual patron Yaroslav of Russia's court in 1046. Edward the Exile was invited home, but he died just after his arrival in London in 1057, leaving a baby son and two daughters; he may have been poisoned by a rival (Harold or William?). Ralph died in 1057, leaving family who were passed over, and his brother Walter ended up imprisoned (1063) and possibly murdered by Duke William. It is possible that Edward turned to Edward the Exile out of disappointment at the military incompetence of his intended successor Earl Ralph, and it is likely that if the Exile (aged around forty when he died) had been alive in 1066, neither Harold nor William would ever have become king.

Siward's death in 1055 led to the experiment of installing a court favourite with no local connections, Harold's brother Tostig, as earl of Northumbria. Probably backed by Edith as well as Harold, this added to royal control as well as Godwin military power; it is not clear that it was to Harold's rather than the king's benefit, and thus part of a plan to control the kingdom. Harold was probably behind the banishment of Leofric's son Aelfgar, now ruling East Anglia again since Godwin's death, in 1055; he allied with Gruffydd ap Llewelyn, defeated the royal army in Herefordshire, and forced his recall. He succeeded Leofric as earl of Mercia in 1057 (Harold's brother Gyrth thus took over East Anglia), was banished again in 1058, and fought his way back aided by the Welsh and probably a Norwegian mercenary force. He then died around 1062/4, and was succeeded by his son Edwin. Much effort has been concentrated on the way the Godwins were able to regain their earldoms by force in 1052, but Aelfgar's success is equally significant. Great earls in exile were thrice able to outface the king – a sign of the weakness of the central institutions, and of local loyalty by the regions' warriors to earl rather than king? If Aelfgar had been alive in 1066, it is probable that he would have opposed Harold taking the throne.

The military success of 1063 in Wales restored the domination of England in southern Britain, with a tried and well-motivated army which was to fight two major battles in three weeks hundreds of miles apart in 1066. In 1065 another war broke out with the south Welsh kingdom of Glamorgan/Morgannwg, after a raid on a hunting-lodge that Harold (as earl of Hereford) was building in Gwent at Portskewett for the king. But the reign ended in another internal military and political crisis, as in 1065 a Northumbrian revolt deposed the allegedly oppressive Earl Tostig in his absence. Even the *Life* of the king composed for Edith, a source sympathetic to Tostig, who she may have preferred to Harold, admitted he could be harsh and thoughtless in his zeal for justice; he apparently introduced new, West Saxon laws to the north and was also subject to blood-feuds for executing prominent nobles (two at his court in 1065, despite a safe-conduct.) A claimant to the earldom called Cospatrick, from the line of the early eleventh-century Earl Uhtred, the 'Bamburgh kindred' who had ruled Bernicia from *c*. 885 to 960, was murdered at the king's court in December 1064; Edith and Tostig were supposed to have been behind it.

The rebels chose Earl Edwin's brother Morcar, an untried youth, as their new earl, winning Mercian military support as they marched south ravaging (October 1065); Harold met them at Oxford and agreed to accept their wishes and have Tostig exiled. Whether or not he had his own motives in removing Tostig ahead of a struggle for the crown is unknown, but the surrender made Edward violently angry and it is possible that this brought on his final illness within a few weeks. Another enigmatic episode of the years 1064–5 is the supposed visit Harold made to Normandy, as recounted in the Bayeux Tapestry and in Norman – but not English – sources. The Norman writers after 1066 said Edward required Harold to take an oath to William as heir, to arrange a smooth succession; the Tapestry (made by English workers under Norman supervision) is silent, but shows Edward warning Harold. Alternatively, it is suggested that Harold was blown ashore in Normandy accidentally during a storm, or went to negotiate his hostage kinsmen's release despite Edward's warnings not to trust William. The episode is hardly likely to have been invented, but there is no proof that Edward ever looked on William as his heir except (at most) in 1051-2. The *Life* written for Edith says that Edward's health declined after Tostig's exile, in his depression or rage at not being able to help him. He was too ill to attend the dedication of Westminster Abbey on 28 December 1065, although he was only a few hundred yards away in his palace, and after a short illness he died on the following 4 January. He apparently raved about forthcoming destruction for his people in his final delirium, and recovered enough to bequeath the protection of his kingdom to Harold (as all sources, English and Norman, agree). This was interpreted by all except the pro-Edith *Life* as nominating him as heir, and Harold thus took it and was duly elected king on 5 January, immediately after Edward's burial in the abbey. He was crowned the following day. In practical terms, Tostig, his eventual patron King Harald 'Hardradi' of Norway, and Duke William could all be expected to invade in 1066 and Harold's 'legitimate' rival, Edgar Atheling (son of Edward the Exile), was at most around fourteen; the kingdom needed a proven adult war-leader. Edward probably (not certainly) meant Harold as king rather than regent for Edgar.

Edward was probably aged sixty to sixty-two, the oldest surviving king of his line since Egbert. The disasters that followed made his reign seem a golden age, English and Normans used him retrospectively for propaganda, and the campaign to raise Westminster Abbey's legal status (and revenue from pilgrims) in the twelfth century annexed its founder as its centrepiece. The statesman, politician and leader was sidelined in favour of the saint, and the miraculous stories of the reign were built up. Some were already extant by the biography, *Vita Aedwardi Regis*, soon after his death, represented his widow's desired image of him, and are more likely to be true; others were clearly invented. The biography also hinted at his holy chastity, while including his secular enthusiasm for hunting. Edward, who seems to have been the first royal to touch for the king's evil and clearly appreciated the sacral elements of kingship (from experience in France) as well as the Church, was supposed to have had the gift of foresight, to have seen a vision of Christ at the Mass, and to have been visited by Saint John the Evangelist disguised as a pilgrim. (The site of this was supposed to have been his Essex hunting-lodge at Havering-atte-Bower.) The first of his miraculous healings was recorded in the *Vita Aedwardi Regis* so the embryonic cult was underway soon after 1066, but it was extended by the writings of Osbert de Clare in the early twelfth century and in 1102 his body was found to be incorrupt like that of a saint. Osbert, as prior of Westminster, wrote an updated *Vita* of the king and succeeded in interesting the visiting papal legate,

Alberic, in Edward's cause in 1138; but his own mission to Rome to plead for canonization in 1139 failed. Thanks to support from the new Angevin dynasty, however, in 1161 Edward was canonised, the Plantagenet monarchy finding an ancestral saintly king a prestigious political tool; there was probably a deliberate attempt to upstage the French royal sanctuary at St Denis by promoting a king who was also a saint. The monks of Westminster Abbey played up their link with him and thus their important role in the subsequent coronations, and their abbot kept the coronation regalia – still centred around Saint Edward's Crown 900 years later – at the abbey.

Edgar Atheling's sister Margaret's marriage to Edward's protégé Malcolm III of Scotland brought the lineage of his dynasty back into the Norman royal family when Henry I (who made much of Edward's reign as his supposed model) married their daughter Edith/Matilda. Edward appears on the Wilton Diptych of *c*. 1380 as co-patron of Richard II. In terms of kingship his power was circumscribed by his earls, as was made apparent through the 1050s, and some parallels can be drawn with his father's character and misfortunes; Aethelred too was prone to sudden banishments, defiance by senior officials, and military reverses. But Edward had arrived home in 1041 without experience or a solid base of support, and had to operate in a system created by and for a very different man, Cnut. Unlike Edgar and Aethelred II, he did not have a numerous, strong and cohesive hereditary nobility at his command (as his failure to halt Godwin's comeback in 1052 showed). His reduction of his fleet in the late 1040s arguably made it easier for the Godwins to invade in 1052, but he could not have foreseen that and the heavy level of fleet-taxes imposed by Cnut was deeply resented. His survival as king for twenty-three years despite his lack of English background or training in 1042 was in itself tribute to his qualities.

EDITH (EADGYTH) (Queen/'Lady' of England, 1045–66) The only daughter of Godwin with five brothers, she was probably in her late teens when her father married her to King Edward on 23 January 1045. One of the three great earls who dominated a new sovereign who had lived much of his life in exile and the governor of Wessex, Godwin aimed at placing his grandchildren on the throne. Edith's youth, beauty, good education and skill at embroidery were all said to have recommended her. According to one version Edith was anointed and crowned at her marriage. The king, probably more than twenty-five years older than his wife, is supposed, by his first hagiographer (in the *Vitae Aedwardi* commissioned by Edith *c*. 1067), to have been a reluctant husband who vowed to remain chaste. This may be a guess due to his lack of children, inflated by his later holy reputation and efforts to prove him a virgin by supporters of his twelfth-century candidacy for sainthood. The absence of children may be down to impotency not design, but it has been suggested that he sought to deny Godwin's family the dynastic power which they would obtain over his son as king. There is no hint of any tension between husband and wife in the sources, least of all that her worldliness contrasted with his sharply divergent devoutness.

When he exiled Godwin and his sons in 1051, he separated from Edith. This had adequate political motives; she might pass information to the exiles and Edward's Norman Archbishop of Canterbury, the Godwins' foe, canvassed for a new queen. The fact that Edith was sent to a (high-status) nunnery may indicate a move to divorce her and make her a nun. She either went to Wilton nunnery, a normal residence for royal females in retirement with a school where she was probably educated, or to the stricter Wherwell; the sources disagree on how much of her wealth she was allowed to keep. Her husband's biographer, probably working at her direction, emphasised the mitigating honours; the versions in the *Chronicle* imply that she was stripped of almost all her wealth and attendants. She was restored to court and her royal role when the Godwin family fought their way back to power in summer 1052.

Thereafter she remained secure as the king's wife and favoured companion, though there were no children in the remaining years of marriage; their relationship was subsequently presented as non-sexual and as 'father' and 'daughter'. As she was the commissioner of Edward's first biography (the *Vita Aedwardi Regis*), we can take it that its picture of her as a loyal and devoted wife, a pious and generous religious patron, and a supporter of learning was that which she wished to portray. Her extensive interests in diverse subjects and in education were regarded as noteworthy. The portrayal of her in the *Vita Aedwardi* as more worldly and concerned with the pomp of majesty than her husband may be symbolic, but the sources are clear that she was touchy of her dignity and active in protecting her interests and favourites. While Edward was building his great new church at Westminster, she was rebuilding a companion church for Wilton nunnery, dedicated in 1065, and was remembered as coveting relics from other institutions to add to its prestige.

Edith's support for her brother Harold as the king's effective deputy in 1053–65 is undoubted, but there may have been a closer personal relationship with her brother Tostig, earl of Northumbria in 1055–65. She is supposed to have looked after his interests at court, and was later reported by Florence of Worcester as responsible when Tostig's Northumbrian rival Cospatric, scion of the dynasty which usually occupied the earldom, was murdered at court in December 1064. The revolt which drove Tostig out in summer 1065 followed; Edith's backing may have enabled him to block critics' complaints and so increased local anger. The failure – or unwillingness? – of Harold to force a confrontation with the rebels, and the king's acceptance of their candidate as earl and exile of Tostig, would have been a major blow. The Norman chronicler William of Poitiers goes so far as to say that Edith was so furious with Harold that she preferred William as successor, but this is unsupported by English writers. At the king's death a few months later on 5 January 1066 she was present at his bedside, warming his feet, and was addressed as his 'daughter'. She then retired to Winchester, the traditional dower of late Saxon queens, as her predecessor Emma had done. There is no reason to suppose that this marked any cooling of relations with Harold due to resentment at his failure to back Tostig in 1065, or that Edith had any involvement with the latter's subsequent invasion. She surrendered Winchester when the Norman army arrived in late October or November 1066, and was permitted to keep her dower lands for her lifetime. She played no known part in any of the subsequent revolts, even that in the south-west in 1068 involving her mother Gytha and Harold's elder sons; the *Vitae Aedwardi Regis*, the biography stated to be designed to win her favour and possibly commissioned by her, may have been her main concern. It portrayed her as the ideal wise, pious, and peace-loving queen, an inspiration to all women. She died on 18 December 1075, aged probably in her late forties, and was buried at Westminster Abbey with her husband by permission of King William.

HAROLD (II) GODWINSON (Earl of East Anglia, 1043-51, 1052-3; of Wessex, 1053-66; King of England, 1066) The second son of Earl Godwin and Gytha, born around 1022; the date may have been a year or two earlier or later. His father was probably the son of the senior Sussex thegn Wulfnoth 'Cild', who commanded Aethelred II's fleet in 1009, but was exiled in a plot and turned pirate; his mother was the daughter of the Danish jarl Thorgils Sprakaleg and sister of Jarl Ulf, temporarily a close confidante of Cnut. Despite later Norman sneers about Godwin being low-born the family were probably from the nobility, long based in West Sussex around their main estate at Bosham, though a later theory that Wulfnoth's father Aethelmaer was son of the chronicler Aethelweard and descendant of King Aethelred I seems unlikely. (In the later twelfth century, Walter Map alleged that Godwin was a crafty, social-climbing cowherd.) By the time of Harold's birth his father was a senior commander of Cnut's (possibly transferring from Edmund Ironside's service), and had recently distinguished himself in a war against the Wends in the Baltic. One unproveable story, by William of Malmesbury, *c.* 1125, had it that Godwin had a first wife, Cnut's unnamed sister, who indulged in slave-trading; this may be a mistake. Harold was probably called after his father's Danish patron's grandfather, King Harald Bluetooth; his elder brother Swein was called after Cnut's father, Swein Forkbeard. By around 1020 Godwin was earl of at least part of Wessex, the senior southern Saxon in Cnut's service, and he later became earl of the whole province – thus diverting patronage and loyalty from the direct service of the king, who before 1016 had not alienated this level of power in his 'home' territory. Godwin is also referred to as a senior household official of Cnut's, possibly his bailiff/administrator.

In 1043 Harold was adult enough to become an earl like his elder brother Swein, and received East Anglia where he showed the family's acquisitiveness, building up a substantial landed base (mainly in Essex and Suffolk). He acquired a mistress or common-law wife of renowned beauty, Eadgyth/Edith 'Swan-

Neck', by whom he had three sons (adult by 1068) and two daughters. In 1047 his brother's exile for ravishing the abbess of Leominster probably led to his acquiring Swein's earldom of Hereford and certainly a share in Swein's estates, which he refused to return when the exile sought his reinstatement. This may have sparked off the fatal episode in which the furious Swein, allowed to call on the king at Sandwich to negotiate his return, turned on, kidnapped, and murdered his and Harold's cousin Beorn, Harold's then ally and brother of King Swein Estrithson of Denmark. Swein was pardoned in 1051 after his father's intercession after agreeing to go on pilgrimage to Jerusalem, but never had a chance to demand his earldom back as he died en route home in Anatolia; Harold was left as the presumed heir to Wessex. In autumn 1051 Harold brought his levies to aid his father in the confrontation with the king near Gloucester, and then to the council in London where the family were abandoned by their fellow earls and exiled.

Unlike Godwin, Harold headed west to take ship for Dublin, joined by his younger brother Leofwine – evidently to seek shipping for an invasion. He allied with and received ships from King Diarmait, the link he set up with Diarmait probably lasting to the latter's aid to his sons in 1068, and in 1052 he returned to raid up the Bristol Channel but was defeated at the River Parret by the local levies. He sailed round into the Channel to link up with his father's fleet from Flanders, and the Godwin force was able to proceed unopposed to the Thames to land at Southwark. Backed this time by Earls Leofric and Siward, the family had their lands and earldoms returned; Swein's death on pilgrimage prevented any dispute between him and Harold. Leofric's son, Aelfgar, given East Anglia in 1051, was deprived and turned out to be Harold's main enemy in the next decade.

In April 1053 Godwin died and Harold succeeded to Wessex as the premier earl in England; Aelfgar was restored to East Anglia until his father Leofric died in 1057, when he received Mercia and Harold's brother Gyrth took East Anglia over. In 1055 the death, without adult heirs, of Siward led to Harold's next brother Tostig taking Northumbria, where he had no local connections and his forceful (harsh?) rule was only temporarily able to assert central power over the turbulent, particularist nobles. Harold was to add Hereford to his lands on the death of Earl Ralph in December 1057, and the collection of earldoms make it seem that the house of Godwin were dominating patronage in the kingdom. Harold's collection of lands, mainly in central/eastern Wessex (centred on his family esates at Bosham, Sussex), south-eastern Mercia, and East Anglia, are listed in the Domesday Book and show him as by far the richest subject in England after the king. Unlike Godwin, his relationship with Edward seems to have been harmonious and the king relied on him throughout 1053–66 as his chief minister. Harold's desire for the succession to the childless king has been muddied by post-1066 Norman propaganda, and there is no contemporary suggestion that he poisoned Edward's recently-returned nephew Edward the

Exile in 1057 to improve his chances. The latter's infant son Edgar was still a potential rival, though his chances of being elected until majority were lesser. Harold was probably behind the two attempts to remove his family's rival Aelfgar from the political reckoning. In 1055 the earl was exiled, but fought his way back with the aid of Gwynedd, invading like Godwin had done and defeating local levies in Herefordshire, and in 1058 (now governing Mercia) he was exiled but won his earldom back with a Welsh and Norse army. Harold also travelled to the Continent late in 1056 to negotiate with his brother Tostig's brother-in-law Baldwin of Flanders and arrange the return of Edward the Exile from Hungary.

Harold founded the Abbey of the Holy Cross at Waltham in Essex (dedicated 1060) on lands he had acquired, probably modelling the church on that at Westminster. The foundation was based on the cult of a black crucifix discovered on the Somerset estate of Waltham's previous owner, the son of the exiled thegn Tofi the Proud (at whose banquet King Harthacnut had died in 1042), and the dedication of the new church was attended by the king and prominent nobles and bishops. In 1058 Harold went to Rome in company with the archbishop the Godwins had illegally foisted on Canterbury in 1052, Stigand. The latter duly received his pallium and the questionable status of his episcopate was ended; unfortunately Pope Benedict, who had granted it, was soon deposed and his acts anathematised. Stigand's status remained a major embarrassment and was duly played up by the Normans (countrymen of the archbishop who Godwin had evicted) as evidence of Harold's blatant illegalities and defiance of the new, reformed Roman Church.

Harold's main concerns were military, with (Aelfgar's ally) Gruffydd ap Llewelyn having reunited Gwynedd/Powys with Deheubarth and his aggressive Welsh state raiding Herefordshire. The Welsh had not been halted by the new French knights with their cavalry and castles, Earl Ralph was a poor commander prone to defeat, and in autumn 1055 Harold had to bring troops to the rescue after the exiled Aelfgar and Gruffydd defeated Ralph and sacked Hereford. A second major attack in 1056 led to the death in battle of the new Bishop Leofgar, Harold's personal chaplain; as in 1055, Harold had to negotiate a treaty from an unfavourable position and this time Gruffydd was recognised as ruler of all Wales. Harold took over the earldom of Hereford on Ralph's death late in 1057 and preserved the frontier, but was only able to strike back early in 1063 when he launched a mid-winter cavalry attack on Gruffydd's court at Rhuddlan. The ruler escaped but the sack of his palace was a humiliation, and in spring 1063 Harold ravaged the Welsh coasts by sea while Tostig marched into Gwynedd by land. Gruffydd fled into the mountains, and the defenders were worn down until in desperation some of Gruffydd's men killed him to secure peace and sent his head to Harold. Gruffydd's half-brothers (Bleddyn and Rhiwallon) succeeded to the north as Harold's vassals while the local dynasties returned to Deheubarth and Morgannwg, and all Gruffydd's gains of 1056 were returned.

This major success established Harold's military reputation and gave England the dominance which the Norman barons were able to use to annex new lands after 1066, although a raid from Morgannwg on Harold's new hunting-lodge at Portskewett, Gwent, in 1065 showed that frontier attacks were not over.

The question of the succession dominates interpretations of Harold's behaviour in 1064–5, and the nature of the sources adds problems. Different interpretations have been suggested for the visit Harold made to Normandy which opens the Bayeux Tapestry, some writers suggesting it never took place. Harold may have been driven across the Channel by a gale while out fishing (according to the early twelfth-century English chronicler Eadmer) or been blown off his intended route, but it is more likely that he intended to go to Normandy (though not on a mission to confirm Edward's grant of the succession to Duke William). He may have been negotiating to free his youngest brother Wulfnoth and his nephew, Swein's son Haakon, left behind on the family's exile in 1051 and handed over to William by Archbishop Robert as hostages – and he may have ignored Edward's request not to go. The Bayeux Tapestry, generally believed to have been produced in the 1070s, possibly by Canterbury craftsmen, for Bishop Odo of Bayeux and broadly presenting the Norman interpretation of events, has the king apparently sending him to Normandy but warning or telling him off on his return, as though events had not gone to plan. He was driven ashore on the coast, east of Normandy, of William's vassal, Count Guy of Ponthieu, who held him prisoner until William forced his release; then Harold accompanied William on an expedition into Brittany and earned distinction for his bravery, saving soldiers from quicksands at Mont-St-Michel.

William knighted him, which in terms of Norman custom made him his 'man' and vassal, and before he allowed Harold to return home he persuaded him to swear an oath to support and assist his succession, probably at Rouen (Orderic Vitalis' account). The Tapestry places it at Bayeux, and William of Poitiers places it at Bonneville-sur-Touques. The uncertainty over the site and circumstances argues that it was in private, and it was subsequently alleged that Harold had not realised that there were holy relics under the table on which he was taking the oath until shown them afterwards; his breach of the oath could be portrayed by the Normans as blasphemy as well as perjury. He is supposed to have agreed to marry William's daughter ('Agatha', who did not actually exist) and to hold Dover 'castle', presumably the pre-Norman Roman fortifications, to hand to the duke when the latter succeeded Edward (according to William of Poitiers). He also supposedly promised to marry his sister Aelfgifu/Aelgiva to a prominent Norman; she may be the enigmatic woman of that name shown being gestured at by a cleric on the Tapestry, but it is unclear if she was with him, and if so what she would be doing on an embassy (let alone a 'fishing-trip'). According to Eadmer, c. 1115, Edward complained to Harold on his return that he had allowed the duke to trap him into giving too much away; is this the reason for the men's confrontation in the Tapestry? The absence of the entire visit from the latter may be due to its relatively secret, low-key, or embarrassing nature or just to a temporary lapse in the chroniclers' usually full coverage of events in 1062-4.

Back in England, in August 1065, a revolt in Northumbria expelled the unpopular Tostig, who was accused of extortion and of murdering prominent thegns; the earl was caught unawares while absent hunting with the king and his bodyguards left in York (presumably housecarls) were massacred. The rebels marched into Mercia, winning over the new earl (Aelfgar's son Edwin) by making his brother Morcar their new earl. Harold confronted them at Oxford, but accepted their demands and had Tostig exiled. The possibility has been raised that Tostig (a favourite of Harold's sister Queen Edith) was a potential rival, not supporter, of Harold for the succession and he was glad to be rid of him. But Harold may have reckoned that it was too dangerous to spill his men's blood in a hard-fought battle for such an unpopular figure; even if Tostig was restored to power, the loss of life would benefit England's enemies, not only William but the predatory King Harald of Norway. Tostig left England in a fury, and went to Flanders to prepare a counter-attack. The *Vita* of King Edward, written *c.* 1067 at Queen Edith's request, says that the quarrel between Harold and Tostig was the main reason for the disaster that befell England in 1066, breaking up Godwinson family unity, and describes Harold as more intelligent and calculating than his rash brother.

Edward's health declined after the debacle, and he died on 4 January 1066 at Westminster. He commended his kingdom to Harold, but did this explicitly mean the succession as opposed to regency for Edgar? The latter was, however, only around twelve to fourteen, and invasion loomed from Duke William, Tostig, and the veteran Norwegian warlord King Harald Hardradi; the councillors duly chose the greatest earl and most experienced warrior in England. He was crowned the next day, the first coronation in Westminster Abbey – by the canonically-acceptable Archbishop Ealdred of York, not Stigand, despite later Norman allegations. His overriding task was defence of the kingdom against his rivals and he won over the allegiance of Edwin and Morcar by setting aside Edith Swan-Neck (probably in spring 1066) to marry their sister Edith, widow of Gruffydd. The Normans alleged he abandoned his 1064 (?) engagement to William's daughter. According to John of Worcester, a Norman source normally hostile, he cancelled a number of bad laws and replaced unjust officials. His attitude to the Church as earl and king, using its patronage to promote loyalists like in secular matters, was condemned after 1066 when the Church was vigorously reformed; it was no worse than most contemporary rulers'. His fighting bishop Leofstan of 1056, and the abbots who fell leading their estates' levies at Hastings, were no worse than William's half-brother Odo of Bayeux.

Harold handed over Wessex to his brother Gyrth, and the latter was replaced by Leofwine in East Anglia (with Kent, Middlesex, and Surrey). Both William and Harald threatened invasion that summer, with a possible English naval sortie and clash, while Tostig (William's brother-in-law) raided the South and East Coasts without much effect, being driven off Norfolk and Lindsey, and then sailed north to Scotland to link up with his ally King Malcolm III. As the opportune timing had it, he could now join Harald's invading Norwegian armada in the Orkneys. As is well-known, the contrary north winds kept Duke William's fleet in Normandy that summer while Harald was able to sail south and invade the Humber. Harold kept watch with a large fleet and the county levies on the South Coast, but had to send his men home to take in the harvest on 8 September; the Norwegians and Tostig landed in the mouth of the Humber and set up camp at Riccall, at the start of the Roman road to York. The inexperienced Edwin and Morcar barred their march up the banks of the Ouse towards the city, but were defeated on 20 September at the battle of Gate Fulford; Harald seems to have concentrated his attack on the younger Morcar, and when his ranks broke, drove Edwin's Mercians into the river. The invaders took York, last in an invading Scandinavian's hands in 1016, but capital of the Viking kingdom from 867 to 954 and full of Norse-descended settlers, so hopefully welcoming to the Norse king.

Harold and his 'standing army' of housecarls, the veterans of the Welsh campaigns, marched north from London and took the invaders by surprise. Having secured the submission of Edwin and Morcar, King Harald of Norway and Tostig had moved on east to receive other submissions and were caught unawares on the banks of the Derwent at Stamford Bridge on 25 September. As recounted in Harald's saga, the Norse were caught unawares by the dust-cloud that marked the English advance and thought at first it was more local thegns come to surrender. Once they realised their error they had to scramble to get armed and formed in line while a solitary warrior held the Derwent bridge to hold up the attackers. The resulting battle was a conclusive English victory with thousands of invaders killed, among them both Harald (struck by an arrow as he charged according to his saga) and Tostig (the latter traditionally in combat with his brother in the final stages of the battle). According to the saga, before the battle a parley saw Harold offering to restore Tostig's lands if he abandoned his ally; King Harald asked what he would be offered and was told 'seven feet of English earth, for he is taller than other men'. Having pulled off as swift an advance as at Rhuddlan with a far larger army, Harold and his men now destroyed the main Scandinavian fighting machine under the era's premier warlord, a veteran of the Byzantine Varangian Guard who had first fought against Cnut's men at Stiklestadr in 1030; it ended the Sacndinavian claim to rule York, present since 865, permanently. The survivors under Harald's sons, fleeing to their ships at Riccall, were allowed to leave for home, but only filled about a dozen out of Harald's 300 ships.

The north winds that aided the Norwegian flight now brought Duke William's fleet into Pevensey Bay, probably on 27 September, and the other invader set about ravaging his rival's home county to lure him back for battle.

Given the contemporary geography of eastern Sussex, it would seem that he chose to occupy the Hastings peninsula (protected by Pevensey Bay to the west and river valleys to the north and east) as it was easy to seal off, with only one road into it from London along a narrow ridge; the resulting battle duly took place on this ridge. Harold hastened south, gathered as many men as possible in London in a brief halt, and pressed on to Sussex to halt more ravaging. Critics have argued that he should have rested his exhausted men longer, but in that case William might have broken out into Kent. The recent English losses in battle and exhaustion from the march gave William an advantage, and when the main English army and their local reinforcements reached the rendezvous at the 'Hoar Apple Tree' (probably on Caldbeck Hill, Battle) he launched a quick attack and forced battle on 14 October. The armies seem to have been well-matched in numbers, and it is a tribute to the English and their general that they nearly won despite having fought one major battle a fortnight earlier. Harold fought a defensive battle, his infantry shield-wall holding out on a steep ridge against repeated cavalry charges and showers of arrows, although part of his army disobeyed orders in charging downhill after a fake retreat by the Normans and being cut off and destroyed. The sun was waning when the Normans finally broke through, and another hour or so would have forced the invaders to fall back and preserved the English army until enough reinforcements arrived to given them a decisive advantage.

Harold was killed in the final attack late in the day, and this either accompanied or led to the flight of his remaining men. There is a dispute over whether the famous picture in the Tapestry showing a warrior with an arrow in his eye refers to him, or if the king is the man next to him being cut down by a cavalryman. Four Norman knights had apparently sworn to kill him and he was almost hacked to pieces as he lay injured, whether already fatally shot in the eye or not. He was probably between forty and forty-four. His body had to be identified by his ex-mistress/wife Edith Swan-Neck as his face was unrecognisable, and he was buried quietly at Waltham Abbey by his mother Gytha (according to William of Malmesbury) or on the cliffs at Dover by Duke William (according to Norman sources). An early twelfth-century Chester Abbey story alleged that he had survived and lived as a holy hermit into Henry I's reign; as the last Saxon king of England, he became a figure of heroic myth. In practical terms, the kingdom was probably lost at the battle of Hastings: in 1016 a similar disaster at Ashingdon had only led – temporarily – to its division between the loser and the victor, but then Edmund Ironside had survived the battle and now the English had no competent adult war-leader.

Duke William's army must have suffered substantial losses, so he was vulnerable until reinforcements arrived, but when the northern earls Edwin and Morcar – who had lost their last battle, at Gate Fulford, and had had to be rescued by Harold – reached London, they were too weak or hesitant to take the offensive. Edgar Atheling was proclaimed king in London by the earls and Archbishop Ealdred of York, but the earls could do no more than hold the city as William, having conquered Kent, arrived on the south bank of the Thames at Southwark. Probably the serious Northumbrian losses to the Norse at Gate Fulford (and to a lesser extent at Stamford Bridge) added to the defenders' hesitation, though William could not storm London Bridge and had to march upstream to cross the Thames at Wallingford. Once he had achieved the surrender of Winchester with the 'Lady'/ Queen Edith (and reinforcements from Normandy?) and he was on the north side of the Thames, the Atheling and the two earls came to Berkhamsted to surrender to him. Technically, Edgar was thus the last king of Anglo-Saxon England, albeit uncrowned, and was recognised as sovereign in London and Mercia and Northumbria for a few weeks; but the invaders prevailed inexorably once they had destroyed Harold and his army. The resistance, however, was far from over – and Edgar himself would flee to Scotland after the failure of a revolt in 1068, be reconciled to William, and still be alive as late as 1125.

Harold's sons (perhaps twins) by Edith of Mercia were born posthumously at Chester while his successor Edgar Atheling and the leading nobles were surrendering to William; his three illegitimate sons were to invade England from Dublin in 1068. His mother Gytha, who must have been at least in her mid- to late sixties, rallied the defence of Exeter against King William in the Devon revolt of 1068 and then escaped to Flatholm Island in the Bristol Channel and later to Flanders, probably on her grandsons' fleet from Dublin.

One of Harold's daughters by Edith Swan-Neck, Gunnhilde, ended up in Wilton nunnery; the other, Gytha, joined her grandmother in exile in Denmark, ruled by Gytha's brother Jarl Ulf's son, Swein Estrithson (who also invaded England in 1068). She ended up marrying the Russian ruler Vladimir 'Monomakh' of Kiev (r. 1113–25). Through her, the later English sovereigns were descended from Harold as well as William. A controversial political figure who the triumphant Normans called a perjured usurper, he had as much right to the English throne as Swein 'Forkbeard' or Cnut in an era when the legitimate dynastic heir needed political and military backing to succeed. His ambition was matched by his skills and leadership qualities. His defeat at the battle of Hastings (sometimes known in retrospect as 'Senlac') overshadowed a usually successful military career in which his achievement was only matched by Edmund Ironside and Cnut. But for bad luck with the weather in autumn 1066 and the outcome of a knife-edge battle which he nearly won, he might well have founded a dynasty.

EDITH (EADGYTH) (Queen/'Lady' of England, 1066) Edith was first married to her father's ally Gruffydd ap Llewelyn, ruler of Gwynedd and Powys since 1039 and by conquest ruler of Deheubarth (1055). Their greatest ruler since Hywel 'Dda' in the tenth century, he was a natural ally for his neighbour Aelfgar when the latter was expelled from his newly-inherited earldom of Mercia in

1058. Deposed due to the influence of the Godwins, Aelfgar fought his way back with an army sent by Gruffydd and a Norwegian mercenary force and King Edward and Earl Harold had to accept his reinstatement. It is likeliest that Edith's marriage formed part of Aelfgar's alliance with Gruffydd, and took place in 1058 or as soon as she was old enough thereafter. Assuming her to be around her brothers' age, Gruffydd was a generation older. They had one daughter, Nest, married to the Herefordshire baron Osbern Fitz Richard. She was widowed in summer 1063 when Harold's invasion of Gwynedd led to her refugee husband being murdered and his head sent to the earl by followers anxious to secure peace. She then returned to Mercia, where her brother Edwin succeeded Aelfgar in *c.* 1062/4. In January 1066 Edwin and his brother Morcar, the new earl of Northumbria, were faced with their family's rival Harold Godwinson as the new king of England. They chose to come to terms rather than resist. Probably following a meeting some time in the next few months, their uneasy alliance was sealed by Edith being married off to Harold. (It is less likely that they married earlier.) The latter duly put away Edith Swan-Neck, mother of his children, (?) his wife under a Danelaw civil law union not recognised by the Church. Edith was pregnant when her husband was killed at Hastings, and fled from London while her brothers remained there to submit to William I. She gave birth at Chester late in 1066, either to one son (Harold) or twin boys. She presumably remained in the north, beyond the control of King William, and when her brothers' revolt against him failed in 1069, she seems to have fled with her sons. Logically she may have accompanied her brothers' retreating Danish allies back home, and have joined her husband's mother Gytha in Flanders; alternatively, she may have gone to Ireland. Her fate is unrecorded, but it has been suggested that she was the otherwise unplaceable 'Queen Edith' who is recorded as dying at an abbey in Auvergne en route to Rome, probably in the 1080s. This woman is said to have been suffering from 'leprosy', which covers assorted skin complaints, and to have been buried there.

Notes

Introduction

1. Bede, *The Ecclesiatical History of the English People*, ed. Judith McClure and Roger Collins, 1969, book 1, ch. 15.
2. Procopius, *De Bello Gothica*, book iv, ch. 20.
3. Bede, book 2, ch. 5.
4. Gildas, *De Excidio Brittaniae*.
5. *The Anglo-Saxon Chronicle*, tr. and ed. Michael Swanton, 1996.
6. Henry of Huntingdon, *Chronicle*, tr. Thomas Forster, Llanerch reprint 1991; William of Malmesbury, *The History of the Kings (of Britain) Before the Norman Conquest*, tr. Joseph Stephenson, Llanerch reprint 1989.
7. E. Freeman, *The Norman Conquest*.
8. Gildas, ch. 44.
9. Post-Roman land-use in agricultural historians: Petra Dark, *The Environment of Britain in the First Millenium AD* (Duckworth, 2000); F. Pryor, *Britain AD* pp. 135–58.
10. DNA research: see Weale et al., in *Molecular Biology and Evolution*, vol 19 (2002) pp. 1,000–21.
11. Ine's law-code on the Welsh: quoted in Morris, p. 312.
12. Bede's complaint: book 1, ch. 22.

For a general theory and details of the evidence on the evolution of early Anglo-Saxon Kingship, see Thomas Charles-Edwards, 'Early medieval kingships in the British Isles', pp. 28–39 in Steven Bassett (ed.), *The Origins of Anglo-Saxon Kingdoms*, Leicester U.P., 1989; and P. Sawyer and L. N. Wood, *Early Germanic Kingships*, 1977.

1. Early Settlements to c. 560

GENERAL

Original sources

Bede, *Ecclesiastical History of the English People*, ed. Judith McClure and Roger Collins, Penguin Classics edition, 1994.

The Chronicle of Aethelweard, ed. A. Campbell, 1962.

The Anglo-Saxon Chronicle, tr. and ed. Michael Swanton, Dent, 1996:
  Version A: Corpus Christi College, Cambridge.
  Version B (to AD 977) and continuation, C, the Abingdon Manuscript.
  Version D, the Worcester Manuscript.
  Version E, the Peterborough Manuscript.

Gildas, *The Ruin of Britain and Other Works*, ed. and tr. M. Winterbottom, 1978.

The Chronicle of Henry of Huntingdon, tr. and ed. Thomas Foster, Llanerch reprint, 1991.

Nennius, British History and the Welsh Annals, tr. John Morris, 1980.

Roger of Wendover's Flowers of History, tr. J. A. Giles, vol. 1 (from 447), Llanerch reprint, 1993.

William of Malmesbury, *History of the Kings of England: The Kings Before the Norman Conquest*, tr. and ed. Joseph Stephenson, Llanerch, 1989.

Secondary sources

Stephen Bassett (ed.), *The Origins of Anglo-Saxon Kingdoms* (Leicester University Press, 1989).

H. M. Chadwick, *Origins of the English Nation*, 1907.

David Dumville, 'Sub-Roman Britain: History and Legend', in *History*, new series vol. lxii (1977), pp. 173–92.

M. Lapidge and D. Dumville, *Gildas: New Approaches*, 1984.

John Morris, *The Age of Arthur*, 1973 (since criticised for being too accepting of the truth of later legendary accounts of English and Welsh origins).

P. H. Sawyer and Ian Wood (eds.), *Early Medieval Kingship*, 1977; especially David Dumville, 'Kingship, Genealogies and Regnal Lists', p. 72–104.

P. Sims-Williams, 'The Settlement of England in Bede and the Chronicle', in *Anglo-Saxon England*, vol. xii (1980), pp. 1–40.

Ibid., 'Gildas and the Anglo-Saxons, in *Cambridge Medieval Celtic Studies*, vol. vi (1983),
  pp. 1–30.

Sir Frank Stenton, *Anglo-Saxon England*, 1971 edition.

Barbara Yorke, *Kings and Kingdoms in Early Saxon England*, 1990.

KENT

Bassett, op. cit: Nicholas Brooks, 'The Creation and Early Structure of the Kingdom of Kent', pp. 55–74.

Bede, book 1, ch. 15 on the settlement (following Gildas' story).

N. P. Brooks, *The Early History of the Church of Canterbury*, 1984.

H. M. Chadwick, *The Origin of the English Nation*, 1907, pp. 44–5.

David Dumville, 'The Historical Value of the Historia Brittonum', in *Arthurian Literature*, vol. vi (1986), pp. 1–26.

A. Everett, *Continuity and Colonization: the Evolution of Kentish Settlement*, 1986.

V. V. Evison, *The Fifth Century Invasions South of the Thames*, 1965.

Gildas, chapter 23.

S. C. Hawkes, 'Anglo-Saxon Kent AD 425 – 725', in *Archaeology in Kent to AD 1500*, ed. P. Leach, 1982, especially pp. 64–75.

D. P. Kirby, *The Earliest English Kings*, 1991, pp. 30–47.

Ibid., 'Vortigern', in *Bulletin of the Board of Celtic Studies*, vol. xxiii , 1968–70, pp. 37–49.

H. Moisl, 'Anglo-Saxon Genealogies and Germanic Oral Tradition', in *Journal of Medieval History*, vol. vii (1981), pp. 219–23, 235–6.

Morris, op. cit, pp. 37 and 80–1; and pp. 266–71 on the archaeological background.

Nennius, *Historia Brittonum*, chs. 31 and 44–5.

Sims-Williams, op. cit., pp. 21–4.

Sir Frank Stenton, *Anglo-Saxon England*, pp. 14, 18.

J. E. Turville-Petre, 'Hengest and Horsa', in *Saga-Book of the Viking Society*, xiv (1953–7), pp. 273–90.

K. P. Whitney, *The Kingdom of Kent*, 1982.

WESSEX

F. Aldsworth, 'Droxford Anglo-Saxon Cemetry, Soberton, Hampshire', in *Proceedings of the Hants. Field Club and Archaeological Society*, vol. xxxv (1979), pp. 93–182, on the Jutish nature of Droxford.

Bassett, op. cit., Barbara Yorke, 'The Jutes of Hampshire and Wight and the origins of Wessex', pp. 84–96.

A. Campbell, ed., *The Chronicle of Aethelweard*, 1962, p. 12 and 59 on the battle-site of Cerdicesford.

R. Coates, 'On Some Controversy surrounding Gewissae/Gewissei, Cerdic and Ceawlin', in *Nomina*, vol. xiii (1989–90), pp. 1–11.

R. G. Collingwood and N. L. Myres, *Roman Briatin and the English Settlements*, 1937 edition, pp. 403–4 on the theory that the 'Gewissae' were the Hampshire Saxons who later took over the larger settlement-area in the Thames valley.

G. C. Copley, *The Conquest of Wessex in the Sixth Century*, 1954.

D. Dumville, 'The West Saxon Genealogical Regnal Lists: Manuscripts and Texts', in *Anglia*, vol. civ (1986), pp. 1–32.

Ibid., 'The West Saxon Regnal Genealogical List and the Chronology of Early Wessex', in *Peritia*, vol. iv (1985), pp. 21–67: on the dates of Cerdic and Cynric.

M. Gelling, 'Latin Loan-Words in Old English Place-Names', in *Anglo-Saxon England*, vol. vi (1977), pp. 10–11 on 'Portesmutha'.

D. P. Kirby, 'Problems of Early West Saxon History', in *English Historical Review* vol. lxxx (1965), pp. 10–29.

D. P. Kirby, *The Earliest English Kings*, 1991, pp. 48–60.

E. T. Leeds, 'The West Saxon Invasion and the Icknield Way', in *History*, vol. x (1925–6), pp. 97–109.

A. T. Lloyd, 'The Place-Names of Hampshire', in *A Survey of Southampton and its Region*, British Association for the Advancement of Science, 1964, pp. 178–80.

R. A. Pelling, 'The Concept of Wessex', in *A Survey of Southampton and its Region*, pp. 174–6.

Stenton, pp. 20–5, 30–1.

H. E. Walker, 'Bede and the Gewissae: the Political Evolution of the Heptarchy and its Nomenclature', in *Cambridge Historical Review*, vol. xii (1956), pp. 174–86.

SUSSEX

Bassett, op. cit., Martin Welch, 'The Kingdom of the South Saxons: the Origins', p. 75–83.

Bede, book ii, ch. 5 on Aelle.

Stenton, p. 19.

M. C. Welch, 'Late Romans and Saxons in Sussex', in *Britannia*, vol. ii (1971), pp. 97–106.

Ibid., *Early Anglo-Saxon Sussex*, BAR British Series no. 1120, 1983.

2. *c.* 550 to *c.* 620

GENERAL

Original sources
The Chronicle of Aethelweard.
The Anglo-Saxon Chronicle.
Bede, op. cit.
Henry of Huntingdon, op. cit.
Nennius, op. cit.
Roger of Wendover, op. cit.
William of Malmesbury, op. cit.

Secondary sources
Bassett, op. cit.
Kirby, op. cit.
Morris, op. cit.
Stenton, op. cit.
Yorke, op. cit.

KENT
As section 1.
Bede, book 1, chs. 23–33, book 2, chs. 1–4 on Aethelbert and St Augustine.
Gregory of Tours, *History of the Franks*, ed. and tr. Lewis Thrope, 1974, book iv, 19 and book ix, 26 (for the Aethelbert/Bertha marriage).
Stenton, *Anglo-Saxon England*, pp. 58–60.

WESSEX
As section 1 for general development of the kingdom.
Collingwood and Myres, op. cit.
C. J. Copley, *The Conquest of Wesex in the Sixth Century*, 1934.
Henry of Huntingdon, pp. 52–3.
E. T. Leeds, 'The West Saxon Invasion and the Icknield Way', *History*, vol. x (1925), pp. 97–109.
Ibid., 'The Early Saxon Penetration of the Upper Thames Area', in *Antiquaries Journal*, vol. xiii (1933), pp. 229–51.
Stenton, pp. 27–8.
G. M. Young, *Origin of the West Saxon Kingdom*, 1934.

ESSEX
Bassett, op. cit: David Dumville, 'Essex, Middle Anglia and the Expansion of Mercia in the South-East Midlands', pp. 123–40.
Henry of Huntingdon, p. 49.
Stenton, pp. 53–4.
Barbara Yorke, 'The Kingdom of the East Saxons', in *Anglo-Saxon England*, vol. xiv (1985), pp. 1–36.

EAST ANGLIA
Bassett, op.cit: Martin Carver, 'Kingship and Material Culture in Early Anglo-Saxon East Anglia', pp. 141–58.
Henry of Huntingdon, p. 53.
S. Keynes, 'Raedwald the Bretwalda', in *Voyage to the Other World: the Legacy of Sutton Hoo*, ed. C. B. Kendall and P. S. Wells, 1992, pp. 103–23.
Sir F. Stenton, 'The East Anglian Kings of the Seventh Century', in *The Anglo-Saxons: Studies of Some Aspects of their History and Culture Presented to Bruce Dickens*, ed. P. Clemoes, 1959.
Stenton, *Anglo-Saxon England*, pp. 50–3.

MERCIA
Bassett, op. cit: Nicholas Brooks, 'The Formation of the Mercian Kingdom', pp. 159–70; especially pp. 160–2, 'Locating the Mercians'.
David Dumville, 'The Anglian Collection of Royal Genealogies and Regnal Lists', in *Anglo-Saxon England*, vol. v, 1976, pp. 23–50 (for the royal genealogy).

W. Davies, 'Annals and the Origins of Mercia', in Mercian Studies, ed. A. Dornier, 1977, pp. 17–29.
C. R. Hart, 'The Tribal Hideage', in *Transactions of the Royal Historical Society*, 5th series, vol. xxi (1971), pp. 133–57.
Morris, p. 272.
Stenton, pp. 39–42.

NORTHUMBRIA

Bassett, op. cit: David Dumville, 'The Origins of Northumbria: Some Aspects of the British Background', pp. 213–24.
Bede, book 1, ch. 34 and book 2, ch. 2 on Aethelfrith.
David Dumville, 1976, on the royal genealogy.
Ibid., 'On the North British Section of the Historia Brittonum', in *Welsh Historical Review*, vol. viii (1976–7), pp. 354–54.
Ibid., 'The Anglian Collection of Royal Genealogies and Regnal Lists', in Anglo-Saxon England, vol. v (1976), pp. 23–50.
Peter Hunter Blair, 'The Origins of Northumbria', in *Archaeologia Aeliana*, 4th series, vol. xxv (1947), pp. 1–51.
K. Jackson, *The Gododdin: the Oldest Scottish Poem*, 1969.
M. Miller, 'The Dates of Deira', in *Anglo-Saxon England*, vol. viii (1979), pp. 35–61.
Morris, pp. 232–9 on the conflict between Bernicia and Rheged, c. 570–616.
J. N. L. Myres, 'The Teutonic Settlement of Northern England', in *History*, new series, vol. xx (1935–6), pp. 250–62.
Stenton, pp. 37, 74–8.

LINDSEY

Bassett, op. cit: Bruce Eagles, 'The Kingdom of Lindsey', pp. 202–12.
P. H. Blair, 'The Northumbrians and their Southern Frontier' in *Archaeologia Aeliana*, 4th series, vol. xxvi, 1948, pp. 98–126.
B. N. Eagles, *The Anglo-Saxon Settlement of Humberside*, Brit. Archaeological Reports, British series, no. 68, parts i and ii, 1979.

3. c. 620 to c. 655

GENERAL

Original sources
The Chronicle of Aethelweard.
The Anglo-Saxon Chronicle.
Bede, op. cit.
Henry of Huntingdon, op. cit.
Roger of Wendover, op. cit.
William of Malmesbury, op. cit.

Secondary sources
Bassett, op. cit.
Kirby, op. cit.
Morris, op. cit.
Stenton, op. cit.
Yorke, op. cit.

KENT
As section 2.
Bede, book 2, chs. 5–6 on Eadbald.
    Book 3, ch. 8 on Earconbert.
D. P. Kirby, *The Earliest English Kings*, especially pp. 37–42.
Stenton, p. 61.

WESSEX
As section 2.
Bede, book 3, ch. 7 on Cynegils, Cenwalh, and the conversion.
Stenton, pp. 67–8.

ESSEX
As section 2.
Bede, book 3, ch. 22 on the conversion.

EAST ANGLIA
Bede, book 2, ch. 15 and book 3, ch. 18 on the conversion; book 3, ch. 18 on Anna's reign.
    Book 3, ch. 8 for the Frankish connection.
D. Brown, 'The Dating of the Sutton Hoo Coins', in *Anglo-Saxon Studies in Archaeology and History*, no. 2 (British Archaeological Reports, British Series, no. 92, 1981), pp. 71–86.
A. C. Evans, *The Sutton Hoo Ship-Burial*.
S. Keynes, 'Raedwald the Bretwalda', in *Voyage to the Other World: the legacy of Sutton Hoo*, ed. C. B. Kendall and P. S. Wells, 1992, pp. 103–21.

MERCIA
As section 2.
See particularly Nicholas Brooks' article, 'The Formation of the Early Mercian Kingdom', in Bassett, op. cit., chapter 7.
Bede, book 2, ch. 20 on Penda in the early 630s.
    Book 3, ch. 16 on Penda's attack on Bamburgh.
    Book 3, ch. 24 on the end of Penda's reign.
Rachel Bromwich, 'The Character of Early Welsh Tradition', in *Studies in Early British History*, ed. N. Chadwick, 1954, pp. 83–136 (on the Welsh side of seventh-century sources).

D. P. Kirby, 'Welsh Bards and the Border', in *Mercian Studies*, ed. Dornier, pp. 31–42 (also on the Welsh sources).

Canu Llywarch Hen, ed. Ifor Williams, 1945 (on the wars of Cyndylan as Penda's ally).

Morris, pp. 241–4 on Penda and Cyndylan.

Stenton, pp. 39–42, and 82–4 (Penda).

Ifor Williams, 'The Poems of Llywarch Hen', *Proceedings of the British Academy*, 1932, pp. (commentary on ditto).

HWICCE

Bassett, op. cit: chapter 13, Margaret Gelling, 'The Early History of Western Mercia', pp. 184–201.

Stenton, pp. 43–6.

NORTHUMBRIA

As section 2.

The Annals of Ulster, ed. S. MacAirt and G. MacNiocaill, Dublin 1983 (Irish perpsective on Anglian events).

Bede, book 2, ch. 5 on the extent of Edwin's power.

Book 2, chs. 9–14 on Edwin's conversion, chs. 171–8 on Paulinus' bishopric, and ch. 20 on Edwin's death and his family's fate.

Book 3, ch. 1 on Eanfrith.

Book 3, chs. 1–6 and 9–13 on Oswald and his miracles; book 3, ch. 3 on the Iona connection and book 3, ch. 6 on the importance of his connection to Edwin's family.

Book 3, chs. 24–6, and book 4, ch. 5 on Oswy.

Book 3, ch. 14 on Oswine of Deira.

Book 3, chs. 23–4 on Aethelwald.

N. K. Chadwick, 'The Conversion of Northumbria: A Comparison of Sources', in *Celt and Saxon: Studies in the Early British Border*, ed. Chadwick, 1963, pp. 138–66.

Eddi Stephanus, *The Life of Bishop Wilfrid*, chs. 7–8 on Wilfred and Alchfrith of Deira.

Ch. 10 on the Synod of Whitby.

Chs. 11–16 on Wilfred and Oswy.

P. Hunter-Blair, 'The Moore Memorandum on Northumbrian History' in C. Fox and B. Dickens, ed. *The Early Culture of North-West Europe*, 1950, pp. 245–57.

D. P. Kirby, *The Earliest English Kings*, especially pp. 77–82.

Morris, pp. 241–4 on Oswald, Oswy and Cyndylan.

Nennius, *Historia Brittonum*, ch. 63 on Edwin's alleged baptism by Bishop Rhun.

Ch. 57 on Oswy and Riemmelth of Rheged.

Ch. 64–5 on Oswald and Oswy versus Penda.

S. Revill, 'King Edwin and the Battle of Hatfield', in *Transactions of the Thoroton Society*, vol. lxxix (1975).

S. J. Ridyard, *The Royal Saints of Anglo-Saxon England*, Cambridge Studies in Medieval Life and Thought, 1988, on SS Oswald and Oswine.

Stenton, pp. 79–81 (Edwin), 82–3 (Oswald), 84–5 (Oswy).

LINDSEY
As section 2.

4. *c. 665* to *c. 690*

GENERAL
As earlier sections.

KENT
Bassett, op. cit: Brooks article.
Bede, book 3, ch. 29 and book 4, ch. 1 on Egbert.
Book 4, chs. 5 and 26 on Hlothere and Eadric.
Kirby, pp. 121–3 on the late 680s.
G. Ward, 'King Oswine – A Forgotten Ruler of Kent', in *Archaeologica Cantiana*, vol. l, 1938, pp. 60–5.
Barbara Yorke, 'Joint Kingship in Kent *c.* 560 – 785', in *Archaeologia Cantiana*, vol. xcix (1983), pp. 1–20.

WESSEX
As section 3.
Bede, book 4, chs. 13 on Wulfhere's attack in early 660s
    Chs. 15–16 and book 5, ch. 7 on Caedwalla.
Eddi Stephanus, *Life of Bishop Wilfrid*, ch. 42 on Wilfred and Caedwalla.
Kirby, op. cit., pp. 119–22 on Caedwalla.
Stenton, pp. 68–70.

SUSSEX
Kirby, as above.
Bede, book 4, ch. 13 on the conversion and on Wulfhere's involvement with Sussex.
    Book 4, ch. 15 for Caedwalla's attacks.
Eddi Stephanus, *Life of Bishop Wilfrid*, chs. 41 and 42 on the conversion.

ESSEX
As section 2 and 3.
Bede, book 3, ch. 22.
Kirby, op. cit., p. 95–7.

EAST ANGLIA
Bede, book 3, ch. 22.

MERCIA
As section 3.

Bassett, op.cit: chapter 9, David Dumville, 'Essex, Middle Anglia and the Expansion of Mercia in the South-East Midlands', p. 124–40 (on the Middle Angles and Peada).

Bede, book 3, ch. 21 on Peada.
    Book 3, ch. 24 and book 4, ch. 3 on Wulfhere.
    Book 4, ch. 12 on Aethelred's attacks on Kent in 676 and the Northumbrian war of 679.
    Book 5, ch. 24 on the killing of Queen Osthryth.
    Book 5, chs. 19 and 24 on Aethelred's religious interests and abdication.

Eddi Stephanus, *Life of Bishop Wilfrid*, chs. 45–8 on Wilfred and King Aethelred.

H. P. Finberg, 'Mercians and Welsh', in *Lucerna*, 1962, pp. 66–82.

D. P. Kirby, *The Earliest English Kings*, chapters 4 and 5; and pp. 113–16 (Wulfhere) and 117 (Aethelred).

Stenton, pp. 84–5.

HWICCE

Bassett, op. cit: Margaret Gelling, 'The early history of western Mercia', pp. 184–201.

Bede, book 4, ch. 23.

MAGONSAETAN

Bassett, op. cit: Kate Pretty, 'Defining the Magonsaete', pp. 171–83.

Finberg, op. cit.

Ibid., 'The Princes of the Magonsaete', in his *The Early Charters of the West Midlands*, 1961, pp. 216–25.

SURREY

Bassett, op. cit: John Blair, 'Frithuwold's Kingdom and the Origins of Surrey', pp. 97–107.

J. Blair, *Landholding, Church and Settlement in Early Medieval Surrey*, Surrey Archaeological Society.

Dornier, 'The Anglo-Saxon Monastery at Breedon-on-the-Hill, Leicestershire' in *Mercian Studies*, ed. Ibid., 1977, pp. 157–8.

Patrick Wormald, 'Bede, the *Bretwaldas* and the Origins of the *Gens Anglorum*', in *Ideal and Reality in Frankish and Anglo-Saxon Society*, ed. ibid., 1983

NORTHUMBRIA

As section 3.

Annals of Ulster, for Ecgfrith's invasion 684–5.

Bede, book 4, chs. 5 and 24–6 on Ecgfrith.
    Book 4, ch. 12 on Ecgfrith's expulsion of Wilfred.
    Book 4, ch. 21 on the confrontation with Mercia in 679.

Two Lives of St Cuthbert, ed. B. Colgrave, 1940.

Eddius Stephanus, *The Life of Bishop Wilfrid*, ed. and tr. B. Colgrave, 1927:
    Ch. 19–20 on Wilfred and Ecgfrith in the early to mid-670s.

Ch. 24 on Wilfred's exile.

Ch. 34 on Ecgfrith's refusal to allow him back, 680.

Ch. 44–5 on Wilfred and Aldfrith.

Chs. 58–9 on the end of Aldfirth's reign.

K. Harrison, 'The Reign of Ecgfrith', in *Yorkshire Archeaological Journal*, vol. 43 (1971), pp. 79–84.

D. P. Kirby, *St Wilfrid at Hexham*, 1974.

Ibid., 'Bede, Eddius Stephanus and the Life of Wilfrid', in *English Historical Review*, vol. 98 (1983), pp. 101–14.

Stenton, pp. 86–9.

5. *c.* 690 to *c.* 756

GENERAL

As section 5.

W. Levison, *England and the Continent in the Eighth Century*, 1946.

Roger of Hoveden, *Annals of English History*, tr. Henry Riley, part 1 (from 732), Llanerch reprint, 1994.

KENT

As section 5.

Bede, book 4, ch. 26 and book 5, ch. 8 on Wihtred.

Yorke, 'Joint Kingship in Kent'.

WESSEX, EAST ANGLIA

As section 5.

Henry of Huntingdon, pp. 128–9 (Cuthred) and 131–2 (Sigebert) for stories of these kings not supported by any other extant references.

Kirby, pp. 124–6 on Ine; pp. 163–6 on Beonna.

Stenton, *Anglo-Saxon England*, pp. 71–3 on Ine.

ESSEX

Bede, book 4, ch. 11 on the 690s.

    Book 5, ch. 19 on Offa's abdication.

MERCIA

As section 5.

Bede book 5, ch. 19 on Coenred's abdication.

The Life of Saint Guthlac, ed. Colgrave, especially chs. 48–9 on Aethalbald.

Sir Frank Stenton, 'The Supremacy of the Mercian Kings', in *Preparatory to Anglo-Saxon England: Being the Collected Papers of Frank Merry Stenton*, ed. D. M. Stenton, 1970, pp. 48–66.

Stenton, *Anglo-Saxon England*, pp. 202–5.

D. P. Kirby, *The Earliest English Kings*, chapter 6; p. 128 on Coenred and Coelred.

P. Wormald, 'Bede, the *Bretwaldas*, and the Origin of the *Gens Anglorum*', in *Ideal and Reality in Frankish and Early Anglo-Saxon Society*, ed. P. Wormald. 1983

NORTHUMBRIA

As section 5.

Aethelwulf, *De Abbatibus* (early ninth-century), tr. A. Campbell, 1967, for an unflattering later picture of Osred.

S. Alcott, *Alcuin of York*, 1984 – see translations of Alcuin's letters of the 780s and 790s referring to Northumbrian events.

Bede, book 5, chs. 22–3 on the upheavals of 705–29 and on Ceolwulf. He closes chapter 23 on an uncertain note about the future – a hint of Ceolwulf's troubles *c.* 731?

Eddi Stephanus, *Life of Bishop Wilfrid*, chs. 59–60 on Aldfrith's sons.

Kirby, op. cit., chapter 7.

Stenton, p. 146 (on the see of York).

Symeonis monachi opera omnia, ed. T. Arnold, Rolls series, 1882, 2 vols – see vol. I for mid-eighth-century Northumbrian events.

L. Wallach, *Alcuin and Charlemagne*, Ithaca, New York, 1959.

6. *c.* 690 to 796

GENERAL

As section 6.

KENT

Henry of Huntingdon, p. 143.

Kirby, pp. 165–7.

Yorke, 'Joint Kingship in Kent'.

WESSEX, SUSSEX, ESSEX

As section 6.

Asser, *Life of Alfred the Great*, tr. Simon Keynes and Michael Lapidge, 1983; chs. 14–15 on Beorhtric and Eadburh.

Roger of Wendover, *Flowers of History*, pp. 170–1 on Beorhtric and Eadburh.

EAST ANGLIA

S. J. Ridyard, op. cit., on Saint Aethelbert's martyrdom.

Roger of Wendover, *Flowers of History*, pp. 158–9 on ibid.

MERCIA

As section 6.

Annales Cambriae.

Asser's *Life of King Alfred*, ch. 14, for the assertion that Offa built the Dyke.

C. E. Blunt, 'The Coinage of Offa', in R. H. M. Dolley (ed.), *Anglo-Saxon Coins*, 1861.

C. Fox, *Offa's Dyke*, 1955.

D. Hill, 'Offa's and Wat's Dyke – Some Exploratory Work on the Frontier Between Celt and Saxon', in T. Rowley (ed.), *Anglo-Saxon Settlement and Landscape*, British Archaeological Reports, vol. vi, 1974.

Kirby, op. cit., pp. 163–84.

Sir Frank Stenton, 'The Supremacy of the Mercian Kings' in his *Preparatory to Anglo-Saxon England*, pp. 48–62.

Stenton, *Anglo-Saxon England*, pp. 206–23.

HWICCE
Kirby, p. 163-4.

LINDSEY
Kirby, p. 163.

Stenton, p. 48.

Stenton, 'Lindsey and its Kings' in his *Peparatory to Anglo-Saxon England*, 1971, pp. 371–82.

NORTHUMBRIA
As section 6, especially Kirby, pp. 142–62.

Symoni monachis opera, vol. 2, for dates of the various coups and killings.

7. 796 to 860

KENT
S. Keynes, 'The Control of Kent in the Ninth Century', in *Medieval Europe*, vol. ii (193), pp. 111–32.

Kirby, op. cit., chapter 9.

WESSEX
Annales de Saint-Bertin, ed. F. Grat, J. Vielliard, and S. Clemencet, Paris 1964.

Asser, *Life of King Alfred*, ed. S. Keynes and M. Lapidge, 1983.

Especially: ch. 2 on Alfred's childhood and his mother Osburh.

Ch. 12 on the revolt against Aethelwulf in 856.

Ch. 13 on the peace-settlement of 856.

Ch. 17 on Aethelbald's marriage to his stepmother Judith.

C. E. Blunt, 'The Coinage of Ecgbert, King of Wessex, 802–39', in *British Numismatical Journal*, vol. 28 (1957), pp. 467–76.

N. Brooks, 'England in the Ninth Century: The Crucible of Defeat', in *Transactions of the Royal Historical Society*, vol. xxix (1979), pp. 1–20.

David Dumville, *Wessex and England From Alfred to Edgar*, 1992.

Ibid., 'The Aetheling: a Study in Anglo-Saxon Constitutional History', in *Anglo-Saxon England*, vol viii (1979), pp. 1–33.

H. Edwards, *Charters of the Early West Saxon Kingdom*, 1988.

M. J. Enwright, 'Charles the Bald and Aethelwulf of Wessex: the Alliance of 856 and Strategies of Medieval Succession', in *Journal of Medieval Studies*, vol. 5 (1979), pp. 291–302.

S. Keynes, 'The West Saxon Charters of King Aethelwulf and his Sons', in *English Historical Review*, vol. cix (1994), pp. 129–30.

Kirby, op. cit., chapter 9.

J. Nelson, *Charles the Bald*, 1992.

Ibid., 'The Franks and the English in the Ninth Century Reconsidered', in *The Preservation and Transmission of Anglo-Saxon Culture*, ed. J. Rosenthal and P. Salzmach, 1997, pp. 190–208.

Pauline Stafford, 'The King's Wife in Wessex, 800–1066', in *Past and Present*, vol. xci (1981), pp. 7–27.

Ibid., 'Charles the Bald, Judith and England', in *Charles the Bald; Court and Kingdom*, ed. M. Gibson and J. Nelson, 1990, pp. 139–53.

Stenton, pp. 231–5 (Egbert), 244–5 (Aethelwulf).

EAST ANGLIA

Kirby, chapter 9.

H. E. Pagan, 'The Coinage of the East Anglian Kingdom', in *British Numismatic Journal*, vol. lii (1982), pp. 41–83.

MERCIA

For the link between Coenwulf and Hwicce, see Bassett, op. cit., pp. 229–30.

Brooks, 1979.

Hemingi Chartularum Ecclesiae Wigorniensis, ed. T. Hearne, 1723, vol. 1, p. 242 – a ninth-century Mercian regnal list with lengths of reigns.

Kirby, chapter 9.

Ridyard, op. cit., on Saint Kenelm.

Roger of Wendover, *Flowers of History*, pp. 173–4 on Saint Kenelm.

W. Macray (ed.), *Chronicon Abbatiae de Evesham*, Rolls Series, 1863, pp. 325–6 on the Wigmund/Evesham link.

D. W. Rollason, 'Cults of Murdered Royal Saints in Anglo-Saxon England', in *Anglo-Saxon England*, vol. xi (1983), pp. 10–22, especially on Saint Kenelm.

Stenton, pp. 225–31 and 235–6.

NORTHUMBRIA

Brooks, 1979.

Kirby, chapter 9, especially pp. 196–8.

Kirby, 'Northumbria in the Ninth Century', in Metcalf, ed. *Coinage in Ninth Century Northumbria*.

For the disputed dates of the early to mid-ninth-century kings: see *Symeonis Monachi Opera Omnia*, ed. Arnold, vol. I, p. 54 and 284, vol. II, pp. 377, 391; and Roger of Hoveden, *Flowers of History*, vol. I, pp. 281, 284.

8. 860 to 899

GENERAL

Original sources, as previous sections; and:

King Alfred's West Saxon Version of Gregory's Pastoral Care, ed. and tr. Henry Sweet, 2 vols, Early English Text Society, original series, nos. 45 and 50, 1871–2.

King Alfred's Old English Version of Boethius' De Consolatione Philosophiae, ed. Walter Sedgefield, 1899.

King Alfred's Version of St Augustine's Soliloquies, ed. Thomas A. Carnicelli, Cambridge, Mass., 1969.

The Annals of St Bertin, tr. Janet Nelson, Manchester Medieval Sources Series: Ninth Century Histories, vol. 1, 1991.

The Annals of St Neot, ed. David Dumville and M. Lapidge.

WESSEX (mainly ALFRED) AND MERCIA

Richard Abels, *Alfred the Great: War, Kingship and Culture in Anglo-Saxon England*, 1998.

    Chapter 2: 848–58.

    Chapter 3, 858–68.

    Chapter 4, 869–79.

    Chapter 5, 880–91.

    Chapter 6, the 'burh' system.

    Chapter 7, culture and Church.

    Chapter 8, the practice of kingship.

    Chapter 9, 891–9.

See especially ibid., pp. 118–26 on the debate over the authenticity of Asser's *Life of Alfred*; pp. 209–12 on Alfred's coinage.

Aethelweard, ed. Campbell, especially p. 40 on the 871 campaign.

    pp. 42–3 on the 878 campaign.

    pp. 49–52 on the 892–4 war.

Asser, op. cit.: see especially chs. 2 and 23 on Alfred's childhood.

    Chs. 8 and 11 on the journeys to Rome in 853/5.

    Ch. 74 on his much-debated illness.

    Ch. 29–30 on his marriage and the Mercian campaign, 868.

    Ch. 35–42 on the 870–1 campaigns to the death of Aethelred.

    Ch. 43 on the peace of 871.

Ch. 49 on the 876 Dorset/Exeter campaign.

Ch. 49–56 on the crisis of 878.

Ch. 75 on the 'palace school'.

Chs. 77 and 106 on the revival of learning and Alfred's moral/cultural vision.

Chs. 77 and 87–9 on Alfred's personal contribution to learning, and his translations.

Ch. 80 on the submissions of ealdorman Aethelred and the Welsh.

Ch. 83 on the occupation of London, 886.

Ch. 91 on the 'burhs' and the early 890s.

Ch. 91 and 94 on international connections after 880.

Janet Bateley, 'The Compilation of the Anglo-Saxon Chronicle, 60 BC to AD 890: Vocabulary as Evidence', in *Proceedings of the British Academy*, vol. lxiv (1978), pp. 93–129.

E. Conybeare, *Alfred in the Chroniclers*, 1900.

R. H. C. Davis, 'King Alfred: Propaganda and Truth', in *History*, vol. lvi (1971).

Dumville, 1979.

Dumville, 'Ecclesiastical Lands and the Defence of Wessex in the First Viking Age', in ibid., *Wessex and England*, pp. 29–54, and 'King Alfred and the Tenth Century Reform of the English Church', pp. 185–205.

Tony Dyson, 'King Alfred and the Restoration of London', in *The London Journal*, vol. xv (1990), pp. 99–110.

V. Galbraith, 'Who Wrote Asser's Life of Alfred?', in his *An Introduction to the Study of History*, 1864, pp. 88–128.

S. Keynes, 'On the Authenticity of Asser's *Life of King Alfred*', in *Journal of Ecclesiastical History*, vol. xlvii, 1996, pp. 526–51.

D. P. Kirby, 'Asser and his *Life of King Alfred*', in *Studia Celtica*, vol. vi (1971), pp. 12–35.

Beatrice Lees, *Alfred the Great, the Truth Teller: Maker of England, 848 to 899*, 1915.

J. Nelson, op. cit.

J. Nelson, 'A King Across the Sea: Alfred in Continental Perspective', in *Transactions of the Royal Historical Society*, vol. xxxvi (1986), pp. 45–68.

J. Nelson, 'The Problem of Alfred's Royal Anointing', in *Journal of Ecclesiatical History*, vol. 18 (1967), pp. 145–63.

J. Nelson, 'Reconstructing a Royal Family: Reflections on Alfred from Asser', in *People and Places in Northern Europe From 500 to 1600: Essays in Honour of P. H. Sawyer*, ed. Ian Wood and N. Lund, 1991, pp. 47–66.

J. Nelson, 'The Political Ideas of Alfred of Wessex', in *Kings and Kingship in Medieval Europe*, ed. Anne Duggan, 1993.

John Peddie, *Alfred the Good Soldier: A History of his Campaigns*, 1989.

D. Pratt, 'The Illnesses of Alfred the Great', in *Anglo-Saxon England*, vol. 30 (2003), pp. 39–90.

Ridyard, op. cit. (on Queen/Lady Osburh).

Alfred Smyth, *Alfred the Great*, 1993, especially pp. 149–367 on his theory that Asser's *Life* was composed in the early eleventh century by Byrtferth of Ramsey.

Pauline Stafford, op. cit.

T. Wright, 'Some Historical Doubts Relating to the Biographer Asser', *Archaeologica*, vol. 29 (1842), pp. 192–201.

J. M. Wallace-Hadrill, *Early Germanic Kingship in England and on the Continent*, 1977: chapter on 'Charles the Bald and Alfred'; especially pp. 100–08 on Alfred's concept of kingship and pp. 124–51 on Alfred's law-code.

Barbara Yorke, *Wessex in the Early Middle Ages*, 1995.

EALHSWITH

Asser, chs. 29 and 75.

J. Ridyard, *The Royal Saints of Anglo-Saxon England*, Cambridge Studies in Medieval Life and Thought, 4th series, vol. 19, 1988: on Ealhswith.

EAST ANGLIA

Abbo of Fleury, *Passio Sancti Edmundi: Three Lives of English Saints*, ed. M. Winterbottom, 1972, pp. 67–87.

Kirby, p. 164.

Ridyard, op. cit: on Saint Edmund.

Roger of Wendover, *Flowers of History*, pp. 193–9 on Saint Edmund's martyrdom.

D. Whitelock, 'Fact and Fiction in the Legend of St Edmund', in *Proceedings of the Suffolk Institute of Archaeology*, vol. xxxi (1967–9), pp. 217–33.

NORTHUMBRIA

Kirby, pp. 196–8.

VIKING KINGDOMS

Gwyn Jones, *A History of the Vikings*, 1984.

H. R. Loyn, *The Vikings in England*, 1994.

R. Page, *Chronicles of the Vikings: Records, Memorials and Myths*, Toronto, 1995.

P. Sawyer, 'Some Sources for the History of Viking Northumbria', in R. A. Hall (ed.), *Viking-Age York and the North*, CBA Research Report, no. 27, 1978, pp. 3–7.

Alfred Smyth, *Scandinavian Kings in the British Isles, 850 – 880*, 1977.

9. 899 to 959

GENERAL AND VIKING YORK

Original sources as section 9.

M. L. Beavan, 'The Regnal Dates of Alfred, Edward the Elder and Athelstan', in *English Historical Review*, xxxii (1917), pp. 517–31.

A. Campbell, 'The End of the Kingdom of Northumbria', in *English Historical Review*, vol. lvii (1942), pp. 91–7.

C. B. Hart, 'Athelstan Half-King and his Family', in *Anglo-Saxon England*, vol. ii (1973), pp. 115–44.

H. R. Loyn, *The Vikings in Britain*, 1994.

EDWARD THE ELDER
N. Higham and D. Hill (eds.), *Edward the Elder, 899 – 924*, 2001.
Stenton, pp. 320–39.

ATHELSTAN
F. Campbell (ed.), *The Battle of Brunanburh*, 1938.
S. M. Sharp, 'England, Europe and the Celtic World: King Athelstan's Foreign Policy', in *Bulletin of the John Rylands Library*, vol. lxxix (1997), pp. 197–220.
Stenton, pp. 339–56.
William of Malmesbury, pp. 113–24; especially details on pp. 113–16 and 122–4 on the king's birth, upbringing, and accession and the flight and death of his half-brother Edwin, not recorded elsewhere.
M. Wood, 'The Making of King Athelstan's Empire: An English Charlemagne', in *Ideal and Reality in Frankish and Anglo-Saxon Society*, ed. P. Wormald, D. Bullough, and R. Collins, 1983, pp. 250–72.
Ibid., *In Search of England: Journeys into the English Past*, 1999: pp. 86–93 on a lost *Life of Athelstan* used by William of Malmesbury.

EDMUND I
M. L. Beavan, 'King Edmund I and the Danes of York', in ibid., vol. xxxiii (1918).
Stenton, pp. 356–60.

10. 959 to 1016

GENERAL, and EDGAR
Anglo-Saxon Chronicle.
The Chronicle of Aethelweard.
Henry of Huntingdon, op. cit.
Roger of Wendover, op. cit.
William of Malmesbury, op. cit.

EDWARD THE MARTYR
D. V. Fisher, 'The Antimonastic Reaction in the Reign of Edward the Martyr', in *Cambridge Historical Journal*, vol. x (1950–2), pp. 254–70.
S. J. Ridyard, op. cit: on Edward the Martyr.
Roger of Wendover, *Flowers of History*, pp. 266–7.
William of Malmesbury, pp. 102–4.

AETHELRED, SWEIN and EDMUND IRONSIDE
T. M. Anderson, 'The Viking Policy of Ethelred the Unready' in *Scandinavian Studies*, vol. lix (1987), pp. 287–97.

J. Gillingham, 'The Most Precious Jewel in the English Crown: Levels of Danegeld and Heregeld in the Early Eleventh Century', in *English Historical Review*, vol. civ (1989), pp. 373–84.

C. B. Hart, op. cit.

D. Hill, *Ethelred the Unready: Papers From the Millenary Conference*, 1978.

S. Keynes, *The Diplomas of King Aethelred 'the Unready', 978–1016*, 1980.

Ibid., 'The Declining Reputation of King Aethelred the Unready', in *Anglo-Saxon History: Basic Readings*, ed. D. A. Pelteret, 2000, pp. 157–90.

Knytlinga Saga: the History of the Kings of Denmark, tr. H. Pallson and P. Edwards, Odense, 1986.

M. Lapidge and M. Winterbottom (ed.) *The Life of St. Aethelwold/Wulfstan of Winchester*, 1991.

R. Lavelle, *Aethelred II, King of the English, 978–1016*, 2002.

M. K. Lawson, 'Danegeld and Hregeld once more' in *English Historical Review*, vol. cv (1990), pp. 951–61.

H. R. Loyn, op.cit.

K. Mack, 'Changing Thegns, Cnut's Conquest and the English Aristocracy', in *Albion*, vol. xvii (1984), pp. 375–87.

J. Raine (ed.), *Vita Sancti Oswaldi autore anonymo* in *The History of the Church of York and its Archbishops*, Rolls series vol. lxxi (1879), pp. 399–475.

Roger of Wendover, *Flowers of History*, pp. 283–92, on the events of 1005–16, concluding with Edmund II's murder.

P. H. Sawyer, 'Ethelred II, Olaf Tryggvason and the Conversion of Norway', in *Scandinavian Studies*, vol. lix (1987), pp. 299–307.

D. Scragg, *The Battle of Maldon, AD 991*, 1991.

P. Stafford, op. cit ('The King's Wife...')

Snorri Sturlason, *Heimskringla: the Olaf Sagas*, tr. S. Laing, 1964.

W. Stubbs (ed.), *Memorials of St Dunstan, Archbshop of Canterbury: Osbern of Canterbury's Vita Sancti Dunstani*, Rolls series, vol. lxiii (1874), pp. 68–164.

William of Malmesbury, pp. 145–9, 160–70.

Williams, 'Cockles Among the Wheat: Danes and English in the Western Midlands in the first Half of the Eleventh Century', in *Midland History*, vol. xi (1986), pp. 1–11.

11. 1016 to 1066

GENERAL

As previous sections; and:

Adam of Bremen, *Magistri Adama Bremensis Gesta Hammaburgensis ecclesiae pontificum*, ed. B. Schmeidler, Hanover and Lepizig, 1917.

Chronici Monasteriae de Abingdon, ed. J. Stevenson, Rolls Series, 1858.

Ailred of Rievaulx, *Genealogia Regum Angliae et Regis David Scotiae*.

Symeon of Durham, *Opera Omnia*, ed. T. Arnold, Rolls series, 1882.

CNUT AND HIS FAMILY
Henry of Huntingdon, pp. 196–9 (Cnut), 199–200 (Harold I), 200–01 (Harthacnut).
L. M. Larson, *Canute the Great, 995 – 1035*, 1912.
M. K. Lawson, *Cnut: the Danes in England in the early Eleventh century*, 1993.
Roger of Hoveden, pp. 103–7 (Cnut), 107–8 (Harold I), 108–11 (Harthacnut).
Roger of Wendover, pp. 292–300 (Cnut), pp. 302–6 (Harthacnut, with mistakes).
A. R. Rumble (ed.), *The Reign of Cnut: King of England, Denmark and Norway*, 1994.
Snorri Sturlason, *Heimskrinringla: The Olaf Sagas*, tr. S. Laing, 1964.
William of Malmesbury, pp. 169–77 (Cnut), 178 (Harold I), 178–9 (Harthacnut).
Williams, op. cit., 1986.

EMMA
Above for Cnut; and
Frank Barlow, 'Cnut's Second Pilgrimage and Queen Emma's Disgrace in 1043', in *English Historical Review*, vol. lxxiii, 1958.
M. Campbell, 'Queen Emma and Aelgifu of Northampton: Cnut the Great's Women', in *Medieval Scandinavia*, vol. iv (1971), pp. 66–79.
Ibid., 'Emma, reine d'Angleterre: mere denature ou femme vindictive?', in *Annales de Normandie*, vol. 23 (1973), pp. 97–114.
Encomiae Emmae reginae, CS, 3rd series, vol. 72 (1949), ed. and tr. A. Campbell.
F. Lishitz, 'The Encomium Emmae Reginae: A Political Pamphlet of the Eleventh Century?' in *Haskins Society Journal*, no. 1 (1989), pp. 19–50.
Pauline Stafford, *Queen Emma and Queen Edith: Queenship and Power in Eleventh-Century England*, 1997.

EDWARD THE CONFESSOR
Ailred of Rievaulx, *The Life of St Edward, King and Confessor*, tr. J. Bertram, 1990.
Eadmer, *Historia Novorum in Anglia*, ed. M. Rule, 1965 reprint.
Frank Barlow, *Edward the Confessor*, 1970.
Especially: chapter 2, before accession.
    Chapter 3, the accession 1042.
    Chapter 4, 1043–8.
    Chapter 5, 1049–51.
    Chapter 6, the Godwins' return 1052–3.
    Chapter 9, 1053–65.
    Chapters 10–11: 1065–6.
    Chapter 12, the cult of the Saint.
    Appendix A: The *Vita Aedwardi Regis*.
Barlow, *The English Church 1000–1066*, 1979.
Ibid., 'Edward the Confessor's Early Life, Character, and Attitudes', in *English Historical Review*, vol. lxxx, 1958.
Ibid., 'The *Carmen de Hastingae Proelio*', in *Studies in International History*, ed. K. Bourne and D. C. Watt, 1967.

Ibid. (ed. and tr.), *The Life of King Edward Who Lies at Westminster*, attributed to a monk of St Bertin, 1992.

R. Allen Brown, *The Normans and the Norman Conquest*, 1969.

M. Campbell, 'Earl Godwine of Wessex and King Edward's Promise of the Throne to Duke William', in *Traditio*, vol. xxviii (1972), pp. 141–58.

Ibid., 'The Anti-Norman Reaction in England in 1052: Suggested Origins', in *Medieval Studies*, vol. xxxviii (1976), pp. 428–41.

Ibid., 'The Rise of an Anglo-Sxaon 'Kingmaker': Earl Godwin of Wessex', in *Canadian Journal of History*, vol. 13 (1978), pp. 17–33.

David Douglas, 'Edward the Confessor, Duke William of Normandy and the English Succession', in *English Historical Review*, vol. lxviii (1953).

Ibid., *William the Conqueror*, 1964.

E. A. Freeman, *History of the Norman Conquest of England*, 2nd edtion, 6 vols, 1870–79.

P. Grierson, 'The Relations between England and Flanders before the Norman Conquest', in *Transactions of the Royal historical Society*, 4th series, vol. 23 (1941), pp. 71–112.

E. K. Heningham, 'The Literary Unity, the Date and the Purposes of the Lady Edith's Book *The Life of King Edward Who Rests At Westminster*', in *Albion* vol vii (1975), pp. 26–40.

N. Hooper, 'Edgar Atheing: Anglo-Saxon Prince, Rebel, and Crusader', in *Anglo-Saxon England*, vol. xiv (1985).

W. E. Kappelle, *The Norman Conquest of the North: the Region and its Transforamtion, 1000 – 1135*, 1979.

E. John, 'Edward the Confessor and the Norman Succession', in *English Historical Review*, vol. xciv (1979), pp. 241–67.

Liber Eliensis, ed. E. O. Blake, Royal Historical Society, Camden 3rd series, vol. xcii, 1962 (on Edward and Ely pre-1016).

Emma Mason, *Westminster Abbey and its People, c. 1050 – 1216*, 1996.

K. L. Maund, 'The Welsh Alliances of Earl Aelfgar of Mercia and his Family in the Mid-Eleventh Century', in *Anglo-Norman Studies*, vol. xi (1988), pp. 181–90.

S. J. Ridyard, op. cit: on King Edward.

B. W. Scholz, 'The Canonization of Edward the Confessor', in *Speculum*, vol. xxvi (1961).

R. W. Southern, 'The First Life of Edward the Confessor', in *English Historical Review*, vol. lviii, 1943.

Pauline Stafford, *Unification and Conquest*, 1989.

B. Wilkinson, 'Freeman and the Crisis of 1051', in *Bulletin of the John Rylands Library*, vol. xxiv (1938).

Williams, 'Some Notes and Considerations on Problems Connected with the English Royal Succession 860–1066', in *Proceedings of the Battle Conference on Anglo-Norman Studies 1977*, 1978, pp. 58 ff.

Ibid., 'The King's Nephew: the Family and Career of Ralph, Earl of Hereford', in C. Harper-Bill, C. J. Holdsworth, and J. Nelson, eds., *Studies in Medieval History Presented to R. Allen Brown*, 1989, pp. 327–43.

HAROLD II AND HIS FAMILY, AND 1066

Above sources for King Edward, and:

Alfred Anscombe, 'The Pedigree of Earl Godwin', in *Transcations of the Royal Historical Society*, 3rd series, vol. 7 (1913), pp. 129–50. (Introduces the theory that Harold was descended from King Aethelred I.)

Lundie Barlow, 'The Antecedents of Earl Godwine of Wessex', in *New England Historical and Genealogical Register*, vol. lxi (1957), pp. 30–8. (Supports Anscombe's theory.)

D. Bernstein, *The Mystery of the Bayeux Tapestry*, 1986.

A. Bridgeford, *1066: The Hidden History of the Bayeux Tapestry*, 2004.

The Carmen de Hastingae Proelio of Guy, Bishop of Amiens, ed. C. Marston and H. Mutz, 1972.

R. H. C. Davis (ed), *From Alfred the Great to Stephen*, 1981: article by ibid., 'Wiliam of Poitiers and his History of William the Conqueror', pp. 101–5.

The Ecclesiastical History of Orderic Vitalis, ed. and tr. M. Chibnall, 6 vols, 1969–80, especially vol. 2.

The Gesta Normannorum Ducum of William of Jumieges, Orderic Vitalis, and Robert of Torigny, ed. and tr. Eric van Houts, 2 vols, 1992–5.

The Gesta Guillelmi of William of Poitiers, ed. and tr. R. H. C. Davis and M. Chibnall, 1988.

M. K. Lawson, *The Battle of Hastings 1066*, 2002.

M. Lewis, *The Real World of the Bayeux Tapestry*, 2008.

Emma Mason, *The House of Godwin: History of a Dynasty*, 2004.

S. Morilo, *The Battle of Hastings*, 1996.

D. G. Raraty, 'Earl Godwine of Wessex: the Origins of his Power and Political Loyalties', in *History*, vol. lxxiv (1989), pp. 3–19.

Snorri Sturlason, *Heimskringla; the Saga of King Harald (Hardradi)*, ed. Laing, 1964. Especially *Harald's Saga*, para 85: battle of Gate Fulford.

Paras 86–93: battle of Stamford Bridge.

Pauline Stafford, op. cit.

Vita Haroldi: The Romance and Life of Harold, King of the English, ed. and tr. W. de Gray.

Birch, 1883.

Ian Walker, *Harold: the Last Anglo-Saxon King*, 1997.

Especially: chapter 1, the Godwin family.

Chapter 2, 1043–51.

Chapter 3, 1051–2.

Chapter 5, 1053–63.

Chapter 6, the visit to Normandy.

Chapter 7, the 1065 Northumbrian revolt.

Chapter 9, early to mid-1066.

Chapter 10, the Norwegian invasion.

Chapter 11, the Hastings campaign.

The Waltham Chronicle, ed. and tr. L. Watkins and M. Chibnall, 1994.

List of Illustrations

1. Queen Bertha, Canterbury Cathedral. (Elizabeth Norton)
2. The ruins of St Augustine's Abbey, Canterbury. (Elizabeth Norton)
3. A field near Wooler. (Philip Nixon)
4. King Eadbald, Canterbury Cathedral. (Elizabeth Norton)
5. King Alfred, Winchester. (Elizabeth Norton)
6. Winchester Cathedral. (Timothy Venning)
7. Bath Abbey. (Elizabeth Norton)
8. King Edgar, Bath Abbey. (Elizabeth Norton)
9. King Edgar, Powis Castle. (Elizabeth Norton)
10. King Cnut. (Library of Congress)
11. Tomb of Queen Emma and Harthacnut. (Peter Rex)
12. Edward the Confessor. (John Brooks and Jonathan Reeve JR1117slide100011000)
13. Bosham Church. (Timothy Venning)
14. King Edward nominates Harold Godwinson. (With special permission from the city of Bayeux)
15. Coronation of King Harold. (With special permission from the city of Bayeux)

ALSO AVAILABLE FROM AMBERLEY PUBLISHING

The Kings & Queens of Wales
Timothy Venning

The Welsh kings and queens who ruled prior to the Norman Conquest of Wales are shrouded in mystery. This book sets out to identify what we know or can reasonably surmise about these rulers, to disentangle their history, and to assess their achievements.

978 1 4456 0905 8
224 pages, 20 illustrations

Available from all good bookshops or order direct
from our website www.amberleybooks.com